Administrator's Guide to NEW PROGRAMS FOR FACULTY MANAGEMENT AND EVALUATION

Rita Dunn
and
Kenneth J. Dunn

Parker Publishing Company, Inc. / West Nyack, New York

PARKER PUBLISHING COMPANY, INC.

West Nyack, NY

Library of Congress Cataloging in Publication Data

Dunn, Rita Stafford
Administrator's guide to new programs for faculty management and evaluation.

Bibliography: p.
Includes index.
1. School personnel management. I. Dunn, Kenneth J. II. Title. III. Title: New programs for faculty management and evaluation.
LB2831.5.D86 658.3'7'3711 76-25993
ISBN 0-13-008623-1

Printed in the United States of America

With love and affection to our parents:

Mae and Phil Goetz

and

Helen and Mack Dunn

What This Book Offers

This book will serve as a practical guide to many of the newer, more successful techniques for the management and evaluation of faculty. It is written in response to the special needs of school administrators and includes a broad range of proven techniques employed in various organizations and businesses. The important principles established by Maslow, Blake, Herzberg, Drake, Mackenzie, and other well-known industrial psychologists and management consultants are translated into *practical* new programs for immediate use by administrators in education.

As a contemporary handbook, the guide focuses on tested procedures that will strengthen administrative and faculty skills and perceptions and explains the close relationship between management style and staff success in meeting program objectives. It also outlines specific ways to ensure the continuing improvement of management and instructional skills.

In the vital areas of staff selection and placement, the book offers interview guidelines, sample evaluation forms and criteria, and teaching-style appraisal techniques all based on successful personnel practices that match selected candidates with program and student needs.

In addition, the book offers effective strategies for self-, peer, and student evaluation to obtain increased personal motivation and commitment without threat or self-defeating anxiety. Moreover, the exact causes of job dissatisfaction can be identified and either reduced or eliminated, thus promoting greater staff cohesiveness and improved teaching and learning.

Specific techniques are described that will help you fill gaps in skills, meet program goals, and gain better administrator-staff agreement and relationships. Dozens of practical tips are given to improve staff meetings and to manage time and self.

Evaluation techniques are described for typical faculty-administrator responsibilities. Emphasis is on "how-to" instruments and strategies for varied situations, especially the newer approaches to assessing individualized instruction. Identifying your managerial style, measuring your perceptions against those of others, and using the exit interview to improve management are just a few of the contemporary strategies included.

Here are several examples that describe how this guide may be used:

1. You will be able to develop effective, up-to-date selection, supervisory, or evaluative practices and measure your decisions against the practical criteria included in this book. You will also learn of selected industry standards established for questionnaires and other managerial control instruments, along with model procedures used by schools and other organizations.
2. Current program weaknesses can be accurately diagnosed by comparing the required faculty skills and attitudes for specific program objectives with those of present faculty. This will increase your effectiveness in the selection and use of appropriate training devices to promote improvement or plan corrective changes.
3. Administrators who recognize the need to develop new faculty programs will be able to analyze their present administrative procedures to determine what type of change in managerial objectives is feasible or desirable.
4. When recruiting new faculty, supervisors will be able to identify more precisely needed personnel skills and talents through instruments *directly* related to the teaching styles required to meet student needs.
5. Specific faculty strengths and weaknesses will be identifiable through the use of objective instruments. The resulting evaluations can be used to improve teaching performance and to reach appropriate decisions on tenure.

This is much more than a book on personnel policies and procedures: It is an invaluable guide that offers a broad range of *practical programs* designed to improve school organization through the (a) efficient matching of staff skills and talents to student needs and organizational objectives and (b) motivation of faculty to learn and employ necessary diagnostic, prescriptive, and evaluative skills. Finally, it provides a formula for evaluating administrative and teaching styles and then promoting growth toward the identified, specified goals of your school or system, such as the individualization of instruction.

Rita Dunn
Kenneth J. Dunn

Acknowledgments

With special thanks to
Ruth Allen

The interpretive graphic illustrations for this book were created by Edward J. Manetta, Chairman of the Department of Fine Arts/Division of Music, St. John's University, New York. Dr. Manetta, who earned an Ed.D. at New York University, has been the recipient of several scholarships and awards and has had his work exhibited nationally in England and in Italy.

Except where otherwise indicated,
all photographs by

Kenneth Dunn

Other books by the authors:

Practical Approaches to Individualizing Instruction: Contracts and Other Effective Teaching Strategies

Educator's Self-Teaching Guide to Individualizing Instruction Programs

Contents

Part II
FACULTY EVALUATION PROGRAMS

Part I

Faculty Management Programs

1

IDENTIFYING AND MEASURING YOUR PERSONAL ADMINISTRATIVE STYLE

MANAGEMENT STYLE AND ITS IMPACT

Your success as a school administrator strongly depends upon the effectiveness of your managerial style—your way of working wtih teachers, students, parents, and staff members in aiding them to reach the educational goals of the school successfully.

The first, and sometimes the foremost, obstacle to effective managerial style is related to the varying perceptions of the administrator and those with whom he works. For example, a principal may view himself as "open" and in direct communication with the parents of the students who attend his school. Inevitably, there will be a parent who speaks of this administrator as one who "doesn't respond to messages." In reality, however, the situation may be at variance with the perceptions of both the principal and the unhappy parent. (See Figure 1-1)

As an administrator, therefore, you must do what you can to identify your perceptions and those held by staff members who work with you. Next, you should measure these perceptions against reality. The instruments in this chapter will aid you in building an accurate assessment of your managerial style and the perceptions of your style held by others.

A second problem in dealing with managerial style is the confusion between the roles of leadership and management. The school administrator is often called upon to use both, and they often overlap. If you select the wrong approach in a given situation, the results may be poor or lead to the defeat or noncompletion of objectives. To illustrate this improper use of role, a superintendent of schools may exhibit leadership through the positive bond he has developed with his followers (administrative staff). Further, he may possess strong influence over them *conferred on him by them willingly and*

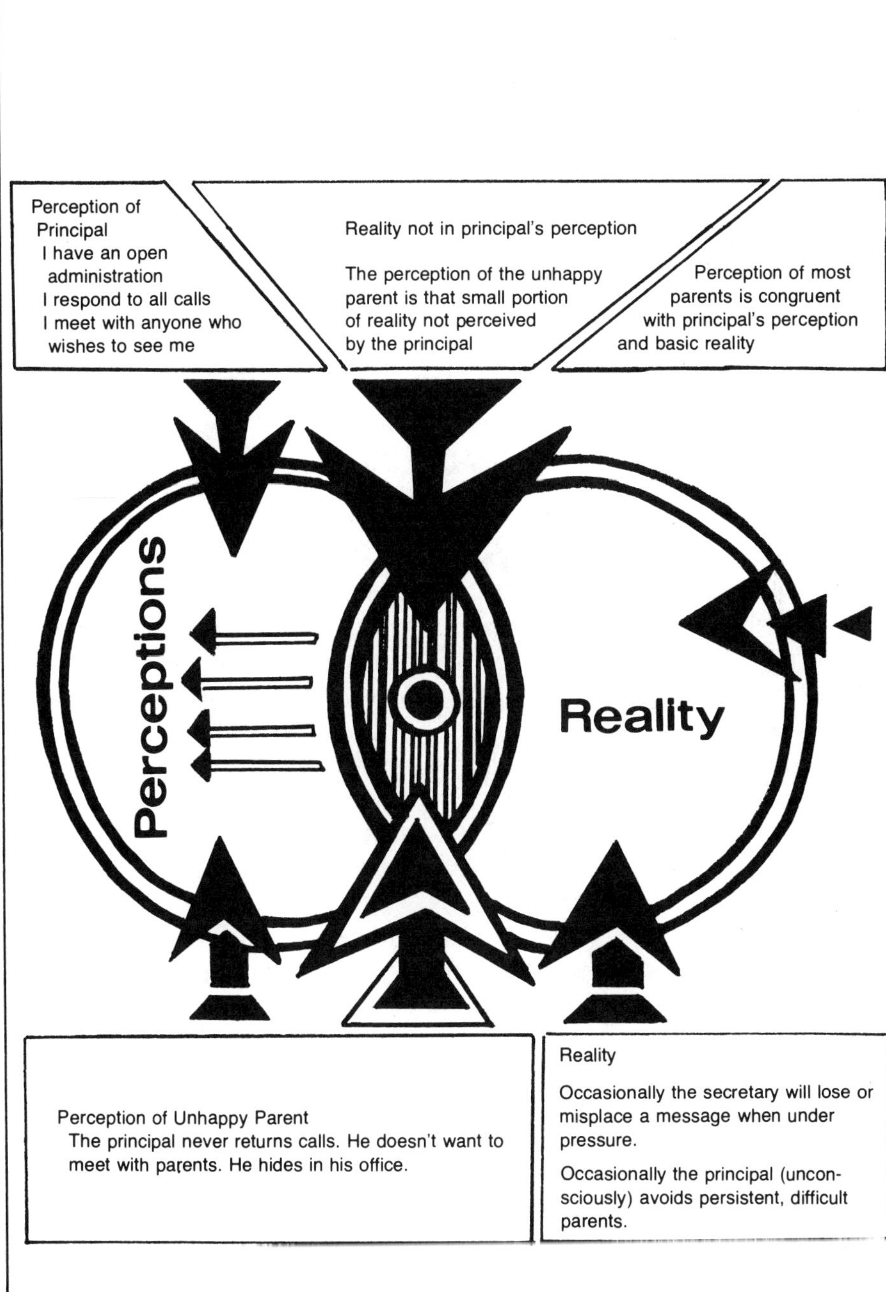

Perception of
Principal
I have an open
administration
I respond to all calls
I meet with anyone who
wishes to see me
Reality not in principal's perception
The perception of the unhappy
parent is that small portion
of reality not perceived
by the principal
Perception of most
parents is congruent
with principal's perception
and basic reality
Perceptions
Reality
Perception of Unhappy Parent
The principal never returns calls. He doesn't want to
meet with parents. He hides in his office.
Reality
Occasionally the secretary will lose or
misplace a message when under
pressure.
Occasionally the principal (uncon-
sciously) avoids persistent, difficult
parents.

Figure 1-1

freely. His appeal is to the emotional and the personal life of the group.[1*] It is his charisma that is responsible for loyalty and influence in this instance.

As a manager, on the other hand, he has a role as a decision maker. The superintendent, principal, or director has the administrative function of choosing the right course of action and committing the group's resources to it.[2] He defines objectives, sets out to achieve them, and evaluates the results accurately. When that charismatic superintendent relies solely on his influence and the loyalty of the group to support an incorrect decision based on intuition or personal desire rather than sound managerial planning, implementation, and evaluation, he has confused leadership with sound management, sometimes with disastrous results.

For example, this beloved superintendent may feel the need for an administrative assistant and gains support for the post through his leadership qualities rather than through sound managerial practice. His supporters say, "Old Bill's done a great job around here for years. It's about time he had some help for the nitty-gritty." Good old Bill tries to steamroll his desire through the Board of Education and the public at budget time and is hurt by their rejection. Further, he begins to lose some of the charismatic sheen he's developed with teachers, board, parents, and lower-level administrators because of their lack of meaningful involvement in deciding managerial issues, the lack of sound planning, and the gap between his desire or need and the objectives they have been working on in other areas.

Moreover, some of the followers may feel they had been exploited in the cold reality of assessing the defeated recommendation because they were influenced to support the added assistant on feelings of loyalty and good will—not on the basis of managerial need, which really had never been demonstrated to their satisfaction.

Alec Mackenzie has devised a useful comparison chart (Figure 1-2) in gaining perspective on these two important but separate concepts.[3]

A third major problem area for some administrators is a lack of understanding of Maslow's hierarchy of needs.[4] This general sociological model (see Figure 1-3) helps any manager to understand employee and administrator behavior in a variety of situations.

Man, throughout history or within a single lifetime, moves through this hierarchy from basic needs toward self-actualization. One way to view this useful model is through a comparison of man in general and teachers as professionals using Maslow's hierarchy. (See Figure 1-4)

The supervisor who says, "No, let me show you how to do it!" to a

---

*Notes appear at the end of each chapter.

	Management	*Leadership*
1) *Classified:*	Science	Art
2) *Based on:*	Body of principles	Innate sense
3) *Arrived at:*	Analytically	Empirically (by experience)
4) *Approach:*	Intellectual	Intuitive
5) *Goals:*	The manager produces them.	The leader obtains acceptance and motivation toward them.
6) *Goal Orientation:*	Toward organizational goals.	Toward personal goals.
7) *Power Derived:*	Positionally	Personally
8) *Method of Influence:*	Authority	Personal example and inspiration
9) *Extent of Influence:*	Limited only to those within his *control*.	Limited to those within his *personal contact*.
10) *Deals with:*	What the organization ought to do.	Motivating the organization to do it.
11) *Works Through:*	Formal organization	Informal organization

Figure 1-2

growing teacher who is on the verge of self-actualization may tumble him or her right back to the safety level *unless* the administrator had been *asked* to help. An approach that encompasses the notion that the supervisor would like to learn of the teacher's success, i.e., "Would you mind showing me how *you* do it?" might be all the support the young teacher needs to reinforce ego and build self-recognition of accomplishment.

The important assessment to make is the relative step that the teacher or staff member has reached in the hierarchy of needs. When this is done, the choice of either support or corrective action becomes apparent and the chances of success are enhanced.

Further, the encouragement of self-actualization will produce positive growth reactions in teachers—or anyone! Maslow lists 13 and points to the many positive after-glow effects on the self-actualizing person:

1. superior perception of reality
2. increased acceptance of self, of others, and of nature
3. increased spontaneity
4. increase in problem-centering (and solving)
5. increased detachment and desire for privacy

6. increased autonomy and resistance to enculturation
7. greater freshness of appreciation and richness of emotional reaction
8. higher frequency of peak experiences
9. increased identification with the human species
10. changed (the clinician would say "improved") interpersonal relations
11. more democratic character structure
12. greatly increased creativity
13. certain improved changes in the value system[5]

MASLOW'S NEED HIERARCHY

Figure 1-3

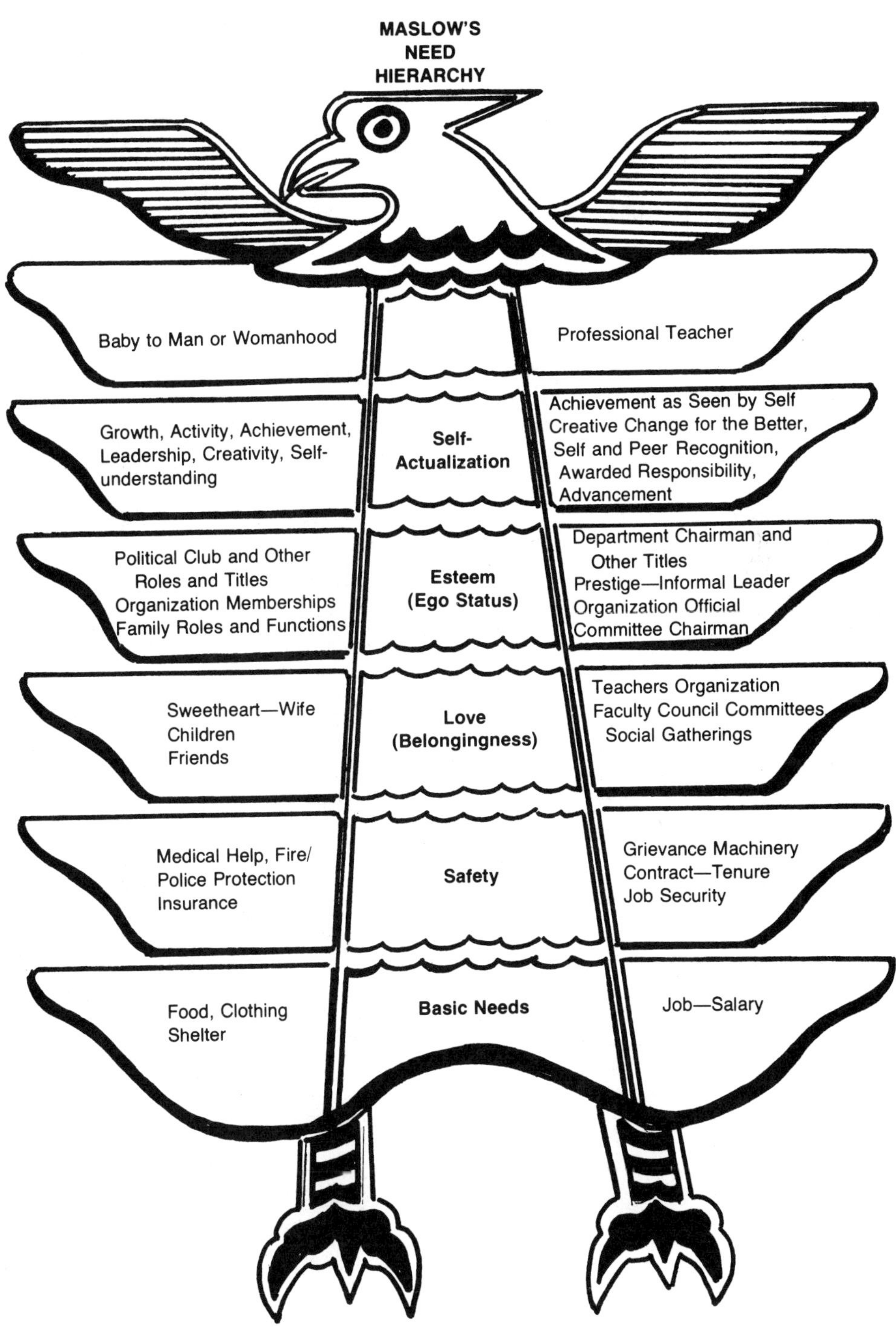
MASLOW'S
NEED
HIERARCHY
Baby to Man or Womanhood
Professional Teacher
Growth, Activity, Achievement, Leadership, Creativity, Self-understanding
Self-
Actualization
Achievement as Seen by Self
Creative Change for the Better,
Self and Peer Recognition,
Awarded Responsibility,
Advancement
Political Club and Other Roles and Titles
Organization Memberships
Family Roles and Functions
Esteem
(Ego Status)
Department Chairman and Other Titles
Prestige—Informal Leader
Organization Official
Committee Chairman
Sweetheart—Wife
Children
Friends
Love
(Belongingness)
Teachers Organization
Faculty Council Committees
Social Gatherings
Medical Help, Fire/
Police Protection
Insurance
Safety
Grievance Machinery
Contract—Tenure
Job Security
Food, Clothing
Shelter
Basic Needs
Job—Salary

Figure 1-4

ANALYZING ADMINISTRATIVE STYLES

Administrators have distinctive and identifiable managerial styles.

Blake-Mouton Grid®[6]

Blake and Mouton developed a useful grid that describes various managerial styles and attitudes on two variables—people and production. (See Figure 1-5)

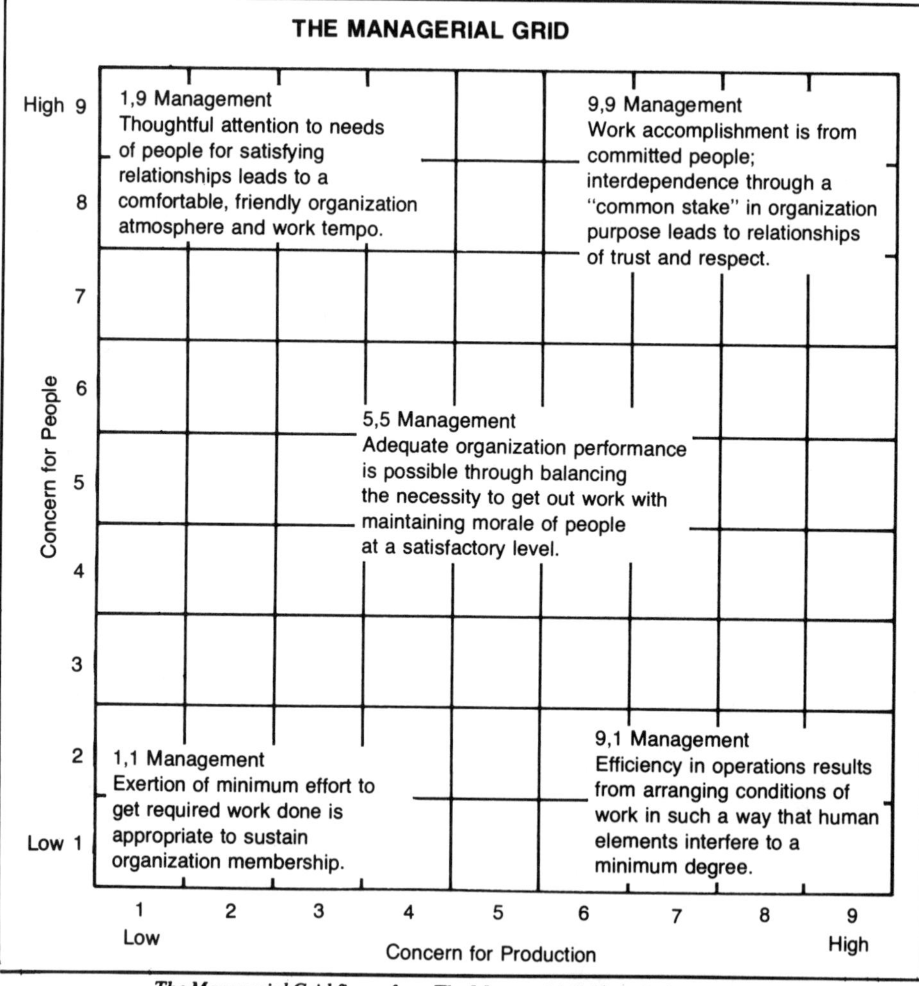

The Managerial Grid figure from The Managerial Grid, *by Robert R. Blake and Jane Srygley Mouton. Houston: Gulf Publishing Company, Copyright © 1964, page 10. Reproduced by permission.*

Figure 1-5

This grid may also be used to assess operational patterns and the managerial styles of administrators. A school principal who consistently considers the needs of his staff above all else (1,9) might be classified as the country club manager. His opposite number is the autocrat (9,1), a tyrant who places results above all other considerations. We find the by-the-book caretaker at 1,1 and the great compromiser at 5,5. The collaborative leader (9,9) registers concern for both people and objectives. (See Figure 1-6)

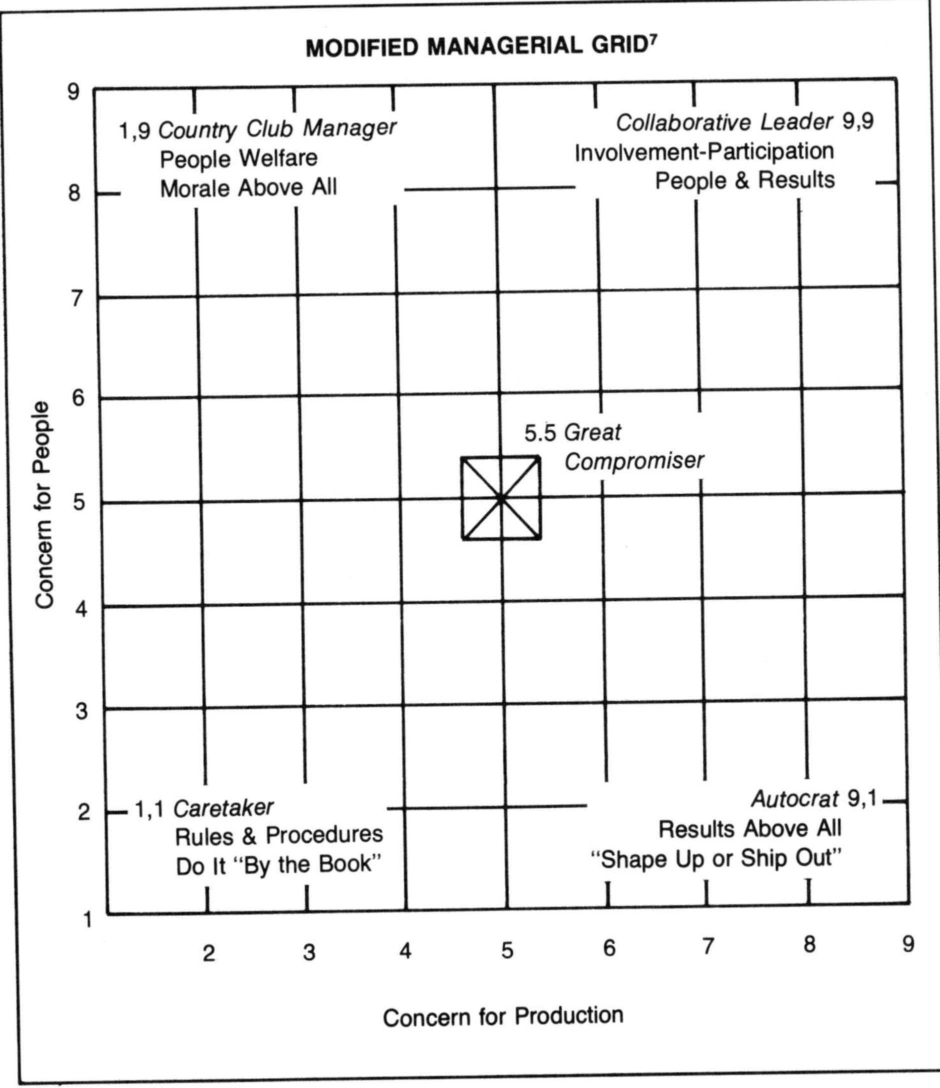

Figure 1-6

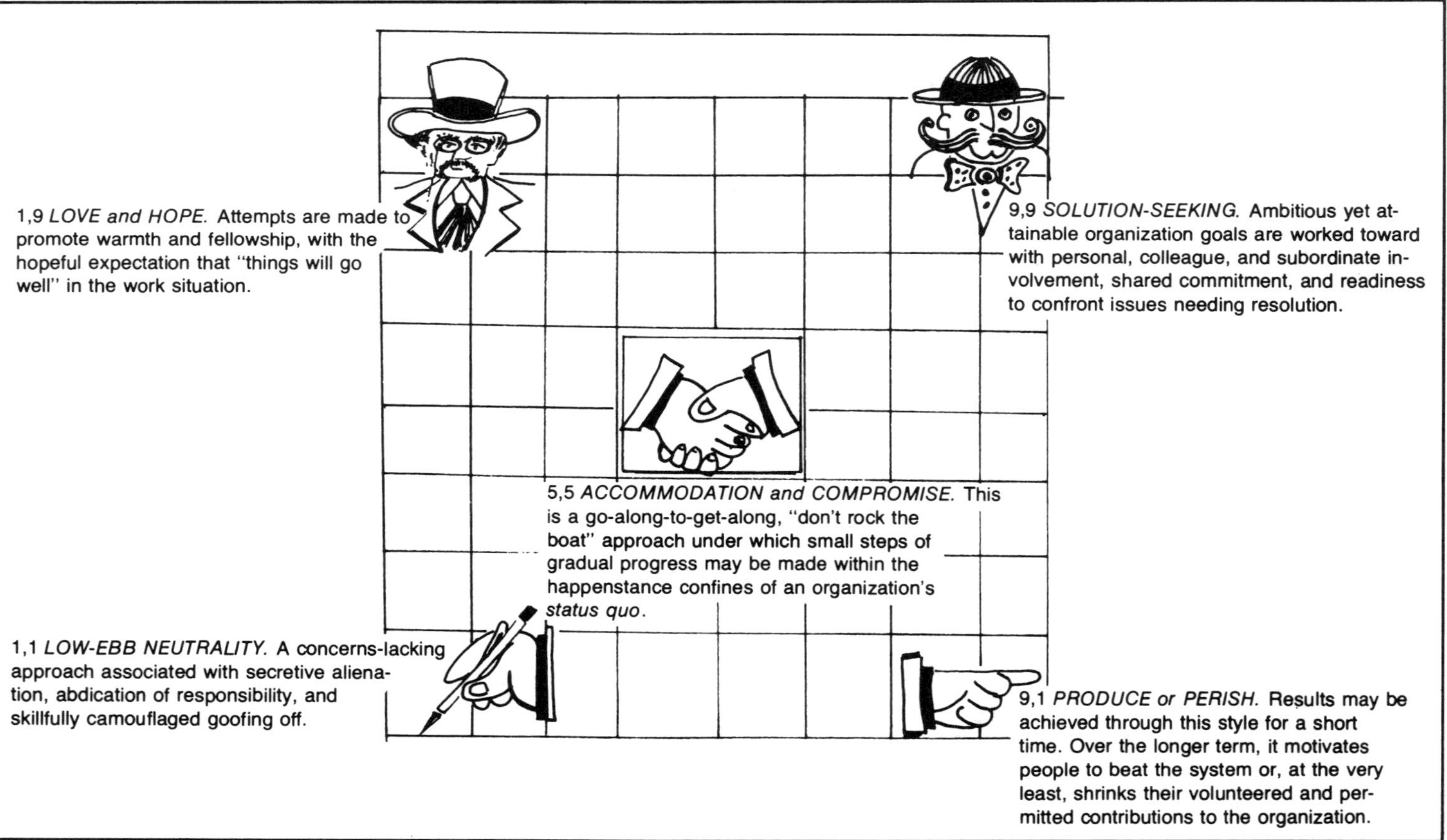

1,9 *LOVE and HOPE.* Attempts are made to promote warmth and fellowship, with the hopeful expectation that "things will go well" in the work situation.
9,9 *SOLUTION-SEEKING.* Ambitious yet attainable organization goals are worked toward with personal, colleague, and subordinate involvement, shared commitment, and readiness to confront issues needing resolution.
5,5 *ACCOMMODATION and COMPROMISE.* This is a go-along-to-get-along, "don't rock the boat" approach under which small steps of gradual progress may be made within the happenstance confines of an organization's *status quo*.
1,1 *LOW-EBB NEUTRALITY.* A concerns-lacking approach associated with secretive alienation, abdication of responsibility, and skillfully camouflaged goofing off.
9,1 *PRODUCE or PERISH.* Results may be achieved through this style for a short time. Over the longer term, it motivates people to beat the system or, at the very least, shrinks their volunteered and permitted contributions to the organization.

Figure 1-6 (cont.)

Your administrative style also may be measured on a scale from autocratic to collaborative:

1. Collaborative
2. Cooperative
3. Participative
4. Bureaucratic
5. Laissez-faire
6. Benevolent Despot
7. Autocratic

Obviously, individual administrators may function on more than one of these levels over a period of time. For example, some bureaucratic managers are autocratic in their daily application of the rules and regulations. Still others allow participation by the staff on some projects but act as benevolent despots when matters of importance to them are involved. And most administrators behave differently during crises as opposed to fair-weather situations.

Nevertheless, you may determine your own general administrative style through the use of the School Administrator's Management Style Inventory (Figure 1-7) and a comparison of how your employees indicate that they perceive you when they respond to the same questionnaire.

It is suggested that you complete and score the School Administrator's Management Style Inventory before reading the next section.

Definition of the Administrative Style Inventory

1. Collaborative. The highest level of democratic administration reflects a continuing responsiveness, a cohesive *rapport*[8] between an administrator or management team and all individuals and groups. Teachers, supervisors, and administrators work together on objectives, plans, procedures, evaluations, and redesigns. Delegation of authority is made more and more to groups; ownership of responsibility is assumed by all members. One forward-looking illustration of collaboration would be represented by a joint management-staff group that is given the responsibility to recommend and implement budget changes in the face of severe cutbacks.

2. Cooperative. A share of management is given to the staff. Those who are concerned are consulted in situations or matters that the administrator believes are of interest to them. The committee is the approach most often used as a function of the cooperative style. Usually the committee has an area of management as a continuing responsibility; thus, the staff has a share of management. For example, it may be school district policy to allow a joint administrative-faculty committee to approve college and other credits for salary scale advancement.

3. Participative. The lesser portion of management allowed staff under this definition usually involves teacher suggestions and ideas. Ad hoc project committees are given problems and asked for recommendations. These are not implemented in every case nor accepted without modification. One manifestation of this style would be the establishment of a search committee for the new elementary school principal. Screenings, visits, evaluations, etc., may be made but an ordered preference list of candidates is usually discouraged. In any event, the final decision is never delegated to the participating committee.

4. Bureaucratic. Under this style of management there is little room for collaboration, cooperation, or even limited participation. The policy book, school manual, department regulations, or other written rules are usually the basic source of management.

Rank is paramount and the hierarchy of command is firmly founded on written authority. Tradition and stability prevail and change is rare; certainly it is almost never instituted from below. A prime reflection of this style is the preoccupation with rank and promotions based on the written rules concerning seniority, recommendations, etc.

5. Laissez-faire. Almost in a category apart from any administrative style continuum is the chaotic approach of the administrator who buries his head in the sands of his organization on a daily basis, who looks the other way when something goes wrong, who allows each staff member to do his or her own thing without concern for either objective evaluation or consequences, who does not promote team decisions, and who even may not assume responsibility in an emergency. As one manifestation of this style, teachers are never certain of specific procedures for controlling severe discipline problems that develop. Each teacher copes, survives, succeeds, or fails based on his or her own sensitive response to a situation.

6. Benevolent Despot. This administrator usually smiles, puts his or her arms around your shoulders as he listens (or pretends to), and then does as he or she wishes. Input or involvement are either accidental and a function of a predetermined decision, or solicited to ensure results as previously projected by this type of autocrat. This manager actually may care about the feelings of the individuals involved and he or she may listen carefully to the facts in the matter. Invariably though, the final decision is the manager's. One illustration of this style is apparent in the ostensibly cooperative verbalizations of the benevolent despot, e.g., "I hear you!" "I understand, but . . .," "Well, we just might follow your suggestion some day soon,'' or ''Let me give that some additional thought.'' It doesn't take long to discover that these are smokescreens for ''full speed ahead—in my direction!''

7. Autocratic. The managed never share in the autocrat's analyses, let alone his decisions. He or she is often aloof, businesslike in outlook, highly directive, and intolerant of any deviation in plans. There is often a semblance of delegation but it is always authoritarian and task-oriented. Too often, power is used directly and arbitrarily to reach goals, implement decisions, and gain acceptance from the staff. For example, the autocrat will keep chronological logs of negative staff behavior to engineer dismissals or to prevent promotions—unless the teacher ''plays ball.'' His motto is ''Shape up or ship out.'' He has little sympathy for individual motivation or input. He knows ''what is best'' for students, parents, staff, and the future of his office or building.

Identifying Administrative Style

Figure 1-7

SCHOOL ADMINISTRATOR'S MANAGEMENT STYLE INVENTORY

Directions:

Rank the alternatives for each of the statements or questions listed below (I-IV) according to the way you would actually respond to that situation or issue. Place a "1" next to the alternative that would be most characteristic of your attitudes or actions for that statement, then place a "2" next to the attitude or action second most characteristic of you, and continue until you have numbered alternatives A-G from 1 through 7 for all four administrative areas. Then use the scoring key to determine your usual administrative style for each of the areas:

1) How I operate, manage or control.
2) My attitude toward handbooks and written regulations.
3) How I respond during a crisis.
4) My attitude toward planning.

Next, use the administrative style inventory to plot your own profile.

Finally, have five of your immediate subordinates respond to the scale by describing you as *they* perceive your attitudes and behaviors. Then compare your answers with theirs. If the two are fairly congruent, your task is one of assessing whether your current style is the most effective one for you. If your subordinates do not perceive your style as you do, it would be important to meet with them for an open discussion of the different perceptions.

I. In the day-to-day operation of my building, I mainly:

______ A Rely on my own ability, knowledge, and experience. I am, after all, the one who is held accountable.

______ B Try to encourage decisions and procedures that are the direct result of interaction and deliberation by the staff members and administrators who are most knowledgeable.

______ C Refer problems and tasks to other administrators for decisions and action.

______ D Let the staff members most directly concerned determine what they would do in given situations. It is really best to allow professionals to be autonomous and responsible for their decisions.

______ E Establish committees to help run the building. We build a strong sense of cooperation that way.

______ F Listen carefully to staff input. After giving their thoughts some consideration, I decide how the building should be operated.

______ G Like to involve the staff in some discussions by appointing ad-hoc committees and groups to study certain problems and to report their findings. I often accept their recommendations.

II. In the use of handbooks, teacher contracts, school board policies, and administrative regulations, my attitude usually is to:

______ A Distribute all written handbooks and procedures to all staff members and rely on staff and standing committees to use them in the proper management of the building and to suggest improvements.

______ B Establish study groups, when needed, to examine written rules and procedures and to recommend changes which I often adopt.

______ C File them and let the people who work for me function according to their personal and professional judgments.

______ D Rely on them as flexible and useful tools in meeting the school's objectives and the needs of students and staff.

______ E Use them to support my goals in maintaining harmony among the staff and firm leadership from my office.

______ F Refer to them often for valuable guidance in many types of situations. To go by the book can prevent all sorts of problems.

______ G Use them when appropriate in the positive and firm directing of my building. It's pretty obvious when a staff member can't follow instructions.

III. In a crisis or emergency I usually tend to:

_____ A Take charge!

_____ B Take over but keep anxiety and distress in individuals to a minimum level.

_____ C Let individuals cope in whatever fashion they can. The overall objectives of my school demand my attention.

_____ D Play it by the rules. Experienced people codified the regulations based on sound practices.

_____ E Speak to a few wise heads before I take the final action.

_____ F Call a meeting of the committees I have established for just this kind of situation.

_____ G Bring together all the key people who are most able and most knowledgeable about the problem and who are likely to recommend and carry out a successful response.

IV. As far as successful planning, innovation, and creativity are concerned, I believe that:

_____ A Professionals should join established committees that are given some firm responsibility for planning and change.

_____ B The district's long-established policies and procedures provide an orderly method of planning the proper maintenance or modification of existing programs.

_____ C A small staff group should be assigned the task of studying proposed changes. Its recommendations will be considered, but not necessarily enacted, of course.

_____ D A leader should listen to any professional who has an idea. After hearing people it's easier to pursue the proper goals for the school.

_____ E The best people most directly concerned with the consequences of the planning should have substantial responsibility and authority to plan change and to carry out those changes.

_____ F Planning and change are the ultimate responsibility of the person chosen to lead the school.

_____ G The staff itself decides its goals and directions on a daily basis. A leader must allow professionals the opportunity to follow their inclinations.

SCHOOL ADMINISTRATOR'S MANAGEMENT STYLE INVENTORY SCORING KEY

INSTRUCTIONS: Place your answers in the appropriate spaces below. (For example: If you answered 1. B with a 2, place the 2 beside 1. B.)

	COLLABORATIVE	*COOPERATIVE*	*PARTICIPATIVE*	*BUREAUCRATIC*	*LAISSEZ-FAIRE*	*BENEVOLENT DESPOT*	*AUTOCRATIC*
Operate, Manage & Control	1. B ______	1. E ______	1. G ______	1. C ______	1. D ____	1. F ______	1. A ______
Handbooks & Written Regulations	2. D ______	2. A ______	2. B ______	2. F ______	2. C ____	2. E ______	2. G ______
Crisis Reaction	3. G ______	3. F ______	3. E ______	3. D ______	3. C ____	3. B ______	3. A ______
Planning	4. E ______	4. A ______	4. C ______	4. B ______	4. G ____	4. D ______	4. F ______
TOTALS	______	______	______	______	____	______	______

Analysis of the School Administrator's Management Style Instrument

Total each of the columns. The *lowest score* is the one that represents your primary administrative style. The next lowest score is likely to be used as a secondary, or back-up approach.

Obviously, few of us always operate in a single style. We are more likely to assume a primary posture on many issues or situations and a secondary approach on others. At other times, style may depend on the individual or groups with which we are dealing and the managerial response required given the situation and the people concerned.

Nevertheless, the answers you gave may reveal some insights into your administrative style and some clues for future modification or improvement in the way you manage planning, the overall operation of your building, and crises.

To analyze your scores, arrange the totals in order with the lowest score at the top, e.g.,

ADMINISTRATOR A		*ADMINISTRATOR B*	
Collaborative	8	Autocratic	7
Cooperative	9	Bureaucratic	12
Participative	11	Benevolent Despot	14
Benevolent Despot	15	Participative	16
Autocratic	17	Collaborative	16
Laissez-faire	24	Cooperative	19
Bureaucratic	28	Laissez-faire	28

The lowest score characterizes your perception of your administrative style. Administrator A views himself as collaborative leader (low score of 8); his second lowest score, 9 for Cooperative, reinforces his basically democratic approach to administration. Administrator B believes in direct, firm leadership from the top (low score of 7 for Autocratic) and probably relies on rules and regulations to manage his school (second lowest score of 12 for Bureaucratic).

Turn back to page 23 if you have not yet read the definitions of each of the styles.

MEASURING STAFF PERCEPTIONS

The same diagrammatic, three-ring approach used in Figure 1-1 applies to your perception of your administrative style, staff perceptions of your administrative style, and reality. It is important, therefore, to determine staff perceptions in obtaining a closer mental match with reality in order to maintain or alter your behavior to attain better results.

Step #1. Ask peers, subordinates, and superiors to fill out the School Administrator's Management Style Inventory (Figure 1-7) as *they* believe you operate in response to the four administrative areas.

Step #2. Compare their answers with yours.

Step #3a. If totals are closely matched, share them with those who completed the form and consider with all of them the desirability of continuing to be the way you and they have described you or of modifying your style (see Step 4) based on common agreement that some changes would benefit you and them.

Step #3b. If there are sizable discrepancies, e.g., you believe you are a collaborative leader and everyone sees you as a benevolent despot, explore with them the specific evidence they offer to demonstrate your friendly but dictatorial rule. Then consider change (step 4), if desirable, with all concerned.

Step #4. Develop a workshop using the Chart of Staff Perceptions of Administrative Style (Figure 1-8). This workshop will tend to increase teacher or other staff awareness of managerial style and their perceptions of how you work and its impact on their behavior. Moreover, open communication about how they like to work, how they like to be treated, their aspirations, and their suggestions for a better school will be enhanced.

Step #5. Keep a record of situations and issues. Note your actions and the subsequent consequences. Review these with staff, peers, and superiors for analysis and suggested modification of your administrative style behaviors.

Workshop Directions: If you decide to sponsor a workshop on this theme, some of the following activities will increase the group's productivity.

1. List the kind of person your administrator seems to be in each of the four areas of control, handbooks, crisis response, and planning. In general tell why you think so.
2. In teams, develop mini-cases describing typical past actions of your administrator that verify your perceptions.
3. Then have the teams develop new situations and issues based on your projection of real events that may occur in the near future. Have your administrator and your team project his likely response.
4. Establish an evaluation team to analyze the answers and predictions.
5. Keep a log of real future issues and decisions. Analyze, with your administrator, his managerial style responses and the consequences.

CHART OF STAFF PERCEPTIONS OF ADMINISTRATIVE STYLE

Administrative Area	Generalized Descriptions						
	Collaborative	Cooperative	Participative	Bureaucratic	Laissez-faire	Benevolent Despot	Autocratic
1) Operation & Control	Responsive management for most decisions; direction after joint commitment to decisions or goals	Committee structure to study, plan, and report on many situations or programs	Temporary groups set up to offer suggestions on some items	Line and staff organizational chart; hierarchy of orders	Lack of direction; people's feelings control direction	Smiles, listens; does as he chooses	Unilateral; highly directive; uncom-promising; expectation of follow-through
2) Use of Handbooks, Policies, Regulations	Flexible use to meet needs of people and to reach objectives	Flexible use or modifications offered by committees	Occasional use or revisions made by ad-hoc committees	Always follows the book; can-not function well without written regulations	Rarely looks at manuals, uses them only to sup-port what his people say at the moment	Highly selective use to persuade people of the wisdom of the administra-tor's decision	Selective use to serve personal view of reaching destination
3) Management of Crises	Cool; brings people and resources to bear, then directive; often successful	Supervisory groups and staff committees used as resources	Certain status staff members called together for advice	Flustered; thumbs through manual; can't find rules to cover situation; makes excuses; often unsuccessful	Solicitous, then asks them what they would like to do; insufficiently directive; often unsuccessful	Very directive; often as successful as not	"Red-necked"; highly directive; often successful
4) Planning	Nancy, who else do we need to involve in Tuesday's work session? What resources do you need to get the job done? Can we agree on a firm deadline?	Bill, which committee is closest to the new program? Who can we add to produce a good study with recom-mendations?	Ruth, let's put together a team to plan that curricu-lum change. Will they be unhappy if we don't follow all of their suggestions?	How did we do it before? What are the state regula-tions? Where is the revised manual?	Well boys, what do you think? Why don't we do this over lunch? Shall we talk about this on the golf course?	Now Barbara, let's not get upset. Go home early, get a good night's sleep, and you'll see that I'm right.	Bob, I want that report in by Friday at 10:00 a.m. Is there anyone on your staff who can't do this kind of job? Do you know what to do?

Figure 1-8

INCREASING YOUR ADMINISTRATIVE EFFECTIVENESS

Several large corporations have developed questionnaires and procedures to increase the effectiveness of their managers and supervisors. The instrument that follows was developed to assist administrators and supervisors in identifying their strengths and areas that might be improved. This questionnaire, to be given to teachers, probes in detail and with some depth into the types of administrative styles described earlier in this chapter.

ADMINISTRATIVE STYLE AND DEVELOPMENT QUESTIONNAIRE

This questionnaire is designed to provide an operational view of your administrator as you see the way he functions in his position. Your responses should be *descriptive* of your administrator's on-the-job *behavior*, not *evaluative*. There are no right or wrong answers to these questions nor are there any standards for comparison.

All teachers in your building will be given an opportunity to respond voluntarily and anonymously to this questionnaire. The results will be reviewed with your administrator by the Administrative Development Committee, which includes peers, central office administrators, supervisors, and teacher organization representatives. Your responses will permit your administrator to see himself as his faculty or staff sees him and may aid him in identifying his strengths as well as those supervisory and administrative behaviors that might be improved.

Please answer all questions as objectively as you can. Return the questionnaire *unsigned* to the Administrative Development Committee.

My Administrator's Name Is ____________________
Title ______________________________
School or Office

I. Teaching Objectives and Improvement

A. How well do you understand your administrator's expectations regarding the teaching improvements he expects *you* to make?

______ 1. Do not understand any of his suggested goals.
______ 2. Only understand a small portion of his goals.
______ 3. Understand some of the things he wants me to improve.
______ 4. Understand most of his goals.
______ 5. Understand exactly what he expects.

B. How reasonable do you feel your administrator's expectations are of you and of your ability to improve along the lines he suggests?

______ 1. He is very unreasonable!
______ 2. He is somewhat unreasonable and makes me reach beyond my ability.

_______ 3. He is reasonable and accurate in his expectations.
_______ 4. He does not challenge me enough.
_______ 5. He does not challenge me at all!

C. How frequently does your administrator discuss your teaching techniques and the resulting student outcomes?
_______ 1. Never.
_______ 2. Occasionally, but not enough.
_______ 3. Enough so that I understand his criticism and suggestions.
_______ 4. Too often! He should allow professionals to set their own growth directions.

D. How well does your administrator help you to improve teaching and learning in your classroom?
_______ 1. Never.
_______ 2. Only occasionally.
_______ 3. About half the time.
_______ 4. Most of the time.
_______ 5. On every occasion.

II. Delegation and Personal Responsibility for the Teacher

A. After your administrator sets an objective for you, how consistently does he allow you the academic freedom to develop or define an approach without *undue* control and close supervision?
_______ 1. Never allows me the freedom to develop my own approach.
_______ 2. Very seldom.
_______ 3. As often as not.
_______ 4. Most of the time.
_______ 5. Always lets me develop a technique according to my style and ability.

B. Considering your teaching responsibilities and related activities, has your administrator clearly outlined the authority you have to make decisions on your own (without checking with him), and those decisions on which you must check with him first?
_______ 1. No.
_______ 2. For some of my teaching responsibilities.
_______ 3. Yes, on most of my teaching responsibilities.
_______ 4. Yes, on all of my important teaching responsibilities.

C. Does your administrator follow up on details of your work and the physical environment or only on the significant major aspects of teaching and learning?
_______ 1. Is concerned only with details and environment.
_______ 2. Is oriented toward details but recognizes some significant aspects.
_______ 3. Spends equal time on details and on significant aspects.
_______ 4. Is more concerned with significant aspects than details.
_______ 5. Focuses exclusively on significant aspects.

D. How often do you find that your administrator modifies your techniques, approaches, or style in accomplishing your work?

_______ 1. Almost all the time.
_______ 2. More often than not.
_______ 3. About half the time.
_______ 4. Seldom.

III. Knowledge of My Performance

A. Do you know how your administrator feels about your performance?

_______ 1. I have no idea how my administrator feels about my teaching performance.
_______ 2. I get very little feedback.
_______ 3. Sometimes I think I know, but I am not really certain.
_______ 4. I usually know how my administrator feels.
_______ 5. I always know exactly how my administrator feels.

B. How aware do you feel your administrator is of the contribution you are making to your students and to the school?

_______ 1. Has no awareness.
_______ 2. There is little awareness.
_______ 3. Is aware as often as not.
_______ 4. Is usually aware.
_______ 5. Really knows and recognizes it.

C. How specific and frank is your administrator when talking with you about your performance?

_______ 1. I get no honest and objective feedback on my performance.
_______ 2. My administrator is often vague or general and does not deal with important aspects of teaching and learning in any detail. Sometimes she/he worries about nonteaching things like the position of shades in the room.
_______ 3. My administrator only likes to talk about successes, but is frank when asked about specific aspects of my teaching.
_______ 4. My administrator usually lets me know what I do well and how I need to improve.
_______ 5. My administrator is honest and objective about all aspects of my teaching performance.

D. When you introduce a new teaching technique, complete a project, or produce learning results that you feel are quite good, how often does your administrator recognize your accomplishments?

_______ 1. Never.
_______ 2. Rarely.
_______ 3. As often as not.
_______ 4. Almost always.
_______ 5. Always.

IV. Assistance When Needed

A. When you encounter student or parent problems hampering the teaching-learning process, is your administrator there to provide assistance and does he do so?

_______ 1. Never.
_______ 2. Occasionally.
_______ 3. As often as not.
_______ 4. Most of the time.
_______ 5. Always.

B. How often, when your administrator's support and backing would be helpful to you, does he provide it?

_______ 1. Never.
_______ 2. Occasionally.
_______ 3. As often as not.
_______ 4. Most of the time.
_______ 5. Always.

C. Does your administrator provide you with the benefit of his/her own experience and knowledge in helping you to improve your teaching performance?

_______ 1. Never on a voluntary basis.
_______ 2. Reluctantly when asked.
_______ 3. Helpful, if asked.
_______ 4. Sometimes offers help.
_______ 5. Always seeks to help without interfering.

D. To what degree and how often does your administrator aid you with specific suggestions that really work successfully in the classroom?

_______ 1. High degree of effectiveness while respecting my individuality.
_______ 2. To a high degree and fairly often.
_______ 3. Moderately and as often as not.
_______ 4. Seldom with any effectiveness.
_______ 5. Never helpful.

V. Personal Learning and Growth

A. Has your administrator had any discussions with you about ways in which you might improve your knowledge or your skills?

_______ 1. None at all.
_______ 2. Occasionally general discussions that really are not constructive.
_______ 3. Only after formal observations.
_______ 4. Only when I experience serious difficulties.
_______ 5. Yes, on a regular basis.

B. Does your administrator provide personal growth opportunities for you such as new assignments, curriculum projects, attendance at inservice classes, conferences, and similar activities?

_______ 1. No.
_______ 2. Occasionally.
_______ 3. Yes, but not as often as would be helpful.
_______ 4. Yes, fairly often.
_______ 5. Yes, whenever possible.

C. Has your administrator discussed with you your aspirations for the future and provided ways in which you can progress toward reaching those personal objectives?
_______ 1. Never.
_______ 2. Occasionally.
_______ 3. Yes, but was not of much help.
_______ 4. Yes, fairly often.
_______ 5. Yes, in a satisfactory manner.

D. Do you generally feel you are "growing" as a teacher and in your knowledge of how to be successful with most types of students?
_______ 1. No.
_______ 2. Very little.
_______ 3. A fair amount; would like more.
_______ 4. Yes, I am growing sufficiently.
_______ 5. Yes, I am growing beyond my expectations.

VI. Communication

A. How often do you feel your administrator communicates information and directions to you that are necessary for you to be a successful teacher?
_______ 1. Never.
_______ 2. On occasion, but not enough.
_______ 3. As often as not.
_______ 4. Most of the time.
_______ 5. Always keeps me informed.

B. How free do you feel to talk with your administrator about things that are important to you—either involving teaching or personal problems?
_______ 1. Not at all.
_______ 2. Somewhat uncomfortable.
_______ 3. Have no feeling one way or another.
_______ 4. Feel free to talk about most of my concerns.
_______ 5. Feel I can talk about anything with my administrator.

C. How often does your administrator ask you for your ideas on things that are important in the department, grade, or school?
_______ 1. Never.
_______ 2. Seldom.
_______ 3. When a problem arises.
_______ 4. On an occasional unscheduled basis.
_______ 5. Ideas and suggestions are solicited on a regular basis.

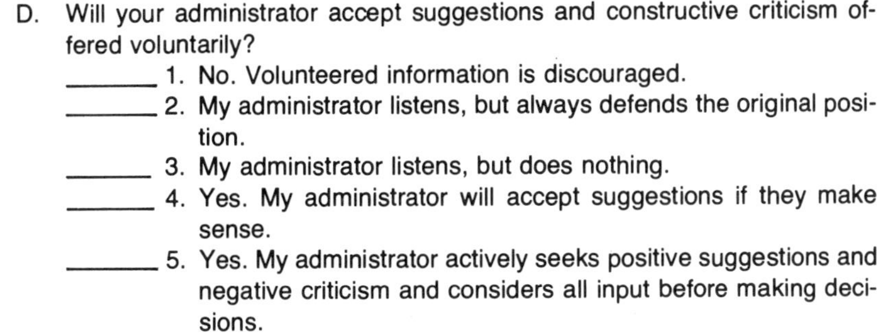

D. Will your administrator accept suggestions and constructive criticism offered voluntarily?

_______ 1. No. Volunteered information is discouraged.

_______ 2. My administrator listens, but always defends the original position.

_______ 3. My administrator listens, but does nothing.

_______ 4. Yes. My administrator will accept suggestions if they make sense.

_______ 5. Yes. My administrator actively seeks positive suggestions and negative criticism and considers all input before making decisions.

VII. General (Answers to the following questions will be summarized in typewritten form to maintain the anonymity of the source of answers.) As you think about your administrator's style, supervisory techniques and methods, what one or two thing(s) does he or she do best and what one or two thing(s) would most increase his or her effectiveness?

THINGS HE OR SHE DOES BEST	WOULD MOST INCREASE HIS OR HER EFFECTIVENESS

The responses to this last question can be eye-opening and require some ego security on the part of the administrator to examine strengths and areas of needed improvement objectively. For example, one principal found that, too often, his secretary did not know where she could reach him. She was too new and shy to tell him. As a result of her willingness to respond on paper (but not face to face), the administrator modified his behavior and this problem disappeared. Another administrator discovered that 80% of his staff wanted more direction from him; they did not appreciate the responsibility that accompanied their decision-making opportunities. His approval was needed to establish accountability at the top. After the initial shock, he converted his surprise into an effective program of visits and action meetings. Everyone felt more secure and less anxious about their involvement.

One of the best approaches to increasing administrative effectiveness is to fill out this form as you believe it will be answered by your teachers and staff. Then compare your guesses of their responses to their actual answers. If the answers are congruent, you have a good perception of their feelings and the reality of your administration. If there are discrepancies, analyze them openly with your staff. Probe for specifics and project better ways to deal with similar issues, situations, or problems in the future. When faculty members recognize *your* willingness to examine your administrative style openly in order to improve, many will begin to identify with you and, similarly, will be receptive to assessing and modifying their teaching styles to increase their effectiveness with individual students.

USING SIMULATIONS TO PROMOTE CONSENSUS

Simulations—structured imitations of real situations, events, or problems—can be very helpful in solving problems, resolving differences, gaining consensus, and in understanding the positions and attitudes of others.

Role playing your own or another administrator's position or attitude in the nonthreatening and gamelike framework of a simulation will reveal underlying issues, attitudes, and the obstacles to the solution of problems or the development of new programs.

Guidelines

Administrators can create effective problem-solving or program-planning simulations through the use of a set of simple guidelines:

1. Use real events, situations, or conditions that are taken from day-to-day experience, expressed attitudes, varied perceptions, and actual happenings in the lives of your administrators and faculty, either past or present.
2. Relate the descriptions, directions, problems, and issues to those that the administrator (or faculty) understand and respond to with interest.
3. Involve faculty, other administrators, students, and parents (if appropriate) in reading, improving, suggesting changes for, and sharpening the reality and intensity of the simulation.
4. Design simulations that involve five to eight administrators or teachers. A combination of participants with different functions may be desirable for some simulations. For example, parents and students might be involved in a simulation designed to improve the curriculum.
5. Create positions and scenarios that involve all of the participants in active roles.
6. Continually revise and modify those simulations that fail, to some degree, in meeting the objectives established for them.

Procedures

One of the administrators—superintendent, assistant superintendent, principal or supervisor etc.—should act as game-master or simulation director and chief consultant for the simulation. He or she can assign groupings and roles or cause them to be self-selected in patterns that take advantage of the strengths, interests, and relationships among the members of the group participating.

After distributing the materials, the director should explain the purpose of simulations in general (if it is the participants' first involvement with one) and the specific objectives of this exercise in particular. He or she should review what the process can do and what it will not do. For example, alternate solutions, planning stages, and problem-solving skills may develop among the group as appropriate goals and decisions or conclusions are reached. Allow ten to 15 minutes of reading and warm-up time. Then begin the simulation and encourage interaction among the participants. The director should join each group for part of each round and observe, suggest next steps, intervene, or aid in timing progress if necessary. Follow the simulation with a group effort to analyze the results. Then brainstorm issues, alternatives, and suggestions for improving group consensus despite differing administrative styles.

Advantages

Simulations are particularly appropriate for a number of administrative goals:

- Developing problem-solving skills
- Designing alternative solutions
- Fostering decision-making ability
- Training administrators to cope with confrontations, differing attitudes, problems, decisions, antagonism, anger, confusion, and other potentially negative emotions
- Developing objective insights into reasons, issues, causes, beliefs, and behaviors
- Learning the techniques of analysis
- Encouraging participation, cooperation, creativity, and a desire to achieve

These goals are more likely to be achieved if specific objectives are understood, if decisions are based on the collaboration of the participants, and if evaluation is built into the follow-up implementation of the plans or solutions that are developed during the simulation.

Simulation for Administrators

The following simulation was developed for a group of principals struggling to implement an individualized instructional program. These administrators found themselves stymied by differences in their administrative styles and basic philosophies.

The simulation succeeded in increasing the principals' sensitivity to differing positions and in improving their ability to work together toward material solutions. One of the reasons for the simulation's success, they reported later, was the opportunity to play roles that represented the attitudes of others and *not* their own. Another thing that enhanced its chance of success was the realistic setting of actual situations and attitudes, slightly fictionalized to permit freedom of expression.

This is the simulation with complete directions. You may elect to use it to achieve one or more of the advantages noted earlier.

FIVE ROLES TOWARD INDIVIDUALIZING INSTRUCTION

To The Participants:

You are about to participate in a simulation designed to engage your powers of positive thinking and to test your ability to resolve philosophical and emotional differences concerning instructional change in your school.

A perplexing and difficult problem has been tossed into your midst by the Superintendent of Schools. He has praised the partial and modest movement toward individualizing instruction achieved at two of the District's ten elementary schools last year and wishes you to press forward with new plans in all buildings. He wants the thrust to reach the five secondary schools as well.

His parting remarks, however, left you and your colleagues puzzled. While exhorting you to action, he decried the pressure being placed on him, the Central Office, and the Board by parents who had been alerted to the individualization practices being introduced to the two schools and who were demanding similar efforts in their children's schools. These mixed signals from "the Captain" seem to say, "Full speed ahead, but don't make waves!" Also, "Run silent and keep a low profile!" How is it possible to individualize learning or make any significant change in your program without involving parents (some of whom will always find something with which to disagree!) and causing concerns to some of the staff?

To further complicate matters, the Assistant Superintendent for Instruction left for a vacation in Hawaii. He was supposed to lead the principals' group toward "the new frontiers" but had not attended the recent preliminary workshops on individualization that provided background information for administrators and selected teachers.

In an attempt to resolve the problem and set some coordinated direction among the schools, a group of five principals of differing philosophies and managerial styles agree to meet.

The simulation assignment is to devise guidelines for moving toward individualized instruction in a manner that:

1. is appropriate for students in your school.
2. is acceptable to the parents in your community.

3. is stimulating and motivating to your staff, and
4. is supported by the Central Office.

Included in the materials before you is a scenario describing your particular role in this simulation. Try to make the goals of your group your very own ("internalize" them) and work toward them throughout the simulation.

Format: (Time allotment at the discretion of the simulation leader)

1. *Round 1:* (warm-up) 10-15 minutes
   During this period the purpose of simulations, and this game in particular, will be explained by the simulation leader.

2. *Round 2:* 25-35 minutes
   Roles will be assigned to participants and materials will be distributed. Each person will wear his identification badge and silently read his own scenario. Then the leader will organize two or more mixed groups consisting of one innovator, compromiser, autocrat, bureaucrat, and country club manager. The remainder of Round 1 will be devoted to a discussion of possible approaches to the implementation of individualized instruction.
   DEVELOP A TENTATIVE PLAN OR SET OF PLANS. You need not reach a final consensus or agreement in this round.

3. *Round 3:* 30 minutes
   A series of national conferences has been called by the U.S. Office of Education to discuss the very issues that confront your group. Those with similar views are to meet in subsections to develop strategies to bring back to each local meeting. YOUR GROUP (those with similar views) are to meet at the following locations:
   Innovators—Hawaii
   Bureaucrats—Washington, D.C.
   Compromisers—St. Louis, Missouri
   Autocrats—Las Vegas, Nevada
   Country Club Managers—Miami Beach, Florida

4. *Round 4:*
   As a group, develop a set of guidelines that will realistically meet the simulation assignment. The final version should be based on total agreement, if possible, or consensus at the very least.

SIMULATION

General Information *Individualizing Instruction*

(See next page for photos and editorial comment.)

THE CITIZEN'S PRESS

Tuesday, July 8, 1975

CITIZENS DEMAND INDIVIDUALIZED INSTRUCTION FOR ALL SCHOOLS; DISSENT NOTED

Leading citizens of this community today supported the immediate adoption of individualized instruction programs for all students when schools open this fall.

Mrs. Joan Librul, spokesman for the pro-individualization group said, "If our children do not learn the way their teachers teach them, then their teachers must teach them the way they learn!" She was loudly applauded by the newly formed NITPICK organization (Now Is the Time to Promote Individualizing Children's Knowledge).

A differing point of view was offered by Mayor Vahst Experienca, who simultaneously serves as President of our local Board of Education. Mayor Experienca vehemently stated, "Students need more discipline, not individualization! All this catering to children has led to increased permissiveness, drugs, and crime. What our children need is basic skills and basic punishment for kids who step out of line!"

The Superintendent has called a series of meetings to resolve community differences and to establish guidelines for improving instructional practices in our local schools.

EDITORIAL

This newspaper submits the following photographs to illustrate the way things were (and ought to be!) and what individualization has done to the minds and habits of our children.

The Bettman Archive, Inc.

THE GOOD OLD-FASHIONED METHOD
LISTEN—OR ELSE!

WHAT INDIVIDUALIZATION CAN
LEAD TO!

Role: collaborative leader

Dan Innovator

You really know how to get the job done! It's difficult to understand why the other schools in the district lag so far behind. In fact, you've had pressure exerted on you from the Superintendent to "cool it" with respect to innovation and progress. He wants a lower profile so that parents won't bombard him and the other principals to catch up with your school.

This is a strange twist. You are the principal who originally pressured the Central Office for support to develop an individualized program extending from students with learning disabilities to those who are talented and gifted. Test scores went up, parents were delighted, students became "turned on," and teachers were happy and productive. Why submerge a program that the other schools should move toward?

Well, you won't. You decide to use your group dynamics knowledge to get the other principals on your exciting bandwagon. You determine to show them how individualization can help them to do a better job and to obtain some of the recognition your school has gained. They have to understand it, of course. This work conference is the place to begin. If the other schools caught up, you could share successful techniques and move forward together.

Role: bureaucrat

Burr O'Kratik

You are not too certain about individualization. The reports that the Superintendent requires on a monthly basis are so exacting that you don't know where you'll find the time for additional tasks. Your reports are always considered "the best." The Superintendent always praises them! They are on time and filled out correctly, and you keep absolute accounts of all expenditures, book losses, and attendance. If you are forced to concentrate on altering instructional practices to produce individualization, who is going to assume the responsibility for all the other things that mandate your continuing involvement?

Not only that, how will you be able to keep track of what your teachers will be doing? How will you be able to evaluate them? When parents come to your office for a pass, how will your secretary be able to look up a schedule and, according to the time of day, tell the parent where the class is and what it should be doing? You'd actually have to begin an entirely new system for scheduling, assignments to teachers, and even grading. You wonder why some people always have the need to change and "make waves"!

Besides, how in the world would you break it to your teachers? They are set in their ways and, actually, you've praised most of them for the fine jobs they are doing. How can you tell them that they are going to have to learn to teach in a totally different way? Why, no district policy has ever required so drastic a change since you can remember! And as far as school regulations go, there is absolutely no reference to anything called "individualization." How would you start? What comes first? What should it look like when it is well done? You think you'll watch the others experiment and fall flat on their individual faces at reporting time. Besides, it will take years before they can reduce this to written guidelines that anyone could follow. You smile. Your retirement forms will be in process by then!

Role: compromiser

Ace Yourkall

You can see the merits of individualization, but you can also see the problems that can occur with changing rules, upsetting teachers and parents, and needing to alter your entire evaluation scheme. Of course, you wonder why teachers can't be more professional and adapt improved methods without being coerced into doing it. One would think that the professional organizations would devote some of their energies toward upgrading instructional practices!

Perhaps the way to start is to find out which teachers are willing to experiment and which ones might need just a little encouragement. There are a few that you will absolutely not approach on the subject of changing; you're glad they are functioning at all! There are a few others who ought to watch the process before they begin to consider a transition. Still, several are really up-to-date people and might welcome an opportunity in which to try some interesting strategies.

You consider suggesting a voluntary workshop for interested staff and permitting those who are won over to move as far as they can. To avoid community conflict, you'll explain the developing program to parents and permit options as to the placement of their youngsters.

You grin. You have a great idea! You're going to establish an "ombudsman hour." Any teacher or parent who is having a problem with a selected child may come to you during that hour to work out a suitable compromise. In that way, you'll be aware of how the new system is progressing and how the faculty and the community are receiving it.

Role: autocrat

Merit Myway

Why is this district wasting time on workshops? Our teachers are supposed to be professionals—and we pay them as if they were nationally recognized experts! More than half of them are earning over $20,000 right now! We should mandate that an individualized program be in operation in every building by next January! Your staff will individualize or they'll be looking for jobs in other districts!—tenure or not! There are ways to deal with those who don't cooperate!

In fact, you'll distribute a notice to that effect this summer! If they need extra training they can read the Dunns' most recent book or meet after school and help each other! That's what they're paid for!

Furthermore, you want to see the results! If the teachers diagnose accurately and then prescribe on the basis of that diagnosis, the kids ought to achieve more academically than they did in previous years. You'll use each student's baseline data as a means for comparing his own growth! No, your teachers are not going to decide whether or not they *want* to individualize; they are going to do what's best for their students!

Role: country club manager

Noble Goodness

Life is so short. Why do Dan and Merit keep urging more and more change? Your teachers are not going to be happy about having to attend the workshops those two are planning. And if they become irritated again, this year's negotiations will be extremely difficult. Moreover, if they are not happy, there's certainly going to be negative carryover into their classrooms!

Well, you're not going to make any decisions until your staff has had a chance to discuss this matter. Then you'll hold a vote on it. You chuckle, realizing that it will take months to even set up a planning session. Once they divide the tasks into committees, the problem can go unresolved ad infinitum.

You suddenly feel yourself becoming angry. The kids appear to be content. The parents have been quiet and off your back for the first time in years. You might have had a relaxing, easy year except for this new, big push for individualization. Central Office forgets that teachers are individuals too, and that their professional organizations use any issue to stir up a frenzy!

No, sir! You are going to have a pleasant group of teachers this year! You are not going to get them all upset. Besides, how does anyone know that individualization is any better than what the staff is doing right now?

You are not going to confront your colleagues. You will smile, nod your head, give the impression that you are sympathetic and supportive, and keep right on doing exactly what you've been doing in the past—and let your teachers do the same. You'll give each of them the option of doing his own thing. In effect, isn't that individualization in a way?

NOTES FOR CHAPTER 1

1. Felix M. Lapez. "The Making of a Manager." AMA (1970): 69-71.
2. "The Making of a Manager."
3. R. Alec Mackenzie. *Notebook Materials.* New York: Institute of Leadership (1972).
4. Abraham Maslow. *Motivation and Personality.* New York: Harper (1954).
5. Abraham Maslow. *Toward a Psychology of Being.* Princeton, New Jersey: D. Van Nostrand Company, Inc. (1962): 23-24.
6. R. R. Blake and J. S. Mouton. *The Managerial Grid.* Houston, TX: Gulf Publishing Company (1964).
7. *The Managerial Grid* (film), Extension Media Center, University of California (1963).
8. Leo B. Moore. "How to Manage Improvement." *How Successful Executives Handle People: 12 Studies on Communication and Management Skills.* Boston: Harvard Business Review (1951-1960): 111-112.

2

DESIGNING AN EFFECTIVE PROGRAM TO EMPLOY THE STAFF YOU NEED

RECRUITING BETTER CANDIDATES

The great turnaround in staff supply that began in 1968 does not guarantee an abundance of quality candidates for the few teaching positions available. Surplus teachers may not have the desired training, teaching ability, positive characteristics, professional growth patterns, or the appropriate match of skills and attitudes needed by your school.

Finding and employing excellent candidates is further complicated by economic pressures to employ beginning, low-salaried teachers. Even these opportunities are limited because of a declining birthrate and a decreasing school population. The net result is a rapidly expanding number of applicants that drastically increases the workload of the personnel office without guaranteeing the superior faculty you seek.

There are several approaches that can be adopted to develop effective procedures for employing staff who match your school's program needs. These methods have evolved from former patterns of recruitment but their important aspects include motivational incentives and wider involvement to increase your chances for success!

FERTILIZING THE GRAPEVINE

The grapevine often has been one of the most productive means of seeking and finding capable or outstanding faculty. Posting staff needs in faculty rooms (see Figure 2-1), telling the very best teachers, and involving grade and department chairmen will pay dividends because sharing responsibility for the development of a fine staff with co-workers will naturally raise their level of concern and expectation. Faculty who become recruiting partners will bend every effort to locate future colleagues who will be a

Figure 2-1

School District Notice of Vacancies

TO: Professional Staff

FROM: Personnel Services

DATE: April 10, 19__

SUBJECT: *VACANCIES IN OUR SCHOOL DISTRICT*

ELEMENTARY

Kindergarten—1/2 Time

Instrumental Music—1/2 Time (1 Year Replacement)

Vocal Music—1/2 Time

For information or applications, please contact Personnel Services, Extension 205/210.

PLEASE POST UNTIL APRIL 18, 19__

credit to the school and a positive reflection of their efforts. Conversely, good teachers are not likely to recommend mediocre, inferior or problem teachers because of an increased sense of personal responsibility and the negative reactions that their poor suggestions would generate. Finally, the sense of trust bestowed on the staff recruiters will build professionalism and responsibility.

OVERCOMING RESISTANCE TO STAFF INVOLVEMENT

Some administrators resist the grapevine because they fear the recruiting of new faculty with attitudes that might parallel those of staff who had caused problems in the past. In this regard, collaborative staff-administrative management must be fostered as an attitude, and should then become a daily reality. A beginning can be made through the joint staff-administrative development of criteria and incentives for successful recruiting. For example, the payment of tuition for college courses, fees for inservice programs, or expenses for appropriate conferences could be some of the search rewards offered the teacher whose candidate is selected. An additional award should be considered for the continuing success of the employee so recommended and hired. Indeed, this indirect approach to merit compensation may be the only one acceptable to faculty.

USING UNUSED SOURCES

An often neglected resource is the community itself. Various organized groups and individuals such as the P.T.A., Rotary, Chamber of Commerce, Town Club, and former employees who have left teaching for industry or through retirement should be informed of openings and their suggestions solicited. Even newly arrived residents might well know of outstanding teachers who might consider moving to your school district.

Again, trust and mutual respect must be established to avoid suspicions of recommendations based only on friendships, "axes to grind," etc. Sound criteria and an interview process controlled by the staff and administration in the final selection process should diminish the potential for conflict.

COPING WITH THE USUAL PLACEMENT SERVICES

University placement offices, newspaper advertisements, employment agencies, and convention, campus, or hotel headquarters interviews have, in recent years, provided more applicants than ever before. The problem, of course, is the relatively small percentage of candidates who match your specific needs.

One technique to reduce endless screening is the careful specification of faculty needs, qualities sought, and the range of experience, abilities, and other characteristics considered necessary for personnel applying to the employing department of the school. Instead of itemizing *minimal* requirements in communications announcing a vacancy, indicate *desired* requirements. Describe the position in terms of the way it would be filled by an *outstanding* professional person. Do not be concerned about the teachers who do not apply because of a lack of confidence. Frequently when people are humble or insecure, they have every right to be! On the other hand, those who overrate themselves will be screened out through follow-up investigations.

A second approach involves the establishment of a personnel screening committee by staff, administration, and possibly community members to reduce long lists and folders to a manageable number of top-flight candidates. Many schools have utilized the building principal and appropriate staff members for this purpose. This suggestion has many advantages. Each principal should be recognized as the educational leader of the building and a faculty council or department group could share the professional responsibility and recognition for one of the most important tasks this administrator has. The results are likely to be better than when a single individual conducts the initial screening process.

ESTABLISHING PROCEDURES FOR RECRUITING

The days of the administrator who "could tell he was talking to a good teacher during a five-minute interview" have passed. No candidate could possibly demonstrate in a single interview the skills, knowledges, and attitudes that are requisites for the multifaceted role that teachers must occupy. Knowledge of teaching and learning has increased dramatically. A higher and higher percentage of students stay in school and all must be dealt with effectively. Economic and social pressures have escalated psychological problems and organizational conflict. Finally, parents and the media have evidenced mounting dissatisfaction with the schools, educational expenditures, and taxes.[1] These groups are becoming increasingly vocal in their appraisals of teachers and the principal is likely to be evaluated, in the near future, on the basis of his selections and evaluations of staff members. Therefore, one of the most important tasks the administrator of today faces is the development and effective use of focused criteria in the selection of staff. In view of increasing citizen scrutiny among city, suburban, and rural sections of the country, department chairmen, supervisors, principals, and superintendents will want to become directly involved in recruitment so that they may select the teachers for whom they may be responsible. While it is not possible to find teachers who match every program need or every evolving personality characteristic of growing and changing students, a more scientific management approach is essential; the use of a basically intuitive selection approach can be damaging to the quality of the school.

DEVELOPING CRITERIA FOR SCREENING AND SELECTION

The direct involvement of faculty councils, administrative teams, citizens, and student representatives should aid in building commitment to the criteria that are cooperatively developed for the selection of staff. In this regard, a limited but representative committee of five to eight members is likely to develop a set of practical and effective personnel characteristics.

A developmental outcome of this approach, of course, is ultimate strong and positive support of and assistance to the selected candidates by those who participated in their selection. Conversely, hiring mistakes are not attributed solely to the administrator, but rather are shared by the committee. Ultimately, the criteria and their interpretation become the logical focus of criticism. Because criteria can be improved, often more easily than overcoming human defense mechanisms, the committee can make collective judgments and can modify them. This approach eliminates the fear of failure often experienced by any single individual who traditionally bears the responsibility for recommendations. Freedom from fear for that individual, usually the building principal, allows him to exercise leadership that is strongly focused on the manager-collaborator role in building a fine staff.

During initial work sessions, the principal, or other group administrator to whom the authority has been delegated, should develop, perhaps through brainstorming,[2] a series of identified personnel needs that are crucial to the individual school at that point in time. The needs list should then be analyzed so that the ways in which each of the necessary characteristics may be recognized easily are identifiable. These characteristics, whether they be specific teacher skills, knowledges, experiences, or attitudes, then become the criteria that the committee will seek when studying applicants' credentials. These general criteria therefore become standardized but kept flexible for specific hiring situations.

One focus of an initial brainstorming-identification meeting would be a work session to state and to analyze necessary criteria. The objective of the first series of meetings, in this case, would be the modification and adaptation of the developing list to the local situation and examination of incoming credentials to identify the relationship between what is needed and what is available. Finally, the definitions of criteria and the procedures to be followed should be determined to implement an improved selection program.

One model set of criteria and the questions and related procedures to be considered follow.

1. Knowledge of Content to Be Taught

Certification standards, completed college courses and grades, the comparative quality of the preparatory colleges, and the answers to a few interview questions about content are insufficient in determining a candidate's knowledge of subject area(s).

If you insist on strong scholarship, investigate in depth:

a. Ask to see college themes, papers, portfolios, or other work developed by each candidate in his/her studies.
b. Discuss the candidate's depth of knowledge, intelligence, and ability to analyze and apply subject content with his/her major professors by telephone, if possible, or by mail if direct voice communication is impractical.
c. Design observation sessions with specific objectives embracing content preparation and presentation. Expect variations, of course, depending upon his or her experience as a traditional, transitional, or individualizing teacher and length of service in the profession.
d. If the vacant position is at the secondary level, arrange for a joint interview with the Department Chairman and the best scholars on your staff in that field. Invite or employ a local first-rate university professor in the particular subject to assist in the interview. You might also be able to obtain local citizen volunteers who are scholarly and work in the same area to participate in an interview session or two.
e. Follow a similar pattern for key elementary subject areas, especially reading, mathematics, the social sciences, and general science.

Obviously, the degree of specialization required, the type of organizational pattern in which the open position exists, and the amount of teaming that is necessary in your school will determine the number and depth of content areas to be investigated.

2. Ability to Teach

Aiding Students to Progress Academically
and to
Achieve Suitable Personal and School Objectives

As with knowledge of content, the usual references, placement folders, and perfunctory interviews are not adequate to assess the candidate's ability to teach or his professional potential. There are several practices, however, that will improve your chances of employing staff that will be successful in your school:

(a) Send a team of two or three teachers, a supervisor or department chairman, the principal, a student, and possibly a parent to spend a day or two at the school where the candidate is currently employed or is in training as a student teacher or intern.

Obviously, the team will vary depending upon the willingness of the employing district staff and the candidate to accept a multiple team including some nonprofessionals. Also, the exact role of each participant should be clearly defined. For example, a parent might be valuable as an observer of interpersonal relationships evidenced between the candidate and his students but not as part of an instructional evaluating team.

Whatever the final makeup of the group, be certain that it meets a sufficient number of times to adequately: (1) identify specific strengths central to the position that is open, e.g., individualization techniques, instructional management skills, creative abilities to develop resources, etc., (2) train in the use of selected observation or interview instruments,[3] and (3) prepare appropriate questions. Students at the candidate's school and his colleagues and administrators may reveal a great deal about the applicant through their answers, facial expressions, body language, and other nonverbal communication.

(b) Invite the candidate to do some demonstration teaching in your school and to spend a day or two talking to teachers, students, and staff members. Again, follow a teamed approach for an assessment of his stay with you.

You should develop a set of employment criteria with the teachers at the grade level or in the department where the vacancy exists. Preliminary questions should be developed with the staff. Those teachers who assist you directly should discuss the needs of the school, the type of program, the kinds of students, and other matters upon which to base a careful assessment of the qualifications for this position. Both formal and informal questions and criteria, such as those described elsewhere in this chapter (see Figures 2-2 and 2-3), should be developed with the staff serving as part of the selection team. It is essential that the team meet with you before, during, and after the candidate's visit to your school.

(c) If it is possible, question the applicant's references who have known him for three or more years and who may have observed him teaching and working with students.

Telephone calls and visits to the applicant's references are essential if an in-depth appraisal is to be achieved. Written evaluations are often too general and positive to permit meaningful differentiation among candidates. Moreover, questions and responses held at a personal level often will trigger new questions and explorations of the candidate's ability that are rarely revealed in a written evaluation. This approach has become more important than previously because of the new federal legislation, Public Law #93, which opens all public records, including heretofore privileged communications, to anyone's view unless a waiver has been signed. In this regard, many states have adopted "Sunshine Laws," the objective of which is to open all records to "the light of day." As a result, those who write recommendations in the future are likely to be extremely careful and general with respect to the references they write to prospective employers.

This procedure should be used to supplement the insights developed through visits and observations. After seeing the candidate teach, new questions undoubtedly will emerge for further investigation with colleagues, current and former principals, references, students, and others.

3. Ability to Team with the Staff and Administration

This potential area for a criterion statement should not be construed as a search for conformist, meek teachers who simply follow directives. To the contrary, employees who team well should be able to disagree and to suggest constructive alternatives. Decisions, once reached, of course, should be supported by all involved unless serious doubts remain in the minds of concerned individuals. If such a situation emerges, the decision should be upheld only when a tight evaluation design is incorporated into that aspect of the program on which agreement could not be reached. Objective outsiders should then assist in an evaluation of the program method or procedure and document the results or outcomes in a report to each team member.

In-depth research into the past behavior patterns of prospective employees is essential. Previous supervisors and colleagues may assist with valuable insights. Caution must be exercised though, because the information gained is only as good as its source. It is important, therefore, to assess the ability and objectivity of those supplying information and evaluations. If a well-respected, highly competent principal or colleague delivered a candid, balanced report of strengths, weaknesses, and potential; it would carry more weight, of course, than a guarded, negatively slanted report from a supervisor or teacher who tended to be psychologically threatened by a bright, action-oriented, innovative, or experimenting faculty member.

Another check on compatibility, in addition to asking questions of former associates, would be a series of informal meetings with appropriate prospective colleagues. This approach will offer several opportunities for unguarded interchange and insights to occur in ways that might not happen in the usual interview situation. Prior to such a meeting, urge the faculty to design questions that seek information about the candidate's background, reasons for wanting to change schools, major professional interests, etc. Caution them not to treat the candidate as a consultant. He should not be expected to supply answers that will cure the school's existing problems.

In all of these arranged meetings an objective perspective must be maintained by those with the final decision-making power. The specific qualities sought must be reviewed during the process to ensure the proper match and the right choice. For example, a "dynamic catalyst" might receive a cool reception from well-intentioned, effective traditional teachers, even though the change-agent type is exactly what the school, department, or grade needs. In fact, some teachers with exactly the characteristics that you, the administrator, know that the staff requires may momentarily become disconcerting to you. Objectivity is served by allowing emotional responses to disperse over a day or two and then to use wise sounding-board personnel to review the applicant's strengths, weaknesses, and perceptions.

SCREENING APPLICANTS TO IDENTIFY THE BEST PROSPECTIVE STAFF MEMBERS

Applicant forms (see Figure 2-4) and placement folders can afford an initial screening procedure, but another step will reduce the field of candidates to those among the very best. Develop a second-stage questionnaire for those applicants who meet the general qualifications through a review of the initial form. This second form should include questions designed to assess quality as measured against the school's stated standards and the itemized needs of the position.

The following questionnaire represents one model of a second-stage application form.

Figure 2-2

SCHOOL DISTRICT QUESTIONNAIRE FOR APPLICANTS

NAME OF CANDIDATE ____________________ DATE ____________________
POSITION SOUGHT ____________________ OVERALL RESPONSE __________

1. List the titles and authors of at least three books published within the past four or five years that have been concerned essentially with new trends, concepts, strategies, instructional techniques or findings in the teaching-learning field. Indicate two or three ideas that appealed to you and that you have adopted as part of your own teaching approach.

	TITLE	*AUTHOR*	*TEACHING IDEA ADOPTED*
1-a.	________	________	________________
1-b.	________	________	________________

1-c. ____________ ____________ ________________________

1-d. ____________ ____________ ________________________

2. Write the title, author, and a short paragraph that describes the essence of the contents of at least three noneducational books that you have read within the past three years. Explain how each has influenced your relationships with students or colleagues.

	TITLE	*AUTHOR*
2-a.	____________________	____________________
2-b.	____________________	____________________
2-c.	____________________	____________________

ANALYSIS AND INFLUENCE ON TEACHING

____________________ ____________________

____________________ ____________________

____________________ ____________________

____________________ ____________________

3. List and describe any new instructional or curriculum practices that you have learned and introduced into your teaching repertoire within the past two years

	TECHNIQUE	*DESCRIPTION*
3-a.	____________________	____________________
	____________________	____________________
3-b.	____________________	____________________
	____________________	____________________
3-c.	____________________	____________________
	____________________	____________________

4. List the names and locations of any schools you have visited and observed in during the past two or three years where you learned something new that you incorporated into your teaching practices. Name and describe those techniques.

	NAME OF SCHOOL	*LOCATION*
4-a.	____________________	____________________
4-b.	____________________	____________________
4-c.	____________________	____________________

	TECHNIQUES' NAMES	*DESCRIPTIONS*
4-d.	________________	________________
	________________	________________
	________________	________________

5. Describe at least one innovative practice that you learned from a colleague and then introduced into your own classroom during the past two or three years.

6. Describe at least one innovative technique that you taught to a colleague during the past two or three years.

7. Explain how you successfully modified or adapted a new technique you had read or heard about or saw during the past two or three years.

8. On a scale from one to six (one being the highest ability to change, greatest flexibility, etc., and six representing a lack of ability to change), estimate your own ability to grow and to increase your professional skills and knowledge.

   8-a. *CHANGE ORIENTATION* *STABILITY ORIENTATION*
   Circle one 1 2 3 4 5 6

   8-b. List specific evidence to support your rating of yourself. For example, which teaching techniques have you abandoned during the past two or three years because you have found them inadequate or unacceptable? Another example would be a listing of unusual, noneducational places you have visited to gain and use new ideas for teaching.

9. List at least three professional magazines to which you currently subscribe or which you read on a regular basis.

   9-a.________________________________

   9-b.________________________________

   9-c.________________________________

10. Explain "individualization of instruction" in a paragraph or two. How does it differ from a traditional program?

11. What is your concept and opinion of an open classroom?

12. Write a short description of the ability level, learning style, interests, talents, study habits, etc. of a typical youngster in the grade, or subject(s) for which you are being considered as a teacher.

    12-a. DESCRIPTION OF YOUNGSTER

    12-b. Write four or five instructional or behavioral objectives that should be completed by this student during the first three or four weeks of the term.

    1. ______________________________
    2. ______________________________
    3. ______________________________
    4. ______________________________
    5. ______________________________

    12-c. List several alternative, multisensory resources that you would suggest this youngster use to achieve the objectives you designed.

    1. ______________________________
    2. ______________________________
    3. ______________________________

    12-d. Develop a short test you would use to determine the degree to which this youngster has mastered these objectives.

13-a. Identify the group of instructional techniques—A, B, or C—that most closely matches your own classroom practices.

13-b. Rate the instructional techniques listed under groups A, B, and C in order of effectiveness from 1 to 6 in each group with one (1) being the best. Briefly indicate why you placed each set in the order you selected.

13-c. Select six of the 18 techniques listed under the groups that you would use most frequently if you could design an ideal learning program for your students. Briefly explain why you selected each one.

	13-a.	13-b. ORDER	EXPLANATION
GROUP A			
• Lectures	☐	______	
• Films or filmstrips		______	
• Discussions (question-and-answer sessions)		______	
• Research assignments		______	
• Class trips		______	
• Homework assignments		______	
GROUP B			
• Large-, small- and medium-sized group instruction	☐	______	
• Committee projects		______	
• Learning stations, interest centers, and/or other instructional areas		______	
• Task cards		______	
• Self-paced materials		______	
• Student-selected activities		______	
GROUP C			
• Contracts, LAPS, or other individualized prescriptions	☐	______	
• Instructional packages		______	
• Multisensory resources		______	
• Self-evaluation assessments		______	
• Programmed learning materials		______	
• Independent study		______	

13-c.	*TECHNIQUES PREFERRED*	*REASON*
1	____________________	
2	____________________	
3	____________________	
4	____________________	
5	____________________	
6	____________________	

It may not be necessary to require an answer to every question in the above model. Conversely, you may wish to add questions or situations to gain a profile easier to evaluate for the specific position. An organized questionnaire designed to elicit in-depth responses, like the one suggested, will certainly improve the likelihood of finding the right applicants for the vacancy available. A bonus will be an early assessment of the attitudes and abilities of the new professional employee.

In evaluating the responses to these questions, the following guidelines are suggested:

Where the teacher candidate is requested to indicate the books or magazines he or she has read, the practices and instructional techniques he has observed and/or adopted, and the schools he has visited, answers will vary extensively among candidates. What is important is that the candidate has read or visited or, minimally, can verify awareness of current professional literature and the major concepts and practices described.

Some teachers will have to omit responses to these questions for they may not have read, adopted, and/or visited at all. Others will provide many sources of readings, observations, and creative efforts. Teachers who are aware of the books in their fields and the innovations that are emerging are more likely to be knowledgeable than those who cannot supply answers to such questions. Responses indicating that specific practices have been used and/or taught to someone else suggest a high degree of professionalism. Responses revealing that selected practices have been modified or improved to fit a local situation suggest teacher creativity. (See questions 1 through 7 and 9.)

Questions referring to the teacher's ability to grow professionally and to change should yield information concerning the candidate's perceptions of his or her ability to respond to the requirements of the vacancy that exists in your school. In addition, where the candidate is asked to cite evidence that verifies his self-perceptions, you will have access to two other important qualities—his ability to engage in self-assessment and to respond accurately and openly to specific questions. The statements may be verified or explored either on the telephone or in writing with the people who are listed as references. (See questions 8a and 8b.)

Questions concerned with individualization of instruction, traditional programs, open classrooms, alternative approaches, and learning styles will reveal knowledge of current trends and the applicant's attitude toward them. The answers may be compared with the descriptions of these concepts provided in chapter 3. (See questions 10, 11, and 12.)

Responses to question 12a will aid you in evaluating the candidate's understanding of the general nature of the age level youngster that he or she would be teaching. A superior applicant will describe some of the differences and exceptions that are likely to be found in the peer group.

Question 12b demonstrates a teacher's ability to convey to students exactly what must be learned and how they may demonstrate that it has been achieved. It also provides some insight into the teacher's knowledge of curriculum appropriate to the age and/or level being considered.

Question 12c, referring to "multisensory resources" is concerned with two items: Does the applicant show familiarity with appropriate learning resources in the area in which he or she will be teaching? Is he or she aware that some students learn through the auditory sense whereas others rely on the visual, or the tactual or the kinesthetic? Therefore, are records, films, filmstrips, tapes, games, packages, and learning kits suggested *in addition* to books or magazines?

Question 12d merely demonstrates that the prospective teacher understands how to develop appropriate test questions related to the objectives that have been assigned.

The answers to questions 13a, b, and c will reveal the candidate's preferred teaching style and depth of knowledge of a variety of instructional techniques. These responses will aid you in matching the skills of the teacher with the learning needs of your students. (See chapter 3.)

An alternative second- or third-stage interview is suggested by the questions enumerated in Figure 2-3 and is appropriate for use with the candidate whose resume appears to match either your program or school needs.

Figure 2-3

SCHOOL DISTRICT INTERVIEW FORM

NAME OF CANDIDATE ______________________ DATE ______________________

POSITION SOUGHT ______________________ OVERALL POTENTIAL ______________________

QUESTION	*PURPOSE—TO IDENTIFY:*	*RESPONSE*	*RATING OR COMMENT*
1) Of which teaching achievement during the past two or three years are you most proud?	Personal pride Self-image Relative worth of achievement		
2) What has been your greatest difficulty in the teaching-learning situation?	Honesty Objectivity Insight Growth needs Importance of gap		
3) What special talents do you have that make you a good teacher?	Enthusiasm Objectivity Talents and skills		
4) How do you know that the children you teach are learning?	Ability to evaluate Sense of the teaching-learning process		
5) What are some of the things you do to achieve rapport with different kinds of students?	Attitude toward children Viability of approaches Ability to diagnose Different response patterns		
6) What would you do with a parent who storms into school one day after hours demanding that his/her:			

Situation	Traits
a) youngster's grade be changed? b) child be transferred? c) youngster be given special assignments because he's "so far ahead" of his classmates? d) child's previously diagnosed learning disability in visual memory retention be remediated immediately by you on a one-to-one basis?	Ability to cope with different types of of parental demands Attitudes toward trends of increasing parental involvement and pressure Sense of humor Sense of reality Ability to provide viable alternatives Ability to modify negative situations toward positive outcomes
7) One of your colleagues who receives many of your students the year after you teach them complains habitually and bitterly about the quality of instruction in your class and the resultant inferior preparation of the youngsters sent to him/her. What would you do?	Ability to cope Attitudes toward staff relationships Strength of purpose Sense of self-worth
8) Your principal seems to give unwanted chores to quiet, uncomplaining staff members. The more aggressive personality types get the best schedules and work assignments. What would you do?	Ability to resolve staff-staff and staff-administrator problems Objectivity Ability to analyze Attitudes toward difficult work
9) Discipline is getting out of hand and every teacher in your wing (on your floor, level) seems to be going it alone by closing his/her door to the outside turmoil. What would you do?	Attitude toward staff teamwork Sense of responsibility Ability to solve problems Ability to provide viable alternatives

QUESTION	PURPOSE—TO IDENTIFY:	RESPONSE	RATING OR COMMENT
10) You have moved ahead of all your colleagues in a particular field such as individualization of instruction. You sense resentment from some staff members and even have been the victim of some minor sabotage ("misplaced sets of objectives"). What would you do?	Attitude toward colleagues Strength of purpose Self-image Tolerance Persistence		
11) Here are two (or three) well-known texts and two (or three) reference books in your field. What are your key objectives in the teaching of __________? How would you describe the approach of each of these texts and references? How would you rate them in their ability to meet your objectives and why?	Content knowledge Worthiness of objectives Knowledge and appropriateness of resources Ability to analyze, apply, and evaluate		
12) This is an analysis prepared by the department chairman in the field in which you are seeking a position. It is intended to clarify a rather subtle aspect of______ and to suggest ways to teach this rather difficult point. Please challenge or support the analysis. How would you teach this concept?	Knowledge of subject Ability to analyze Ability to design Teaching approaches		
13) Alternate question or mini-case situation.	Specific insight		
14) Do you have any questions or comments about the position, the school, or the community?	Ability to focus on important issues or relevant areas		

The following application (Figure 2-4) is one form that includes two vital questions that should be posed to all prospective employees: (1) Would it be possible to observe you at your present job? and (2) Would you be willing to teach a demonstration class in this district? Without affirmative answers to both, an administrator would be wise to avoid any commitment to the applicant.

Figure 2-4

NAME

AND ADDRESS

OF SCHOOL

FOR OFFICE USE ONLY			
L/G/S____			
Rec'd. _/_/_	Sent to: ____		
Intv'd. ____ _/_/_		____	_/_/_
by ____ _/_/_		____	_/_/_
Emp.	Step	Sch.	Sal.
Emp. ____	Step ____	Sch. ____	Sal. ____
Cert. ____	Ref. ____	Trnsc. ____	Bd. App. _/_/_
Notf'd. / /		Accept'd / /	

APPLICATION FOR PROFESSIONAL POSITION
(Please type or print in black ink)

Dr. Mrs.
Mr. Miss ________________ Date _/_/_
(LAST NAME) (FIRST) (INITIAL OR MAIDEN NAME)

Home Address ________________ Phone ( ) ____
(STREET) (TOWN OR CITY) (STATE) (ZIP)

Business Address ________________ Phone ( ) ____

Marital status ____ Spouse's name ____ Ages of children ____
Present occupation ____ Salary ____ NYS Ret. # ____
Date of Birth ____ Height ____ Weight ____ Soc. Sec. # ____

Level/Grade/Subject preference ____
Available date _/_/_/_ Would it be possible to observe you at your present job? ____

Would you be willing to teach a demonstration class in ______________? ______________

Extracurricular activities you will be willing and qualified to sponsor: ______________

May we contact your present employer? ______________ How did you hear about ______________? ______________

Certification: Kind of Certificate	Date	Issued by	Expires	Subjects & Grades

References: Name	Position	Address	Phone
			( )
			( )
			( )

EDUCATIONAL AND PROFESSIONAL TRAINING:

List high school, college and university in chronological order (include documented inservice, travel, and experience approved for salary credit by previous school employer).

Name & location of Institution	Degrees & dates received	Dates from-to	Number of semester credit hours	Areas of Specialization	**Please leave blank**
				TOTAL CREDITS	

EXPERIENCE IN TEACHING and/or EDUCATIONAL ADMINISTRATION (begin with most recent position) (fulltime employment in day school).

Name and address of school	Position grade or subject	Dates from-to	Identify work on curriculum studies or special projects	**Please leave blank**

OTHER TEACHING EXPERIENCE (day-to-day substitute, part-time, evening).

Name and address of school	Position grade or subject	Dates from-to	Identify work on curriculum studies or special projects	

MILITARY SERVICE (refers to active duty)

Branch of service	Dates from-to	Nature of assignment	

BUSINESS EMPLOYMENT OR OTHER OCCUPATION

Name and address of employer	Dates from-to	Nature of position	
		TOTAL STEPS	

Please return this form to:

Placement papers may be obtained from:

(INSTITUTION)

(ADDRESS)

(   )
(PHONE)

(SIGNATURE OF APPLICANT) (DATE)

Too often, administrators make errors in selection. Teachers will sometimes apply to a district whose philosophy, goals, community expectations, and student attitudes may not match theirs, and may still be employed. Rigorous recruiting, screening, interviewing, and selection processes, including the use of planned procedures and the involvement of appropriate staff members and supervisors, will decrease the chances of a mismatch. Both employer and prospective employee will have a comprehensive profile of each other. The prognosis for success is enhanced.

NOTES FOR CHAPTER 2

1. Kevin Ryan and James M. Cooper. *Those Who Can, Teach.* Boston: Houghton Mifflin (1975): 337, 351; Neil Postman and Charles Weingartner. *The School Book.* New York: Delacorte Press (1973): 73-74; Norman E. Hankins. *Psychology for Contemporary Education.* Columbus, Ohio: Charles E. Merrill (1973): 2-4.
2. Rita Dunn and Kenneth Dunn. *Practical Approaches to Individualizing Instruction.* West Nyack, New York: Parker Publishing Company, Inc. (1972): 191-207; G. Ray Muggrave. *Individualized Instruction: Teaching Strategies Focusing on the Learner.* Boston: Allyn and Bacon (1975): 21-27.
3. Rita Dunn and Kenneth Dunn. *Educator's Self-Teaching Guide to Individualizing Instructional Programs.* West Nyack, New York: Parker Publishing Company, Inc. (1975): 227-266; Charles W. Beegle and Richard M. Brandt. *Observational Methods in the Classroom.* Washington, D.C.: Association for Supervision and Curriculum Development (1973).

3

INCREASING FACULTY MOTIVATION AND SKILL

UNDERSTANDING BASIC STAFF MOTIVATION

"Think back about your professional life over the past year or so. What is the one thing of which you are most proud for that period of time? Now, what is the one thing in your job or career about which you are least happy?"

These are the types of questions that Herzberg repeatedly asked of employees and executives at all levels. The results confirmed his basic insights that job satisfaction and job dissatisfaction are not opposites; they are completely separate factors, like seeing and hearing.[1]

In other words, the reverse of things that tend to make people unhappy in their jobs do not necessarily make them happy! An obvious example would be a salary increase to a worker who is unhappy with his income. The raise is soon forgotten; indeed the next salary level is yearned for. An achievement by that teacher is likely to have a more lasting effect than increased income on his attitude and happiness.

The authors have posed the aforementioned questions to hundreds of teachers and principals. The results invariably supported Herzberg's thesis that the factors which make people happy are related to what they *do* and *achieve*—the job content and personal accomplishment or growth. What makes them unhappy, on the other hand, are factors related to the *situation* in which workers do their job—working conditions, job environment, and context. "What makes people happy is what they do or the way they're utilized, and what makes them unhappy is the way they're treated."[2]

The following are typical responses of teachers and administrators to the two basic questions cited above.

List the Thing You Are Most Proud of or Happy About in Your Job

- I instituted a new program in science.
- I improved staff-administration relationships.
- I changed my style of teaching—I began to individualize.
- I started a program of personal objectives and achieved every one!
- I wrote separate contracts for eight students, and they learned!
- I was given responsibility for planning this workshop, and it is rated tops by the participants.

List the Thing You Are Least Happy About in Your Job

- I was passed over for the principalship.
- We're required to write reports, reports, meaningless reports! No one reads them or uses the data or follows the recommendations.
- My salary—they've changed the formula to hold us down!
- The administration changed signals and announced the program revision as a final decision.
- My efforts are fragmented. I can't focus on a single task and get the time and support to complete one assignment well.

To make your staff aware of those factors that actually motivate them, try posing the above two questions at a faculty meeting. Participants at the session immediately will become interested in this shift in focus away from long lists of "administrivia" and how their job situation blocks them from growing and doing toward how they feel about their jobs and how they might function better.

BUILDING JOB SATISFACTION—ELIMINATING JOB DISSATISFACTION

Robert Ford applied Herzberg's theory to his work with the American Telephone and Telegraph Company and reported the results in a fine book on job enrichment.[3]

Ford found that the many usual attempts of companies to make employees feel better about their jobs or employers did not result in increased productivity, improved quality, lower turnover, better morale, or reduced costs. Ineffective attempts to build job satisfaction included each of the following:

- Reduced hours and longer vacations
- Increased wages
- Benefit packages
- Profit sharing
- Off-hours programs

- Better training of supervisors in:
  - Human relations skills
  - Sensitivity toward others
  - Art of leadership
  - Work analysis, planning and control
- Increased employee communication
  - One-way (company magazines, booklets, movies)
  - Two-way (attitude surveys, discussion groups)
- Employee counseling services
- Job participation
- Organizational planning[4]

Unfortunately, situational factors have not motivated people either; thirty-five years of effort in this regard have revealed effects of only short duration and have succeeded solely in establishing minimum job acceptability standards rather than productivity standards!

The translation of these findings from industry to school systems and the classroom is direct and obvious. The impact of increases in salary and benefits to teachers or administrators after contract negotiations last about two weeks! Then, as all workers do, eyes and emotions turn up to the next level or contract demand. Maintenance factors are not the basic cause of satisfaction. In fact, these "hygiene" items, e.g., policies, rules, administration, supervision, working conditions, and salaries or fringe benefits, often cause feelings of *dissatisfaction*.

Things that cause employees to become satisfied, on the other hand, deal with:

- Actual employee achievements
- The recognition received for that achievement (not to be confused with recognition as a human relations gesture)
- Opportunities for increasing knowledge of and capability at a task
- Available opportunities for advancement[5]

The application of job satisfiers to faculties of school systems are suggested in this chart:

Motivators (Long-Range Satisfiers)	*Suggested Techniques*
Responsibility and personal achievement	Allow innovative approaches without direct supervisory control (but with accountability), e.g. nonsequential teaching, alternative program designs, independent study assignments, etc.

Motivators (Long-Range Satisfiers)	*Suggested Techniques*
Responsibility and recognition	Increase each teacher's accountability for his or her own work through the use of written self-evaluations and self-establishment of measurable objectives and other types of goals to be assessed by him or her at specific checkpoints during the year.
Responsibility, recognition, and achievement	Give a teacher or team of teachers total responsibility for a group of students, a unit of work, interdisciplinary curriculum development or module design, etc. If achievement is evident, increase the amount of responsibility and broaden the areas in which teacher judgment is sufficient for the decision-making process. Give additional authority (with accountability) to teachers to make decisions on programs, courses, techniques, or recommendations.
Internal recognition	Institute a system of periodic reporting concerning test results, student growth, parent satisfactions, outside praise, etc. and have these sent directly to the teacher rather than to the principal, department chairman, or other supervisor.
Growth and learning	Introduce, suggest, or assign new and more difficult tasks such as individualizing instruction, or designing studies for the gifted and/or learning disabled to be developed, implemented, and reported on by an individual teacher or group.
Responsibility, growth, and advancement	Identify teachers with specific strengths and assign them as consultants, liaison persons, visitors to other projects or schools, or as interns, trainees, or assistants with responsibility to learn and to help others.

Increasing the availability of long-range motivators should be accompanied by the removal of dissatisfiers such as poor policies, poor supervisory practices, poor salaries, and undesirable working conditions. Lists of such items can be long but brainstorming with the faculty will reveal the most serious ones rather quickly. These might include overcrowding, lack of space, lack of consistent rules for discipline, insufficient funds for supplies, no home base for roaming teachers, etc.

Remember, the removal of these problems will not compensate for boring or static jobs without growth, recognition, achievement, responsibility, and advancement.

Tennis as an Example of the Task Itself

The tennis player often is motivated to play repeatedly because of a great backhand passing shot he achieved or a good serve or a great "get." It is the chance for *achievement* that drives him back to compete against himself. The *responsibility* is the player's; he seeks the *opportunity to grow* to the limits of his ability. His successes bring instant *internal* and *external recognition.* His standards are internalized and he comes back week after week (or more often) because he is interested in the *task itself.*

He may become unhappy with the poor state of the clay on the court, the taped lines, the unreasonable club rules, the lack of screening, the manners of the other players, i.e., the *situational* conditions, the *dissatisfiers.* But he works at removing those with the officials in charge and keeps returning to play tennis because of the motivation within the task.

Administrators should work at providing similar long-range motivators for their staffs. These are some basic questions that you might consider:

- What objectives can I set jointly with this teacher?
- What goals am I willing to let him set by himself?
- What advanced training or skill could he or she absorb and benefit from at this time?
- Is there anything that he is required to do that could be given to an aide or secretary?
- Can anything he does be automated out of his task?
- What advanced job or task could he work toward? How can I help him?
- What is being done for him that he can do for himself?
- Can his assignment be combined with another he would like?
- Is he responsible for any total unit, module, or program?
- What thinking can he do for himself? What authority should be given him so that he may better fulfill his responsibilities?

APPRAISING FACULTY TEACHING STYLES

Identifying potential areas of growth and long-range motivators should begin with an appraisal of each individual faculty member's teaching style. Teachers should aid you in completing the instrument included later in this section.

There are nine major elements that comprise a person's teaching style. These include each of the following.

1. Instructional Planning

Instructional planning encompasses the diagnosis, learning prescriptions, and evaluations completed for each student or group of students. Knowledge of each student's ability, learning style, interests, skill development, ability to retain information, concept formation, etc., is essential to the diagnosis. The prescription includes the design and/or use of objectives, materials, techniques, and multisensory learning activities at various levels. Evaluation encompasses pretesting, student self-assessment, and teacher assessment based on the original objectives established for each student.

2. Teaching Methods

Teaching methods usually refers to the instructor's behavior in the learning environment—the way he or she groups students for learning, designs and/or assigns resources, uses interaction techniques with students, and employs basic approaches to the teaching and learning of each student. Since the advent of individualization strategies, teaching methods also applies to the specific materials through which youngsters may achieve independently, such as contracts, instructional packages, or programmed learning.

3. Student Groupings

Student grouping is defined as the way a teacher assigns or permits learning to occur through small groups, pairs, individuals, large groups, varied groupings, or through one-to-one tutoring. Because different youngsters respond to varied sociological interactions, a teacher should have "at her fingertips" a series of alternative grouping strategies that provide a wide range of interesting activities.

4. Room Design

Room design reflects the ways in which the teacher divides, decorates, and designs learning spaces or areas to match the learning needs of his or her students. The various types of furniture arrangements, alcoves, "offices," work areas, etc., and how they comprise the instructional environment are included in this element.

5. Teaching Environment

The teaching environment includes time schedules, the different types of instructional stations and centers, the optional learning activities that are available, and provisions that are made for mobility, multilevel resources, and nutritional intake.

6. Evaluation Techniques

Evaluation techniques encompass the methods used by the teacher to assess the progress of individual students. Testing, observations, performance assessments, and self-evaluation are part of the assessment of each student.

7. Educational Philosophy

Educational philosophy refers to the attitudes a teacher holds toward key program descriptions, such as open education, a student-centered curriculum, a basic skills approach, etc.

8. Teaching Characteristics

Teaching characteristics are defined as the values and standards a teacher holds and the operational approaches used to transmit those values and standards. The degree of flexibility, the importance of what is learned, and the amount of direction given to students are examples of teaching characteristics.

9. Student Preference

Student preference describes the types of youngsters whom the teacher prefers to have as students. Characteristics of students are itemized, such as the gifted, the learning-impaired, the motivated, the nonachieving, etc., to permit easy identification.

The following instrument may be used to reveal each faculty member's actual teaching style at the time it is administered and should serve as the first step toward the eventual matching of teachers and students.

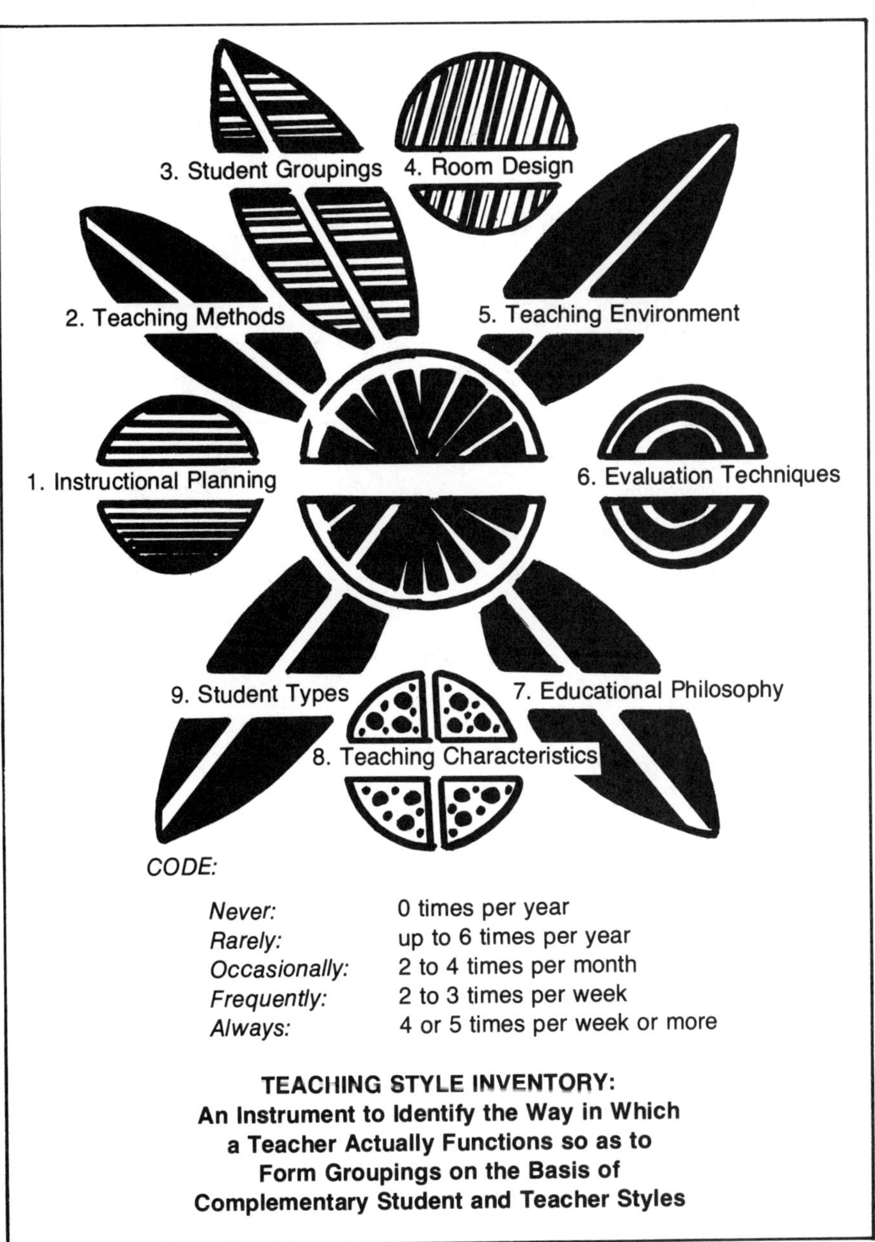

TEACHING STYLE INVENTORY:
An Instrument to Identify the Way in Which a Teacher Actually Functions so as to Form Groupings on the Basis of Complementary Student and Teacher Styles

Figure 3-1

Figure 3-2

Question I: *Instructional Planning*

Directions:

Circle the number that best describes how often you use each of the following planning techniques.

	Never	Rarely	Occasionally	Frequently	Always
	1	2	3	4	5
a) Diagnosis and prescription for each student	1	2	3	4	5
b) Whole class lessons	1	2	3	4	5
c) Contracts, learning activity packages, or instructional packages	1	2	3	4	5
d) Creative activities with student options	1	2	3	4	5
e) Programmed materials or drill assignments	1	2	3	4	5
f) Small-group assignments	1	2	3	4	5
g) Task cards or games	1	2	3	4	5
h) Objectives, varied for individuals	1	2	3	4	5
i) Peer tutoring or team learning	1	2	3	4	5
j) Role playing or simulations	1	2	3	4	5
k) Brainstorming or circles of knowledge	1	2	3	4	5
l) Students design their own studies	1	2	3	4	5

Question II: *Teaching Methods*

Directions:

Circle the number that best describes how often you use each of the following teaching methods.

	Never	Rarely	Occasionally	Frequently	Always
	1	2	3	4	5
a) Lecture (whole class)	1	2	3	4	5
b) Teacher demonstration	1	2	3	4	5
c) Small groups (3-8)	1	2	3	4	5
d) Media (films, tapes, etc.)	1	2	3	4	5
e) Class discussion (question-answer)	1	2	3	4	5
f) Individualized (diagnosis and prescription for each student)	1	2	3	4	5

Question III: *Student Groupings*

Directions:

Circle the number that best describes how often you use each of the following types of groupings.

	Never	Rarely	Occasionally	Frequently	Always
	1	2	3	4	5
a) Several small groups (3-8 students)	1	2	3	4	5
b) Pairs (2 students)	1	2	3	4	5
c) Independent study assignments (student works alone)	1	2	3	4	5
d) One-to-one interactions with the teacher	1	2	3	4	5
e) Two or more of the above groupings at one time	1	2	3	4	5
f) One large group (entire class)	1	2	3	4	5

Question IV: *Room Design*

Directions:

Circle the number that best describes how often you use each of the following classroom designs.

	Never	Rarely	Occasionally	Frequently	Always
	1	2	3	4	5
a) Rows of desks	1	2	3	4	5
b) Small groups of 3-8 students	1	2	3	4	5
c) Learning stations or interest centers	1	2	3	4	5
d) A variety of areas	1	2	3	4	5
e) Individual and small-group (2-4) alcoves, dens, "offices"	1	2	3	4	5
f) Three or more of the above arrangements at the same time	1	2	3	4	5

Question V: *Teaching Environment*

Directions:

Circle the number that best describes your present instructional environment.

	Never	Rarely	Occasionally	Frequently	Always
	1	2	3	4	5
a) Varied instructional areas are provided in the classroom for different, simultaneous activities	1	2	3	4	5
b) Nutritional intake is available for all students as needed	1	2	3	4	5

	Never	Rarely	Occasionally	Frequently	Always
	1	2	3	4	5
c) Instructional areas are designed for different groups that need to talk and interact	1	2	3	4	5
d) Varied time schedules are in use for individuals	1	2	3	4	5
e) Students are permitted to choose where they will sit and/or work	1	2	3	4	5
f) Many multisensory resources are available in the classroom for use by individuals and groups	1	2	3	4	5
g) Alternative arrangements are made for mobile, active, or overly talkative students	1	2	3	4	5

Question VI: *Evaluation Techniques*

Directions:

Circle the number that best describes how often you use each of the following evaluation techniques.

	Never	Rarely	Occasionally	Frequently	Always
I use:	1	2	3	4	5
a) Observation by moving from group to group and among individuals	1	2	3	4	5
b) Teacher-made tests	1	2	3	4	5
c) Student self-assessment tests	1	2	3	4	5
d) Performance tests (demonstrations rather than written responses)	1	2	3	4	5
e) Criterion-referenced achievement tests* based on student self-selected, individual objectives	1	2	3	4	5
f) Criterion-referenced achievement tests* based on small-group objectives	1	2	3	4	5
g) Standardized achievement tests based on grade-level objectives	1	2	3	4	5
h) Criterion-referenced achievement tests* based on the individual student's potential	1	2	3	4	5

*Criterion-Referenced Achievement Tests: The questions on these tests are based directly on the objectives assigned to or selected by the students.

Question VII: *Educational Philosophy*

Directions:

Circle the number that best describes your attitude toward each of the following approaches and concepts.

	Strongly Disagree	Disagree	Undecided	Support	Strongly Support
	1	2	3	4	5
a) Open education	1	2	3	4	5
b) Diagnostic-prescriptive teaching	1	2	3	4	5
c) Multiage groupings	1	2	3	4	5
d) Matched teaching and learning styles	1	2	3	4	5
e) Alternative education	1	2	3	4	5
f) Student-centered curriculum	1	2	3	4	5
g) Behavioral or performance objectives	1	2	3	4	5
h) Humanistic education	1	2	3	4	5
i) Independent study	1	2	3	4	5
j) Individualized instruction	1	2	3	4	5
NOTE THE REVERSED NUMBERS					
k) Traditional education	5	4	3	2	1
l) Whole-group achievement	5	4	3	2	1
m) Grade-level standards	5	4	3	2	1
n) Teacher-dominated instruction	5	4	3	2	1

Question VIII: *Teaching Characteristics**

Directions:

Circle the number that best describes you as a teacher.

I tend to be:	Not At All	Not Very	Somewhat	Very	Extremely
	1	2	3	4	5
a) Concerned with *how* students learn (learning style)	1	2	3	4	5
b) Prescriptive (with student options)	1	2	3	4	5
c) Demanding—with high expectations based on *individual* ability	1	2	3	4	5
d) Evaluative of students as they work	1	2	3	4	5
NOTE THE REVERSED NUMBERS					
e) Concerned with *how much* students learn (grade-level standards)	5	4	3	2	1

	Not At All	Not Very	Somewhat	Very	Extremely
	1	2	3	4	5
f) Concerned with what students learn (grade-level curriculum)	5	4	3	2	1
g) Lesson plan oriented	5	4	3	2	1
h) Authoritative to reach group objectives	5	4	3	2	1

*When teachers respond that they are "concerned with *how* students learn," the inference is that they permit options in the learning environment because of their awareness of individual differences. An observer should, thus, be able to see students working alone, with a peer or two, or with the teacher; sitting on chairs or on carpeting; using self-selected resources of a multisensory nature (if available); mobile (if necessary and without disturbing others), etc.

When a teacher indicates that he or she tends to be "prescriptive" but permits some student options, observers should be able to locate written objectives that include selected choices.

"Evaluative . . . as (students) work" suggests that observers will be able to see the teacher moving among the students while checking their progress and questioning them.

"Concerned with . . . grade-level curriculum" suggests that observers will see that objectives, lessons, and/or assignments tend to respond to a suggested or required grade-level curriculum.

"Authoritative to reach group objectives" suggests that observers will see the identical objectives, lessons, and/or assignments for every student in the same class.

SCORING KEY

Questions I through VIII are weighted according to the relative importance of each item. Simply multiply the weight assigned to the technique by the number selected for the frequency.

Example:

I a) Diagnosis and prescription for each student—3—Occasionally

Item	Weight		Frequency		Score
a	5	X	3	=	15

Complete each item and the total for each question. Then chart the totals on the Teaching Style Profile. This analysis and the predictor profile will aid you in matching students and teachers.

WEIGHT KEY

5. Highly Individualized
4. Somewhat Individualized
3. Transitional
2. Somewhat Traditional
1. Traditional

I Instructional Planning

Item	Weight X Frequency = Score
a	5
b	1
c	5
d	3
e	4
f	3
g	3
h	4
i	3
j	3
k	3
l	5

I: Total Score ______

II Teaching Methods

Item	Weight X Frequency = Score
a	1
b	2
c	3
d	3
e	2
f	5

II: Total Score ______

III Student Groupings

Item	Weight X Frequency = Score
a	3
b	3
c	5
d	2
e	4
f	1

III: Total Score ______

IV Room Design

Item	Weight X Frequency = Score
a	1
b	3
c	4
d	5
e	4
f	5

IV: Total Score ______

V Teaching Environment

Item	Weight X Frequency = Score
a	5
b	4
c	4
d	5
e	4
f	4
g	4

V: Total Score ______

VI Evaluation Techniques

Item	Weight X Frequency = Score
a	4
b	2
c	4
d	4
e	5
f	4
g	1
h	4

VI: Total Score ______

VII Educational Philosophy

Item	Weight	X Frequency	= Score
a	4		
b	5		
c	3		
d	5		
e	4		
f	3		
g	4		
h	3		
i	4		
j	5		
k	1		
l	1		
m	1		
n	1		

VII: Total Score____

VIII Teaching Characteristics

Item	Weight	X Frequency	= Score
a	4		
b	5		
c	4		
d	3		
e	1		
f	1		
g	1		
h	1		

VIII: Total Score____

Place the "Total Score" that you obtained for each of the previous categories on the line pertaining to that item by making a dot on the line closest to the appropriate numeral.

TEACHING STYLE PROFILE

	Individualized	Somewhat Individualized	Transitional	Somewhat Traditional	Traditional
I: Instructional Planning	210	168	126	84	42
II: Teaching Methods	80	64	48	32	16
III: Student Groupings	90	72	54	36	18
IV: Room Design	110	88	66	44	22
V: Teaching Environment	150	120	90	60	30
VI: Evaluation Techniques	140	112	84	56	28
VII: Educational Philosophy	220	176	132	88	44
VIII: Teaching Characteristics	100	80	60	40	20

After you have placed a dot on each line indicating the total score you obtained for each category, link each dot in succession. This chart should provide you with a graphic representation, or profile, of your present teaching style.

Question IX: *Student Types*

Directions:

Rate the degree of success you tend to have with each type of student.

CODE:

5. Almost Always Successful
4. Frequently Successful
3. Occasionally Successful
2. Rarely Successful
1. Almost Never Successful

A. Learning Rate

_______ Quickly achieving
_______ Average achieving
_______ Slowly achieving
_______ Nonachieving

B. Motivation Scale

_______ Motivated
_______ Conforming
_______ Persistent
_______ Responsible
_______ Apathetic
_______ Unmotivated
_______ Nonconforming
_______ Not persistent
_______ Not responsible

C. Emotional Stability

_______ Emotionally stable
_______ Active-mobile
_______ Quiet-passive
_______ Emotionally troubled

D. Learning Potential

_______ Gifted
_______ Creative
_______ Far above-average I.Q.
_______ Average I.Q.
_______ Below-average I.Q.
_______ Learning-impaired

E. Verbal Communication Ability

_______ Articulate
_______ Average verbal ability
_______ Below-average verbal ability
_______ Bilingual
_______ Non-English speaking

F. Independence Level

_______ Peer-oriented
_______ Adult-oriented
_______ Independent
_______ Authority-oriented

A resume of a teacher's response to this inventory will indicate the kinds of youngsters who might function well and grow under his/her guidance.

TEACHER SUCCESS WITH STUDENT TYPES/PREDICTOR PROFILE

A: Learning Rate_______________________________________

B: Motivation Scale_______________________________________

C: Emotional Stability_______________________________________

D: Learning Potential_______________________________________

E: Verbal Communications Ability____

F: Independence Level____

List all of the types of students that received 5's under Question IX for each of the categories A through F. You now know how to identify faculty teaching styles and the students with whom individuals believe they are successful. The only remaining step (below) is to identify individual youngsters' learning styles and to then match the right student with the right teacher—for him or her.

IDENTIFYING STUDENT LEARNING STYLES

Newly selected faculty may be somewhat more aware than current staff of student learning styles, profiles, individualized instruction, learning stations, and other approaches designed to assist each student despite the differences that exist among them. This awareness may be due to several factors:

1. The new employees are recruited, screened, and selected because of their ability to work effectively with differing individual student learning styles, abilities, interests, levels, rates of learning, etc.
2. Teachers with recent college training are more likely to have had exposure to the latest research and its applications concerning individual learners than veteran staff members.
3. Teachers coming from other districts and regions have the advantage of exposure to different approaches and experiences.

In any event, current and new staff members should be brought to a commonality of understanding with respect to learning styles—the key to the effective use of faculty and improved instruction.

Research indicates clearly that students can recognize their own learning styles[6] and that they perform better if taught and tested[7] in their preferred manner of learning. It is essential, therefore, to group students for instruction by matching them with teachers and programs that permit them to learn in the ways they learn best.

Learning style is "the manner in which at least 18 different elements from four basic stimuli affect a person's ability to absorb and retain."[8] The combinations and variations among these elements suggest that few people learn in exactly the same way, just as few people think exactly alike.

When people concentrate, they are affected by at least four different stimuli or sets of stimuli: (1) the physical environment, (2) the emotional framework in which they are functioning, (3) the sociological setting, and (4) their own physical being and needs. (See Figure 3-3)

Figure 3-3

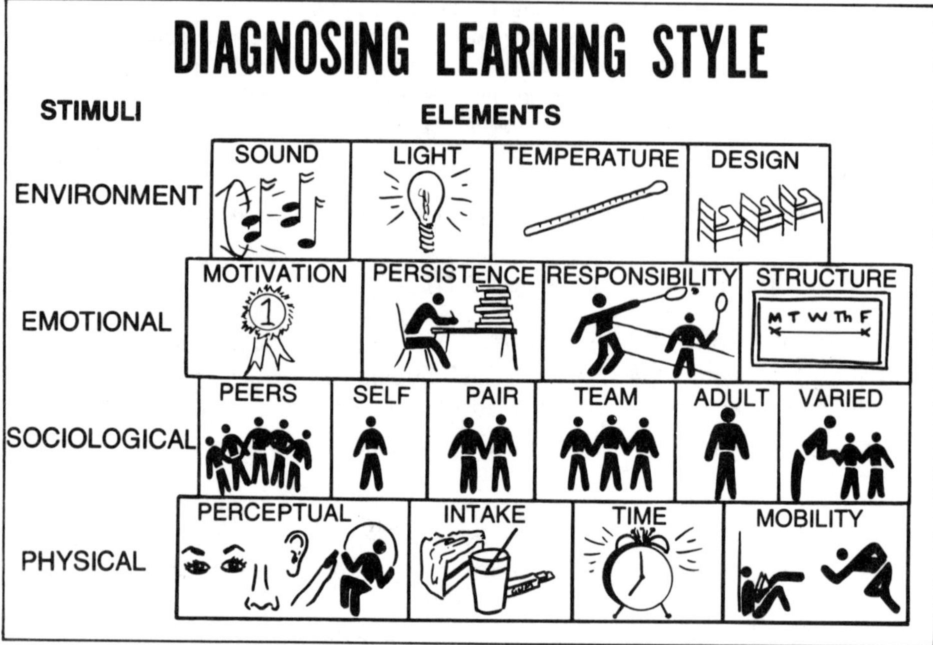

Designed by Dr. Rita S. Dunn
Dr. Kenneth J. Dunn

Environment and Learning Style

The environmental factors that affect how much a student is able to achieve at a given time include the elements of sound, light, temperature, and design.[9]

Some people can block out surrounding noises and function effectively in spite of them. Others can adjust to selected kinds of sounds, depending on the task. A larger group appears to need virtual silence if the learning to be accomplished requires concentration or is difficult for them. Another group appears to be unable to study or concentrate without discussing the materials to be learned; this group, in effect, *requires* sound.

The way in which a room is illuminated also appears to affect the learning process. Whereas some people can function with ease only when the environment is well lit, the same degree of lighting is considered excessive by some and insufficient by others. If lighting is incorrect for the individual, it can prevent concentration either by overstimulating him or lulling him into drowsiness.

Temperature is an element that yields easily observable differences in the degree to which people can learn. Some require a warm environment before they can study; others find that the same degree of heat that relaxes some people unnerves them. Some students can function well only in a cool area, whereas others become nervous in the same degree of temperature that facilitates learning for their peers.

The way in which an environment is designed also produces differences in the amount of learning that individuals are able to achieve. Selected students indicate that they require a formal study area with tables and chairs such as might be found in a library or a kitchen. Others state that they cannot sit in a highly structured area for any length of time and continue to concentrate; these people require a relaxed setting and find that they can continue to work for comparatively long periods of time when the furniture and surroundings are informal. This very informality, however, often causes drowsiness or daydreaming in the group requiring the structured design.

Emotional Aspects of Learning Style

Most teachers intuitively understand that youngsters who come to school motivated, persistent, responsible, or in need of little structure should be worked with differently from the unmotivated, the unpersistent, the irresponsible, and the student who must be supervised closely, given short assignments, kept within eye's sight, and frequently encouraged and/or praised.[10] Historically, however, we address each class as a whole and rarely vary the assignments, the requirements, the tests, the instructional methods, or the grading system so that they correspond to what students are capable of producing.

Students who want to learn, who complete assigned tasks, and who accomplish specified objectives require instructional programs that promote increased independence and self-paced growth. Conversely, students who give up easily when confronting difficult tasks, who have short attention spans and few curriculum interests, who prefer social activities to academic achievement, and who need constant or frequent interaction with an adult who teaches, supervises, guides, and oversees will not profit from participation in a program that permits them to self-select tasks, pace themselves, interact with peers at their discretion, or self-schedule activities. Certainly the student and the program to which the student is assigned should be carefully matched.

Sociological Aspects of Learning Style

Students react differently to their peers, adults, and the learning process itself. Some prefer to study alone and can achieve more in this manner than when working directly with either other youngsters or adults. Some students require direct and virtually continuous interaction with an authority figure, whether it be the teacher, an expert, an outside resource, or a paraprofessional. There are, however, youngsters who become "uptight" or intimidated by adults in general and find that they can learn more easily when working with a friend or two, or even a small group. This tendency is found among many people and is often manifested by an inclination to work within a committee structure or on task forces.

Students who profit from close student/teacher interactions should not be assigned to a system wherein independent or peer-group studies are emphasized. Obviously, too, students who successfully achieve through interaction with their classmates and enjoy this process should not be placed in a program that requires either extensive self-teaching or teacher-dominated instruction.

Many youngsters will enjoy variations in the instructional process; teachers can design their methods to include such alternatives. It is necessary, however, to avoid placing students in programs that require a preponderance of specific sociological strategies if the youngster's learning style indicates disharmony with the basic pattern.

Physical Aspects of Learning Style

To a major extent, students are not free agents; they are controlled by their physical needs. Only the strongly motivated learner can achieve when his physical requirements are at variance with the learning system.

Some people learn well through hearing; for these a lecture, a discussion, a record, or a cassette will facilitate achievement. Some must experience visually what should be learned. Both of these groups comprise only a portion of the student community, and sometimes their abilities to advance academically through the use of auditory or visual strategies are mutually exclusive; sometimes they are complementary or reinforcing.

Other students experience extensive difficulty when trying to learn without a tactual or kinesthetic involvement with their objectives. This is often true of youngsters who do not learn to read through either a phonics or word-recognition approach. When exposed to touch or "doing" methods, however, they frequently overcome the difficulties they had when taught through auditory or visual techniques. Using a multisensory approach to teaching often will overcome perceptual problems that certain students experience in a traditional program emphasizing lectures or discussions.

Another physical problem that confronts selected students is the need for nutritional intake at regular intervals. Whether this is a physical need to replace the energy being expended by concentration or a means of releasing nervous energy, some students frequently need to eat, drink, chew gum, or even bite on objects while engaged in the learning process. Obviously, a conservative program will not permit breaks for intake, whereas a more informal one may.

The time when a person is most alert and, therefore, best able to absorb learning varies with the individual.[11] Some students work most effectively early in the morning, others excel later in the day, and still others are proverbial "night owls." A highly structured program divided into time blocks for concentrated study in specific disciplines will not be conducive to achievement for youngsters who may not be alert at the arbitrarily scheduled time. If timing is an important learning style factor for a particular student, his chances for academic success would be improved if he were placed in a flexible program, so that the subjects with which he experiences the most difficulty can be studied when he is most mentally alert.

Finally, the physical need for mobility evidenced in many youngsters may easily inhibit their learning efforts.[12] Students who are not able to remain in their seats or in a restricted environment for long periods of time find it difficult to function in a traditional program. Conversely, youngsters who are at ease in one position for intervals of 45 minutes or longer sometimes find the constant (or frequent) movement that occurs in informal programs disconcerting.

Therefore, before a student is assigned to either an instructional program or a specific teacher, his learning style profile should be matched with the program's characteristics and the particular teacher's instructional style and an effort should be made to match the student to the appropriate teacher and type of learning environment.

MATCHING LEARNING STYLES TO TEACHING STYLES

The following sample of one of the categories in an instrument that has yielded a high degree of reliability in identifying individual students' learning styles demonstrates one way in which to begin analyzing how to plan the instructional environment, resources, and strategies for learners. Figure 3-4 represents the instrument's category of "Mobility"[13] and is but one of the eighteen elements that are diagnosed by the Learning Style Questionnaire.[14]

Figure 3-4

MOBILITY	True	False
1. When I study I often get up to do something (like take a drink, get a cookie, etc.) and then return to work.	____	____
2. When I study I stay with it until I am finished and then I get up.	____	____
3. It's difficult for me to sit in one place for a long time.	____	____
4. I often change my position when I work.	____	____
5. I can sit in one place for a long time.	____	____
6. I constantly change position in my chair.	____	____
7. I can work best for short amounts of time with breaks in between.	____	____
8. I like getting my work done and over with.	____	____
9. I like to work a little, stop, return to the work, stop, return to it again, and so forth.	____	____
10. I like to stick to a job and finish it in one sitting if I can.	____	____
11. I leave most jobs for the last minute and then have to work on them from beginning to end.	____	____
12. I do most of my jobs a little at a time and eventually get them done.	____	____
13. I enjoy doing something over and over again when I know how to do it well.	____	____
14. I like familiar friends and places.	____	____
15. New jobs and subjects make me nervous.	____	____

Consistency Key:

Needs Mobility	*Does Not Need Mobility*
True	True
1	2
3	5
4	8

Needs Mobility	*Does Not Need Mobility*
True	True
6	10
7	11
9	13
12	14
	15

Totals:

Needs Mobility	*Does Not Need Mobility*
True	True
___	___
7	8

Once each of the eighteen elements of learning style have been diagnosed, the cumulative findings are recorded on a profile form that reveals the unique responses of the individual student[15] through a composite overview (see Figure 3-5).

Figure 3-5

LEARNING STYLE PROFILE

Name__________ Teacher__________ School__________
Grade__________ Counselor__________ Date__________

Comments Based on Highest Ratios Noted on Questionnaire

I. Environmental
- Sound __________
- Light __________
- Temperature __________
- Design __________

II. Emotional
- Motivation __________
- Persistence __________
- Responsibility __________
- Structure __________

III. Sociological
- Appears to Work Best with:
  1. __________
  2. __________
  3. __________

IV. Physical
- Perceptual Preferences __________
- Nutritional Intake __________
- Time __________
- Mobility __________

Checked by __________

More recently, computer technology has been used to aid the teacher in both diagnosing and prescribing for individuals on the basis of student learning style preferences. After conducting a factor analysis of those items that yielded a consistency score of 90% or better on the Learning Style Questionnaire described on the previous pages, Price and the authors developed a shortened form. In this new computerized instrument, the Learning Style Inventory,[16] questions concerned with each of the eighteen elements are scrambled, although selected ones reappear repeatedly to provide a means of determining individual consistency of responses (see Figure 3-6). This form requires a minimum of teacher time, yet provides the teacher and principal with an invaluable guide for properly matching the ways students learn with appropriate resources, methods, environmental structures, and prescriptions for each individual. When combined with the information in chapter 3 that describes the appropriate learning style for each instructional program, you can match the right student with the right teacher.

Figure 3-6

SAMPLE QUESTIONS FROM THE LEARNING STYLE INVENTORY (LSI)

69. I remember things best when I study them early in the morning.
70. I remember things best when I study them before dinner.
71. If I could go to school anytime during the day, I would choose to go in the early morning.
72. When I can, I do my homework in the afternoon.
83. I like to be given choices of how I can do things.
84. When I really have a lot of studying to do, I like to work with two friends.
85. I like to study by myself.
86. The thing I like doing best in school, I do with one friend.
87. The thing I like doing best in school, I do with a grown-up.
88. If I have to learn something new, I like to learn about it by having it told to me.

Obvious advantages of the Learning Style Inventory include (1) rapid scoring via the computer, (2) prescription that is provided on the computer printout and which is based on the Learning Style Inventory diagnosis yielded for the individual student, (3) individual diagnosis and prescription sheets that may be included in each youngster's cumulative record folder for permanent reference by present and future teachers and for a basis of discussion with parents or the student, (4) an overall class summary indicating the number of individuals that respond to similar learning style elements to facilitate grouping and environmental redesign, and (5) a summary that also indicates the number of students who require specific methods, resources, environmental strategies, etc. (see Figure 3-7).

Figure 3-7

LEARNING STYLE INVENTORY-INDIVIDUAL SUMMARY PAGE 1
DUNN, DUNN AND PRICE

Smith, Jack SEX M ANY DATE
ANY SCHOOL NAME—ANY TEACHER NAME GR 11 CL 1

LEARNING STYLE	REFERENCE
CONSISTENCY SCORE 0.85	
1. NEEDS QUIET.	SEE MANUAL PAGE 6.
3. REQUIRES BRIGHT LIGHT.	SEE MANUAL PAGE 6.
6. NEEDS WARM ENVIRONMENT.	SEE MANUAL PAGE 6.
9. SELF-MOTIVATED.	SEE MANUAL PAGE 6.*
10. ADULT-MOTIVATED.	SEE MANUAL PAGE 6.
11. TEACHER-MOTIVATED.	SEE MANUAL PAGE 6.*
15. RESPONSIBLE.	SEE MANUAL PAGE 7.*
17. NEEDS STRUCTURE.	SEE MANUAL PAGE 7.
19. PREFERS LEARNING ALONE.	SEE MANUAL PAGE 8.
20. PREFERS LEARNING WITH ONE PEER.	SEE MANUAL PAGE 8.
27. TACTILE PREFERENCES.	SEE MANUAL PAGE 9.
33. FUNCTIONS BEST IN AFTERNOON.	SEE MANUAL PAGE 9.

*Examples from the Manual

9. SELF-MOTIVATED	ENCOURAGE USE OF CONTRACT ACTIVITY PACKAGES, INSTRUCTIONAL PACKAGES, AND PROGRAMMED LEARNING; PERMIT SELF-PACING AND ACHIEVEMENT BEYOND GRADE LEVEL; ENCOURAGE USE OF SELF-CORRECTIVE AND SELF-ASSESSMENT MATERIALS.
11. TEACHER-MOTIVATED	ESTABLISH DEN AREA NEAR TEACHER; PRAISE OFTEN; INCORPORATE REPORTING TO TEACHER INTO PRESCRIPTION; INCLUDE IN SMALL-GROUP INSTRUCTIONAL TECHNIQUES WHEN TEACHER IS INVOLVED.
15. RESPONSIBLE	BEGIN BY DESIGNING SHORT-TERM PRESCRIPTIONS; AS THESE ARE COMPLETED SUCCESSFULLY, GRADUALLY INCREASE THEIR LENGTH, BEING CERTAIN TO KEEP THEM ON THE STUDENT'S LEVEL OF FUNCTIONAL ABILITY.

Once a learning style profile is completed for each student, using either the Learning Style Questionnaire or the Learning Style Inventory (LSI), it is relatively easy to determine the instructional strategies, resources, and environment that should facilitate a youngster's academic achievement. The next step is to match that student with the teacher whose Teaching Style Inventory data indicates that he/she can provide the academic climate that complements the student's learning style. For example, a highly motivated, independent, competent, relative "loner" requires a teacher who individualizes his approach and is knowledgeable about the use of contract activity packages, programmed learning, instructional packages, and other techniques that will permit him to work independently. The teacher also would have to use the student's profile sheet to determine which of the three strategies tends to be more appropriate for that youngster, dependent upon whether he/she is an auditory, visual, tactual, or kinesthetic learner.

If funds are available, it is suggested that computer printout prescriptions be placed in the hands of teachers who are capable of using alternative strategies. This will aid in designing the educational environment and program to the point where maximum teaching effectiveness will be achieved.

PLACING STUDENTS AND TEACHERS IN APPROPRIATE INSTRUCTIONAL PROGRAMS

Both students and teachers should be placed in appropriate instructional programs—programs that provide opportunities for teaching and learning in an educational environment that allows them to function according to the strengths revealed in each individual's teaching or learning style diagnosis.

The accompanying charts (see Figures 3-8, 3-9, 3-10, 3-11) suggest the basic philosophy represented by selected instructional programs and the related skills that are required of students participating in them. The skills are then correlated with the learning style elements that the student should have to function effectively in that program. Finally, the third column indicates the teaching style characteristics that are generally associated with each of the described programs.

Figure 3-8

INSTRUCTIONAL PROGRAM: TRADITIONAL CLASSROOM

Philosophy:

The teacher is responsible for helping students to achieve minimal grade-level standards. Children are expected to "pay attention," "try," "work," "take their work seriously," and "be good"—all of which presupposes that they are each able to achieve through the method(s) selected by the teacher. Most of the instruction is through lecture and questioning, occasionally supplemented by media. Lesson plans are written by the teacher for the principal as indications of what the class will be taught. Grades are determined by the student's achievement on group tests. All students learn sequential blocks of subject matter at the same time. A few students are permitted some enrichment if it does not interfere with the curriculum to be covered. For all, self-selection of subject content and method of learning are rare.

Required Student Skills	*Learning Style Characteristics*	*Teaching Style Characteristics*
The student is required to:	The student should therefore:	The teacher:
1. pay attention for consecutive intervals of 20-50 minutes each.	be motivated.	is whole-class lesson oriented.
2. sit still for consecutive intervals of from one to three hours.	not require mobility.	essentially dominates the instruction or lesson.
3. refrain from needing a drink, a break, or using a lavatory except during specified times (recess, lunch, etc.).	not require intake, except at "correct" times.	is unaware of individual physical needs.
-or-	-or-	-or-
raise his hand, interrupt the teacher, and publicly request permission to do any of the above during instructional time.	not be embarrassed because of being different from peers.	is structured and directive.
4. concentrate on studies for several hours during the school day and engage in homework after school.	be persistent.	is concerned with how much students learn.

Required Student Skills	*Learning Style Characteristics*	*Teaching Style Characteristics*
The student is required to:	The student should therefore:	The teacher:
5. retain information by listening.	be an auditory learner.	is lecture- and whole-class oriented.
6. learn at a table and chair or desk.	function easily in a structured environment.	employs rigid and traditional physical arrangements.
7. learn at his desk wherever it has been placed.	be unaffected by sound, light, and temperature.	assigns seats.
8. accept that what is taught is necessary, valuable, and interesting.	be authority-oriented.	is oriented to group and grade-level standards and content.
9. conform to externally established standards and rules.	be authority-oriented.	dominates instruction and behavior.
10. accept being marked on a competitive basis regardless of inherited ability or environmental background.	be authority-oriented.	employs group and grade-level standards.
11. learn whenever a subject is being taught.	be unaffected by time.	uses scheduled lesson plans.
12. keep working at an item until it is mastered.	be persistent.	focuses on sequenced material that must be covered.
13. maintain a positive self-image and creativity while following directions, controlling normal body needs, learning in a way that prohibits use of personal learning style, studying what may be irrelevant and uninteresting, and avoiding conflict.	be authority-oriented.	is authoritarian to reach class or grade-level objectives.

Figure 3-9

INSTRUCTIONAL PROGRAM: OPEN CLASSROOM

Philosophy:

Students are permitted to determine their curriculum, resources, schedule, and pacing. Youngsters may remain with a topic as long as it interests them and may study alone, with a friend or two, or in a small group. Since children learn in very individual ways, the teacher is responsible for providing an environment rich in multimedia resources and for encouraging student involvement with the materials. Objectives, if used, are determined by the child and may vary from student to student and on a continuously changing basis. Grades are not given, but evaluations are made in terms of the child's demonstrated growth. A positive and "happy" attitude is considered very important for student progress.

Required Student Skills	*Learning Style Characteristics*	*Teaching Style Characteristics*
The student is required to:	The student should therefore:	The teacher:
1. learn without continuous direction and supervision.	be motivated.	provides multiple resources.
2. avoid an essentially social, rather than academic, experience.	be responsible.	permits wide options to the student to learn and produce as he or she chooses.
3. discipline himself to concentrate and to learn self-selected ideas, data, and values.	be motivated and responsible.	believes in students designing their own studies.
4. study in the midst of movement, discussion, and varied activities.	be unaffected by sound, structure, and the mobility of others.	believes in varied, continuing, interactive learning activities.
5. interact positively with other children.	be peer-oriented.	provides varied options for working with one or more peers.
6. retain information without drill reinforcement.	have no need of imposed structure.	believes that students want to learn and will study as much as they are able.

Figure 3-10

INSTRUCTIONAL PROGRAM: ALTERNATIVE PROGRAMS

Philosophy:

Students are given curriculum choices, decision-making responsibilities, and selected and optional objectives and are expected to gather and retain information independently. Students are usually permitted a voice in their program development. Since alternative programs differ widely, the degree to which options are provided concerning objectives, resources, activities, and evaluations is dependent on the individual program, not the student.

Required Student Skills	*Learning Style Characteristics*	*Teaching Style Characteristics*
The student is required to:	The student should therefore:	The teacher:
1. learn without continuous direction and supervision.	be motivated.	provides multiple materials and serves as a resource person or guide.
2. determine the scope, sequence, and depth of undertaken studies.	be responsible.	believes in student selection of objectives and procedures.
3. self-assess his progress and potential accurately.	be self-oriented.	supervises self-evaluation by student.
4. discipline himself to study and achieve.	be motivated and responsible.	develops student self-reliance through consultation.
5. retain information without drill reinforcement.	have no need for imposed structure.	provides opportunities for independent study, individual or small-group assignments, and other self-instructional and reinforcement procedures and materials.

3-1 3-2 3-3 3-4 3-5 3-6

Photos 3-1 through 3-6. Although the objectives and processes of alternative schools vary widely, one of the major goals of the faculty who designed this program was to create an environment where "kids *want* to achieve and become involved in a learning community." (Photographs courtesy of the Alternative School, Mater Christi High School, Long Island City, New York.)

3-7

3-8

Photos 3-7 and 3-8. One way of eliciting enthusiastic student participation is to encourage them to conduct research for, design, and *teach* mini-courses on topics in which other youngsters are extremely interested. Above, three students are planning a short series on "The Rights of Minorities." Once students volunteer to take a course, they are required to attend and complete it. (Photographs courtesy of the Alternative School, Mater Christi High School, Long Island City, New York.)

3-9

3-10

Photos 3-9 and 3-10. A group of senior girls were concerned about their inability to dance discotheque style. They drafted one of the Alternative School's best dancers to teach a mini-course on the latest steps. (Photographs courtesy of the Alternative School, Mater Christi High School, Long Island City, New York.)

Photo 3-11. Although mini-courses may be student initiated, designed, and taught, they always involve direct faculty participation and supervision. Topics that have been studied in this manner include the effects of tobacco, alcohol, and drugs; escaping reality; auto repair; stereo repair; and how to be a master bowler. (Photograph courtesy of the Alternative School, Mater Christi High School, Long Island City, New York.)

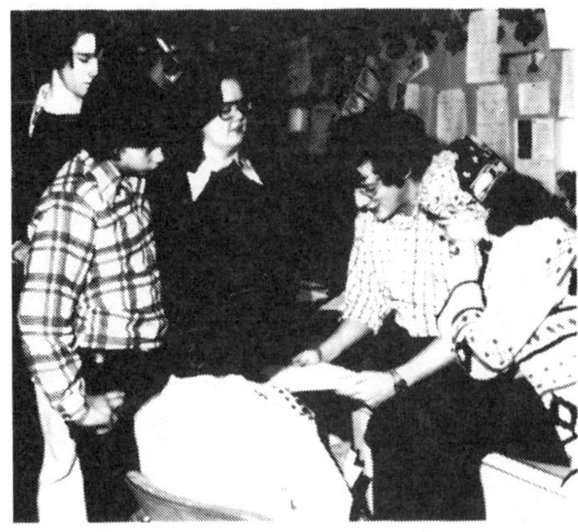

3-11

Photo 3-12. Mini-courses, however, comprise only a fraction of the program's offerings. Mornings are devoted to the development of basic skills that are taught through different instructional strategies. Here Bill Therway and his science students are discussing a stroboscopic light demonstration. (Photograph courtesy of the Alternative School, Mater Christi High School, Long Island City, New York.)

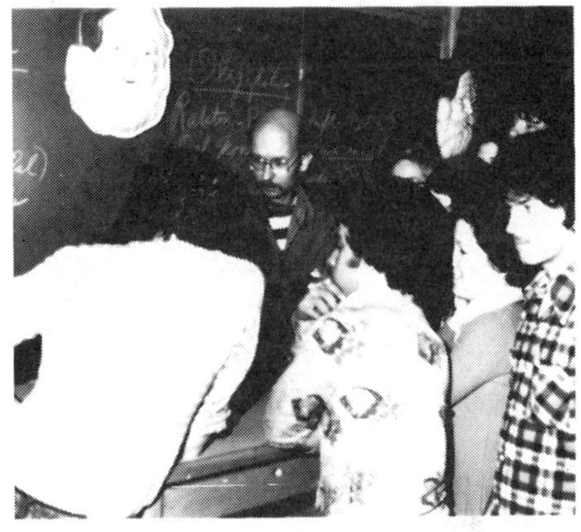

3-12

Photo 3-13. This is a large-group instructional session on *Law*, one of the required subjects in this program. Youngsters are encouraged to apply their knowledge of legal statutes to personal, community, or governmental issues that directly affect their lives. (Photograph courtesy of the Alternative School, Mater Christi High School, Long Island City, New York.)

3-13

3-14

Photo 3-14. Students are urged to identify how they learn best and then to pursue their studies in ways that complement their learning styles. Here students are working together toward the completion of common objectives. (Photograph courtesy of the Alternative School, Mater Christi High School, Long Island City, New York.)

3-15

Photo 3-15. Individuals who prefer to study alone are provided access to quiet areas where they may proceed to learn at their own rate. (Photograph courtesy of the Alternative School, Mater Christi High School, Long Island City, New York.)

3-16

3-17

Photos 3-16 and 3-17. Students who prefer learning through interaction with an adult find their teachers available for individual, paired, and small-group activities on a daily basis. John Gilroy, pictured here, and each of the other faculty members often schedule weekend and evening activities in which they and their students continue academic studies off campus. (Photographs courtesy of the Alternative School, Mater Christi High School, Long Island City, New York.)

3-18

3-19

Photos 3-18, 3-19, and 3-20. One of the major activities of this alternative school is the development of a theme—an interdisciplinary curriculum that involves all students in research, writing, discussions, and projects related to a specific focus, such as "In Search of the American Dream," "Media and Communications," "Urban Man," and "The Future of Society." The students in the photographs are sharing information and developing individual and group reports. (Photographs courtesy of the Alternative School, Mater Christi High School, Long Island City, New York.)

3-20

3-21

3-22

Photos 3-21 and 3-22. Students are permitted to take breaks when they feel the need and may listen to music in either their home base room or in a lounge that boasts leather chairs and space for dancing. They also may interact freely with their peers and help each other to learn. Students and teachers are all on a first-name basis. Despite this informality, they are given a great deal of responsibility for achieving at a pace that is both comfortable for them individually and is compatible with the teacher's expectations. (Photographs courtesy of the Alternative School, Mater Christi High School, Long Island City, New York.)

3-23

3-24

3-25

Photos 3-23, 3-24, and 3-25. Although youngsters may be found studying in halls, in corners of both empty and crowded rooms, on staircases, and in the lounge, they study and learn with what can only be described as "gusto!" They measure their academic progress in terms of how much and how well they learn *after* entering the alternative school and verbalize extreme pride and pleasure in belonging to this program. (Photographs courtesy of the Alternative School, Mater Christi High School, Long Island City, New York.)

3-26

Photo 3-26. Youngsters become so involved in and enthusiastic about their studies that classes continue—without adult supervision—when a teacher is absent. This group was involved in a literature-creative writing course and, when the teacher could not be present, one of the youngsters assumed the responsibility for monitoring the readings and critiques. (Photograph courtesy of the Alternative School, Mater Christi High School, Long Island City, New York.)

Photo 3-27. This young lady created characters and a situational plot that so absorbed her, she "could not wait" to share it with her peers. (Photograph courtesy of the Alternative School, Mater Christi High School, Long Island City, New York.)

3-27

3-28

3-29

Photos 3-28 and 3-29. Classmates listened intently, critiqued positively, and participated with such decorum that visitors questioned their behavior. In response, students stated that they were there "because they want(ed) to be!" that they "enjoyed learning," and that they "often did not want to go home from school." (Photographs courtesy of the Alternative School, Mater Christi High School, Long Island City, New York.)

3-30

Photo 3-30. Despite the fact that both national and state commissions* have recommended the development of alternative programs that respond to "the great diversity of students and needs . . . within the schools,"† innovative or "different" approaches to learning are often suspect and required to produce continuously higher academic achievement and more positive student attitudes than are evidenced in traditional educational settings. This program, described by John Azrak and John Penha (above) in their book *The Learning Community: The Story of a Successful Mini-School* (New York: Paulist Press, 1975), has been lauded by Neil Postman, noted New York University professor and author, as an "important contribution to the science, as well as the art, of teaching." The faculty states, however, that they never know whether the Learning Community will be in existence from year to year despite demonstrated success by students who had not done well in a traditional setting.

**The National Commission on the Reform of Secondary Education,* B. Frank Brown, Chairman. *The Reform of Secondary Education: A Report to the Public and the Profession.* New York: McGraw-Hill Book Company (1973); and *The Rise Report: Report of the California Commission for Reform of Intermediate and Secondary Education.* Sacramento, California: California State Department of Education (1975).

†*The Rise Report:* xiii.

Figure 3-11

INSTRUCTIONAL PROGRAM: INDIVIDUALIZED CLASSROOM

Philosophy:

The teacher is responsible for diagnosing, prescribing for, and guiding each student through the learning process. Recognizing the different elements of learning style, she permits students to work anywhere in the environment, in any sociological pattern that they choose. When a student evidences his ability to follow objectives that have been assigned to him, he is permitted to continue working as he prefers and is gradually permitted more and more options in objectives, resources, activities, and evaluation. When a student does not appear to be able to work independently, structure is added to his prescription so that he works to varying degrees under the direct supervision of the teacher. Multimedia, multisensory resources are available to students, who may select from among them. Objectives are written on an individual basis and may be contributed to or developed by the student. When progress is not satisfactory, the teacher becomes increasingly directive. Grades are determined as a result of criterion-referenced testing related to each youngster's enumerated objectives.

Required Student Skills The student is required to:	*Learning Style Characteristics* The student should therefore:	*Teaching Style Characteristics* The teacher:
1. identify those objectives, resources, activities, and assessment devices that need to be fulfilled. This will be done with a minimum of direction by students who can function independently and with the teacher for students who need guidance.	be permitted more options when he demonstrates responsible behavior and fewer options when he is unable to make choices that lead toward academic progress.	engages in diagnostic and prescriptive teaching.
2. identify the resources through which his objectives may be achieved. These will be itemized by the student. When student progress is not apparent or appropriate, resources will be prescribed by the teacher.	learn through resources that complement his perceptual strengths.	provides appropriate multisensory resources at various levels to facilitate the instructional planning.

Required Student Skills The student is required to:	*Learning Style Characteristics* The student should therefore:	*Teaching Style Characteristics* The teacher:
3. complete individual prescriptions. When this is not done, the instruction will become formalized and more traditional. As the student evidences achievement, options in the mode of instruction will become available. As options increase with evidenced achievement, achievement should continue to increase.	be given long-term prescriptions when he is motivated and/or persistent and short-term prescriptions when he does not follow through on prescriptions successfully.	is a manager of the teaching-learning process and is flexible and guiding with some students and directive and authoritarian with others.
4. self-assess his progress. Students who are able to evaluate their academic growth objectively are permitted to continue doing so. Students who are unable to do so are evaluated by the teacher frequently.	be assigned evaluation procedures that correspond to his ability to self-assess his growth.	uses different types of assessment devices with different types of students.

We educators have historically failed to look at youngsters as they really are—individual people who are very different from each other. When we consider learning, we look at it narrowly, asking how one acquires information. Howe states that "we have failed to interest ourselves significantly in how youngsters feel and behave and how they attain perspective and wisdom,"[17]—and he is correct.

The direct implication of improving teacher effectiveness is the provision of alternative strategies through which students may achieve their own or the school's or society's objectives through optional resources that facilitate their acquisition of knowledge, attitudes, and/or skills. After they have had opportunities in which to learn in ways with which they feel comfortable, students should be taught to self-assess themselves so that they are each aware of how much they have progressed and how much further they need to go. Ongoing opportunities should be available to them for further study and growth.

For those students who are unable to exercise good judgment and who evidence that they are not self-directed, motivated, responsible, persistent, or in need of little imposed structure, varying amounts of direction should be added to their learning cycle. They should be encouraged to make choices and be responsible for those choices so that, eventually, they will learn how to choose learning options that will benefit them.

This kind of learning situation—one that develops a student who will become a lifelong learner—requires new skills and attitudes for the teaching profession. The effective teacher of today's youth should be able to diagnose youngsters accurately and identify the way(s) in which individuals are most likely to achieve. He or she must then use that diagnosis to develop a course of study for each learner—a prescription that may vary drastically (or slightly) from those of other students. The teacher should help the student to build independence skills that will aid him in learning on a continuing basis long after he leaves school.

Some people are capable of change; others are not. For the teacher who is able to examine what teaching really should be and who can then acquire the skills that are requisite to becoming a superior teacher, the future holds great promise. The teacher who cannot improve outdated skills of essentially teacher-dominated instruction for everyone must be given opportunities to grow or be placed with students whose learning styles require structure and direction.

Students and teachers should be paired so that they stimulate one another. The right teacher should be available to each youngster and, similarly, the students with whom a teacher is most effective should be assigned to that person. We strongly advocate permitting students to choose their teachers, especially at the secondary level. It is possible that each school will have some teachers for whose classes few will register. That is perhaps the most direct means of demonstrating to a teacher that he or she is viewed as being ineffective by more persons than the administrator who supervises instruction. If, when teachers and students are paired on the basis of mutually complementary learning and teaching styles, no one wants to be a student of certain teachers, it will be obvious to all that that teacher's effectiveness has already been determined—and publicly recognized. Conferences of administrator and teacher for the purpose of joint goal-setting toward change would then be in order.

NOTES FOR CHAPTER 3

1. William F. Dowling and Frederick Herzberg. An Interview with Management Review, "Managers or Animal Trainers" (July 1971): 3.
2. "Managers or Animal Trainers": 4.
3. Robert N. Ford. *Motivation Through the Work Itself.* New York: American Management Association (1969).

4. *Motivation Through the Work Itself*: 22.
5. *Motivation Through the Work Itself*: 24.
6. Beatrice J. Farr. "Individual Differences in Learning: Predicting One's More Effective Learning Modality" (Ph.D. dissertation, Catholic University of America, 1971). University Microfilm, Ann Arbor, Michigan (July 1971): 1332A.
7. George Domino. "Interactive Effects of Achievement Orientation and Teaching Style on Academic Achievement." ACT Research Report, No. 39 (1970): 1-9.
8. Rita Dunn and Kenneth Dunn. *Educator's Self-Teaching Guide to Individualizing Instructional Programs.* West Nyack, New York: Parker Publishing Company, Inc. (1975): chapter 3.
9. *Educator's Self-Teaching Guide to Individualizing Instructional Programs*: 75, 77.
10. Barbara Blitz. *The Open Classroom: Making It Work.* Boston: Allyn and Bacon (1973): 93, 194-196.
11. D. Braddeley, J. E. Hatter, D. Scott, and A. Snashall. "Memory and Time of Day." *Quarterly Journal of Experimental Psychology,* 22, 4 (November 1970): 605-609; Sidney Trubowitz. "The Tyranny of Time." *The Elementary School Journal.* 73, 1 (October 1972): 1-6; Blitz. *The Open Classroom:* 61. Also Jerome Kagan, Howard A. Moss, and Irving A. Siegel. "Psychological Significance of Styles of Conceptualization." Society for Research in Child Development, Monographs, #86, 17 (1963): 927-940. For time adaptations in industry, see "Germans Setting Own Office Hours." *New York Times* (July 12, 1971): 1, 10; Harriet Mann, Miriam Siegler, and Humphrey Osmand. "The Many Worlds of Time." *The Journal of Analytical Psychology,* 13, 4 (1968): 33-56; "Flextime Seems to Lessen Tension." Puerto Rico: *The San Juan Star* (February 19, 1973): 36.
12. *The Open Classroom:* 74, 194.
13. *Educator's Self-Teaching Guide to Individualizing Instructional Programs:* 109.
14. *Educator's Self-Teaching Guide to Individualizing Instructional Programs:* 95-109.
15. *Educator's Self-Teaching Guide to Individualizing Instructional Programs:* 110.
16. Learning Style Inventory (LSI) Price Systems, P. O. Box 3271, Lawrence, Kansas 66044.
17. Ruth Weinstock, ed. *The Greening of the High School.* Dayton, Ohio: Educational Facilities Laboratory and Institute for Development of Educational Activities, Inc. (1973): 79.

4

TRAINING SELF AND STAFF TO MANAGE TIME

ACCOMPLISHING MORE WITH LESS EFFORT

The image of the efficiency expert with a stopwatch doing a time-and-motion study as he watches a worker's every move is a stereotyped myth that should be discarded. Contemporary time-management experts like Alec Mackenzie[1] ask executives, workers, and even those who work at home (like housewives), what they want to accomplish or do, why they want to find time, and approximately when. The time-management consultant then proceeds to show them how to find the time they desire.

For example, an overworked executive indicates that he would love to play golf at 4:00 p.m. on Friday afternoon, a harried housewife reveals that she longs for an hour a day for herself, and a teacher implores that he would like to spend only two evenings a week, instead of four, grading papers and preparing lessons. The consultant, in these and similar cases, aids individuals in managing their time and, therefore, in controlling their lives. Assigning priorities, avoiding distraction, overcoming procrastination, eliminating interruptions, and improving meetings are just a few ways in which to gain time. Finding time requires no more than some training or skill acquisition based on the successful studies and experiences of others. Helping you to accomplish more with less effort is the subject of this chapter.

ACQUIRING TECHNIQUES THAT IMPROVE MEETINGS

Mackenzie, Webster, and others offer a variety of suggestions that require no more energy than putting them into practice. Too often the problem is that school administrators, like other executives, believe they *know* how to conduct efficient meetings. Occasionally, when an administrator admits that the last meeting was interminable and resolved little, he mumbles that he has "no choice" and then calls people together again with a laundry checklist of items that is quickly clogged with the same suds of endless discussion that made the original meeting unsatisfactory.

Most meetings should not last longer than one hour; certainly they should not exceed two hours. The following questions are guaranteed to aid you, as they have their authors, in eliminating, shortening, and improving meetings:

1. Have you considered all alternatives to meetings?
   Strong justification for calling a meeting, *especially* those that are regularly scheduled, should be apparent to all participants if the meeting is to be held.
   1.1 If there are no valid objectives for a meeting, *cancel* it.
   1.2 If there are more important objectives to be dealt with by a number of participants, postpone the meeting.
   1.3 If the objectives require brief discussions and a decision, arrange a conference call.
   1.4 If objectives can be reached through some form of contact to develop consensus, send liaison representatives.
   1.5 If the items are basically informational, telephone or send a simple memo.
2. Have you planned the meeting for maximum effectiveness?
   2.1 Use a participating agenda. Attendees should receive a form to offer agenda items that are important, relevant to the entire group, and have specific objectives, e.g.,
   ..to decide something
   ..to inform others
   ..to coordinate an activity
   ..to analyze data or situations for future decisions
   ..to create something
   ..to resolve a problem
   This approach aids in building a meaningful and purposeful agenda.
   2.2 Be certain to select the right time, place, and people for the meeting. Limit attendance to those who should be there and only for the time period they are needed.
   2.3 Each item should include a time estimate suggested by the participant who included the item. The agenda should follow the Pre-Agenda Form (Figure 4-1) sent to attendees for their input. The same form may then be used for taking minutes to forward to all concerned for subsequent action and decisions, or as information to be used.
3. Have you considered all of the common-sense time-savers available?
   3.1 Start on time! (A must)
   3.2 Give each item a time limit.

Figure 4-1

PRE-AGENDA FORM

Before Meeting

Topic or Question: (brief description)	*Time Required* e.g. 10 min.	*Submitted by:* name, title	*Action Required* e.g. (decision requested, information, report, suggestions required, follow-up)
Example:			
1. Negotiation Planning	10 min.	R. Schilling Asst. Supt.	Review of contract; Procedures for submission of negotiation items
2. Budget Guidelines	30 min.	K. Dunn Superintendent	Outline of board criteria; Response required

Minutes after the Meeting

Topic or Question	*Actual Time*	*Persons Responsible for Taking Action*	*Action Required*
(brief description)	e.g. 15 min.	names, titles	brief description, time limits, communications requirements
Example:			
1. Negotiation Planning	6 min.	All Principals	Submission of suggested changes in the teacher's agreement by paragraph and subsection—to be brought to next management meeting (date: one week hence)
2. Budget Guidelines	40 min.	All Principals, Asst. Supt.	Initial review of staff, program, equipment, and supply budgets; Submission of budget reduction so as to meet guidelines required (date: two weeks hence)

3.3 Watch the clock and stay on the topic. Some executives have placed large one-hour clocks that move from 60 to zero in a position where the leader or timekeeper can use it to move the group into the next item when the time is up for a topic. This technique aids the group in focusing on the agenda item and in speeding the decision-making process.

3.4 Try a stand-up conference. This is especially effective when an unexpected or unnecessary visitor stops by to see you. Meet him at the door and discuss the matter standing up. He won't stay long. Some executives have carried this principle to the conference room—they have the chairs removed. Conference time is shortened considerably.

3.5 Stick to the agenda. Preplanning and setting priority items will help. Continually screen out suggestions that apply to only a few people and those items that can be handled in another way.

3.6 Prevent interruptions. Avoid telephone call intrusions, secretarial requests, visitors, etc., except for serious problems or emergencies.

3.7 Try brainstorming (see the next section), small-group task analysis, or wall charts for small groups within the meeting to solve side issues, emergency problems, or projected consequences.

3.8 End on time!

4. Is everyone clear on what was accomplished and who is responsible for future action?
   It is important to reaffirm agreement and assignments.
5. Have you evaluated the session?
   Future meetings will be better if participants take some time at the end of each session to discuss the completed agenda, the nature of advance information, presentations, ways of reducing the number of topics and of dealing with major matters of concern or high-priority objectives.
6. Have you followed through on the results of the meeting?
   Clear and concise minutes should include information concerning decisions, responsibilities, time deadlines, etc., and should be distributed within 48 hours.
   Follow-up progress reports, descriptions of actions taken, notice of the formation of task groups, and implementation and evaluation data should be reported to all concerned on a regular basis. And—disband committees and groups as soon as they complete their objectives and receive appropriate recognition.

BRAINSTORMING TO BETTER SOLUTIONS

Brainstorming (sometimes called "greenlighting") is one of the most effective ways to save time, release creativity, ensure wide participation, and *motivate*. This technique provides several of Ford's key motivators,[2] such as:

—*More responsibility* for action or potential action based on teacher or administrator suggestions,
—*Achievement* personally recognized as an act of creativity or contribution to change or improvement,
—*Recognition* by self and others who see the value of brainstorming suggestions,
—*Growth* in creativity, rapid analysis, recognition of relationships, projection of positive consequences, and
—*Advancement* to a higher order of task either as a direct outgrowth of suggestions or as a participant in meaningful planning; the brainstorming task itself calls upon creativity, associative ability, and abstract as well as practical planning.

Other Advantages of Brainstorming

In addition to increasing motivation, there are a series of practical advantages associated with the process and results of brainstorming. Brainstorming is:

—*Stimulating*. It offers a unique, freewheeling, exciting, and rapid-fire technique that builds enthusiasm in most of the participants.
—*Positive*. Less-articulate or verbal people can participate constructively without being "put down." Those who usually dominate endless discussions also are stimulated to get their ideas out and on the record.
—*Focused*. Stories, recollections, editorial comments, speeches, rejoinders, arguments, and other nonconstructive time-wasters usually associated with most committee work are eliminated.
—*Spontaneous and creative*. The natural sounding board established in this process builds momentum through the associative linkage of ideas that releases each individual's reactive and creative powers.
—*Efficient and productive*. Dozens of ideas, obstacles, and suggestions are listed in a matter of minutes. Next steps can be brainstormed as well as more specific ideas for too general a suggestion (subset brainstorming).
—*Involving—participation builds group ownership of recommendations*. The participants feel the cohesiveness of the group as they join mental hands in the collective process of generating ideas. As the items are born, they are inbued with individual and group ownership and creation through their written appearance on the brainstorming sheets. The group's production takes on value as written testimony to its efforts.
—*Ongoing and problem-solving*. The results are permanently recorded and may be modified, added to, analyzed, and reproduced for future action and reference. The Next Steps section acts as a springboard to problem solution.

Guidelines for Brainstorming

The Leader

The brainstorming leader also acts as a recorder. His or her functions include recording all suggestions, asking for clarification or repetition, synthesizing longer phrases or statements into key ideas, and keeping the group focused on each single question or topic. The leader should not comment, editorialize, or contribute; his efforts should be concentrated on producing an effective and productive session.

The Setting (Figure 4-2)

From five to eight participants should form a fairly tight semicircle of chairs facing the leader and three to five large sheets of lecture pad paper or newsprint, doubled-folded to prevent strike-through marks. These sheets, approximately 20-24 inches wide and 30-36 inches high, should be attached to the wall with masking tape and placed a few inches apart at a reachable height for recording. The leader should use a broad-tipped felt marker for instant visibility by the entire group. A timekeeper should be appointed for the two- or three-minute brainstorming segments, but the timekeeper may participate in the brainstorming. It is useful, too, to have an overhead projector or additional sheets available for subset brainstorming, explorations, analysis groups, etc.

Figure 4-2

The Rules for Participants

1. Concentrate on the topic or question—"Storm your brain."
2. Fill the silence—call out what "pops into your head."
3. Wait for an opening—"Don't step on someone's lines."
4. Record the thoughts in short form (leader).
5. Record *everything*, no matter how "far out" (leader).
6. Repeat your contribution until it is recorded.
7. Be positive—no "put downs," negative body language, or editorial comment by any participant.
8. Stay in focus—no digressions or tangents.
9. Use short time spans—one to three minutes.
10. Analyze later—add, subtract, plan, implement.
11. Brainstorm from general to specific through subsets.

To demonstrate brainstorming for the first time, begin with a simple one-word topic such as the listing of synonyms for the word "leader" or naming the characteristics of a leader. The group is likely to respond with approximately twenty to thirty substitutes that have the same meaning as the selected noun or a like number of positive or negative adjectives for its characteristics. Within a short time the participants will warm to their task and associative linkages will appear, e.g., "boss—principal—father—mother—king—ruler—despot—dictator," etc. Under "characteristics," you might try the "qualities of a good principal" and record the thirty or thirty-five God-like attributes sought by teachers of candidates for that new administrative opening.

Move on to a creative topic such as the avoidance of clichés in compositions. Try brainstorming "as quiet as a ______ ______ ing." Instead of "as quite as a mouse," you will have delighted groups calling, "as quiet as a snowflake falling," "grass growing," "eyelid closing," "a principal thinking," "student sneaking," "headache throbbing," "butter-flying," "mind-worrying," "cat stalking," "child sleeping," etc.

Now you are ready to try problems of concern to you or, perhaps more important, issues or topics that trouble the staff. You can brainstorm those and ask teachers or other administrators to select the topic(s) they would like to brainstorm.

The Process

You are now ready to try an actual problem in two parts—(1) the negative aspects (−) and (2) the potential solutions (+).

The following sample is a partial list of actual responses from teacher brainstorming groups:

(−) *What's wrong with homework assignments as we know them?*	(+) *What can we do to improve them?*
too long, resources unavailable	vary length
busy work, not taken seriously	mark each one
not done, not individualized	design on simpler and more complex levels
not marked, not stimulating	individualize assignments
irrelevant, doubtful benefit	provide choices
done by parents, copied	relate to real world
not clear, not returned to students	assign only to students who need them, prepare specific directions, develop creative alternatives

Obviously, several "what we can do" responses require specificity. For example, part, or all, of the group should subset brainstorm examples of what constitutes a creative or an individualized assignment.

Now try a three-part brainstorming session based on the problem topics elicited from the group.

(+) *Positive Description or Projection of an Ideal Program*	(−) *Obstacles or Preventions*	(+) *Next Steps*
Examples:		
(1) What would constitute an ideal disciplinary climate for our school?	What's keeping us from having good discipline?	What can we do about it?
-OR-	-OR-	-OR-
(2) What should an ideal program of study skills include?	What might prevent us from establishing this program?	What are our next steps?

A more global topic requires a five-part brainstorming session:

(+)	(−)	(+)	(−)	(+)
What is our total goal? e.g. new school, revised curriculum, reorganization plan	What will prevent us from achieving it?	What are some viable programs that will aid us in reaching our goal?	What will prevent these programs from materializing?	What are our next steps?
-OR-	-OR-	-OR-	-OR-	-OR-
What would constitute a totally individualized program for all students?	What would prevent us from achieving total individualization?	What are some programs we should establish to reach this goal?	What will block these programs?	What are our next steps?

Continue to move from general to more and more specific responses and suggestions. Brainstorm these until concrete suggestions emerge. These should be reported to all and tried as potential viable programs or solutions.

Brainstorming with students and parents has proven very successful. Students will reveal what they believe their school should be like and how to improve discipline, the school cafeteria, or any area that affects them. Parents will be happy to pinpoint problems, high-priority items, concerns, or what they like about the schools, to name but a few topics. You might also brainstorm the almost limitless use of this technique for instructional purposes with department chairmen and teachers.

Brainstorming Case History: A Writing Skills Program

Brainstorming can be used to involve parents in developing a program that responds to an individual community's concerns. The technique can be efficient as well as effective. The following lists of brainstorming items were developed by parents, teachers, and administrators as part of a one-hour segment at a regular public school board meeting.

A REPRESENTATIVE SAMPLE OF A BRAINSTORMING SESSION

Board of Education Meeting June 23

QUESTION: What would be the ideal English composition program?

PARTICIPANTS: 15-20 parents, 2 teachers, 2 administrators, and 1 board member in each of five groups. Underlined = Highest priorities

Elementary	Middle School—Group A	Middle School—Group B	High School—Group A	High School—Group B
Corrected and taught for grammar and spelling—in all subjects	Repetition of basics	High standards and expectations	Compulsory writing	Good mix of structure and free form
Outlining, notetaking, and proofreading	Content (subject matter)	Regular assignments	Grammar/punctuation	Frequent assignments
Teacher's comment on content and form	Writing on regular basis (at least twice per week)	Two grades (with constructive correction for content and grammar)	More writing/rewriting	Read and write
Organization and articulation of ideas	Standardization across the classes	More reading—better writing	Clarity of expression	Interest-related
Pleasure of writing—creatively written and oral communication of ideas should generate excitement	Organization of thoughts	Basic language skills and application:	Pride in work	Carefully graded assignments
Not composition alone—include grammar	Basics!!! Grammar	Sentence structure	Good critical review (without devastation)	Exposure to good literature
Frequent short writing assignments	Consistency	Grammar	Creative writing	Conferences with teachers
Children should be taught to proofread	Leadership by teacher	Spelling	More uniform	Wide exposure to varied courses
	Creativity	Punctuation	More control in mini-course balance	Good models
	Reading for ideas	Vocabulary	Writing on any subject	Meaningful and not artificial
	Learning style elements	Paragraph structure	Develop good work habits	Guidelines to proper form
	Separating the important from unimportant	Appearance	Learning techniques of formal writing	Cater to varied learning styles
	Expressing feelings	Analysis	Learning to proofread	
	Research papers	Proofreading	Exposure to broader range of writers	

Elementary	Middle School—Group A	Middle School—Group B	High School—Group A	High School—Group B
Creative Grammar and spelling not priority in creative writing in primary grades Individualized writing assignments Purposes of writing Relevance for children of particular age level Storytelling Balance of creativity and form		Essays in other subjects Correction Stimulation Communication with home Rewriting Resource writing Outlining	Having something to say Filling wastebaskets	Communication of ideas Ability-grouped

QUESTION: What might prevent us from having this program?

Elementary	Middle School—Group A	Middle School—Group B	High School—Group A	High School—Group B
Fear of inhibitions on part of students/teachers Teacher confusion if program were not clearly outlined Teacher's rejection of creativity Lack of continuity from K-12	Poor teaching Poor students Inadequate supervision Overcrowding Poor use of English by teachers Lack of imagination Assuming something is learned	Teacher apathy Differing philosophies Lack of leadership Lack of coordination Conflict of goals between departments Lack of parental support Poor reading ability Too much TV	Teacher getting off subject Teacher/student laziness Lack of discipline (both parties) Fun of teaching literature over writing Teacher preparedness	Too much structure Not enough structure Poor teaching Disinterested students and/or teachers trying to do too much Too many courses Not enough challenge Lack of money

Elementary	Middle School—Group A	Middle School—Group B	High School—Group A	High School—Group B
Absence of options on part of teachers	Nothing	Poor adult example	Student preparedness	Poor guidance
Individual differences: teachers, children, and parents	Lack of money	Lack of student interest	Expectations too great?	Lack of program articulation
Communication from teacher to parent on assignments, goals, program	Lack of pupil/teacher discussion of papers	Lack of discipline	Time	Nonuniform supervision of program
Teacher's fear of inadequacy	Lack of encouragement and supportive attitudes	Dryness of grammar skills	Lack of student/teacher motivation	Lack of student and teacher accountability
Lack of teacher workshops	Concern of parents, teachers, and community	Lack of opportunity for verbal expression	Rationalization	
Lack of time devoted to English program	School Board deaf ear	Time—for detailed correction at home	Really difficult	
Communication between teacher and teacher	Lack of follow-through		Sequencing through grades (what to teach, when)	
Too many subjects	Lack of publications (within school building)		Insufficient readers	
Failure of teacher to set high standards	Time wasted with games		Poor teacher-to-parent follow-through	
Too short a day	Time needed for thorough correction, encouragement, etc.		Lack of money	
Too much acceleration			Imbalance between student need and teacher effort	
Parental unwillingness to accept program			Lack of student desire	
			Lack of courses (filled courses)	
			Poor student choices	
			Poor guidance	
			Parental apathy	

QUESTION: How can we achieve this program?

Elementary	Middle School—Group A	Middle School—Group B	High School—Group A	High School—Group B
By changing obstacles to positive statements	Standardize English program K-12	Accountability for curriculum	A	Offering more sections of better courses (e.g. AP English)
More communication between school and home	Better communication among schools	Implementation	Make them work	Better teachers—balance of strengths
More communication among elementary schools	Standardize English usage throughout all departments	Greater care in hiring	Make them write more	Planning
Continuing evaluation of curriculum guide for English	High-quality teachers	Articulation among three school levels	Everyone (other teachers/parents et. al.) encourage more writing	Attention to clarity of expression
Teachers using various approaches	Supervision of program	Coordination K-12 guidance for implementation of curriculum	B	Coordination with social studies program
Curriculum outline	Allow for individual teacher's creativity	Competency-based program	Evaluation of composition importance in teacher's total course program	Consistency among grade levels
Students' newspaper/magazine	Attention to guidelines for grade level	More supervision	Program planning	Coordination with foreign language program
Comprehensive criticism—peer-to-peer, teacher-to-student	Thorough study of English curriculum in all schools	More detailed curriculum	Trace back deficiencies to where they occurred	Better guidance
Having children write their own absence notes (signed by parent)	Intense vocabulary program	Greater emphasis on reading and vocabulary	Guidelines for formal papers	More money
Old-fashioned spelling bees	Emphasis on word derivation for spelling	Aggressive communication with home re expectations	Volunteer aides (trained by faculty) to assist in paper grading	Greater motivation
	Leadership at all levels	Fewer superficial communications		Grading of elements of composition
	Exchange of pupils and teachers in mid-year	Carrying out of goals		Conference on strengths and weaknesses

Elementary	Middle School—Group A	Middle School—Group B	High School—Group A	High School—Group B
Vocabulary testing	Penmanship development	Recognition of good writing	Standards of excellence across grade levels and disciplines	Mandatory courses for those found deficient in various elements
Goal achievement	Parts of speech learned	Praise for a job well done	C	Aggressive communication to home
Strong administrative involvement	Testing in sixth grade	Consider lay readers	Papers be corrected and returned with comments	Special courses on grammar
Continued emphasis on dictionary use	Diagramming sentences	Appropriate matching of teacher/pupils	Ongoing critical evaluation of teachers	High standards of excellence
Volunteers to help correct	High moral values expressed by teachers	Individual attention	Review of teacher's writings as part of job interview	
Utilize multimedia approach		Less "sugar-coating"	Sensitivity to needs of individual students—draw them out	
Teacher willingness to help student after school		Less visual instruction	Making use of AV aids on individual basis	
Writing workshops for children		More screening	Creativity is not all important	
Freer use of library			Program for pinpointing and correcting student deficiencies	
More time			D	
Awards for achievement			Thorough review of grammar basics	
Rewards for trying				

These brainstorming items, elicited in the late spring, were subjected to rigorous analysis. A group of six teachers, one principal, and the superintendent met for a total of five days during the summer to consider the listings, the subsequent input from colleagues in the schools, and their own analyses as well as those of other administrators.

The district's faculties subsequently designed the following guidelines with specific procedures and action patterns to ensure the continuing improvement of writing skills in their schools.

Writing Skills Guidelines

I. INTRODUCTION

All teachers, within the limit of their subject areas, are responsible for the improvement of student writing. The emphasis in these materials is on the skills essential to develop both effective creative and expository writing at all grade levels. . . .

II. INSTRUCTIONAL GOALS

A. Objectively Measurable Goals
   1. Improvement in standard mechanics
      a. spelling
      b. punctuation
      c. capitalization
   2. Improvement in standard usage
   3. Ability to write complete sentences
   4. Ability to write coherent and well-developed paragraphs
   5. Ability to write coherent and well-developed compositions
   6. Ability to use appropriate research techniques

B. Developmental Goals
   1. Knowledge and use of the forms and types of expository writing
   2. Awareness of elements of style—tone, stance, purpose, and effect
   3. Improvement in logical relations
   4. Improvement in vocabulary

C. Attitudinal Goals
   1. Increased respect for language
   2. Increased appreciation of the value of writing
   3. Increased willingness to write

III. PROCEDURAL GUIDELINES

A. All elementary classroom English and social studies teachers should:
   1. assign and correct written work frequently.
   2. use corrected written work in follow-up procedures wtih individual students.

3. assign and correct appropriate research projects on a regular basis.
4. provide opportunities for students to learn logical relationships, respect for language, and elements of style.
5. evaluate improvement in instructional goals through periodic accountability.

B. All other teachers should assign and correct written work as appropriate to their subject areas.

C. All teachers should visit and exchange teaching techniques, methods, papers, systems, and ideas.

D. The administrative staff should:
1. establish a unified evaluation program to measure progress toward the instructional goals.
2. communicate goals and programs to parents.
3. encourage parental support for the instructional goals.

NOTE: Teachers at each grade level should devise activities appropriate to each student's needs. For example, in the primary grades some skills may be developed through oral instead of written exercises.

IV. SAMPLE METHODS OF EVALUATION BY TEACHERS
(as appropriate to grade level and subject matter)

A. For Objectively Measurable Goals:
1. Dictation
2. Proofreading and correction
3. Multiple choice
4. Oral response
5. Examination of work samples

B. For Developmental Goals:
1. Cumulative folders of student writing
2. Objective testing

V. SUGGESTIONS FOR PROGRAM EVALUATION

A. Examination of Cumulative Folder Program
B. Development of Writing Skills Scales
C. Design of Long-range Evaluation, e.g., spelling, complete sentences, paragraph development, etc.
D. Establishment of Internal and External Assessment of the Ongoing Program

VI. WRITING SKILLS K-12
Minimum Curriculum Standards in Writing

Major responsibility for teaching (T) each item is at the level indicated. Individual needs will require maintenance and reinforcement (R) in subsequent years.

A teacher should introduce or teach a specific item earlier if individual students or groups are ready for the advanced work. Individual elementary schools may wish to designate specific grade levels or, in some instances, a different initiation (T) range as appropriate to their detailed teaching manuals.

Instruction at all levels includes development of methods such as outlining, revising, and proofreading. Editing skills are taught as appropriate at the upper levels.

WRITING SKILLS K-12

	K-3	4-6	7-8	9-12
CAPITALIZATION				
I	T	R	R	R
Names of people, animals	T	R	R	R
First words	T	R	R	R
Times	T	R	R	R
Places	T	R	R	R
Holidays	T	R	R	R
Notes and letters	T	R	R	R
Titles of people	T	R	R	R
Groups		T	R	R
Outlines		T	R	R
Languages	T	R	R	R
Clubs	T	R	R	R
Business letters		T	R	R
Deities		T	R	R
Titles	T	R	R	R
Quotations		T	R	R
Documents		T	R	R
Directions		T	R	R
Direct address		T	R	R
PUNCTUATION				
End of sentences	T	R	R	R
Commas, time-place	T	R	R	R
Informal letters	T	R	R	R
Apostrophes	T	R	R	R
Commas in series	T	R	R	R
Business letters		T	R	R

	K-3	4-6	7-8	9-12
PUNCTUATION (cont.)				
Other uses of the period	T	R	R	R
Outlines		T	R	R
Possessives		T	R	R
Quotations		T	R	R
Appositives		T	R	R
Direct address		T	R	R
Interjections		T	R	R
Introductory words/phrases		T	R	R
Underlining		T	R	R
Hyphens		T	R	R
Colons			T	R
Semicolons			T	R
USAGE				
Subject-verb agreement		T	R	R
Pronouns		T	R	R
Verb forms		T	R	R
Adjectives-adverbs			T	R
Position of modifiers			T	R
Pronoun-antecedent agreement			T	R
Tense use				T
SENTENCE				
Sentence sense	T	R	R	R
Coordination (compounding)		T	R	R
Sentence types		T	R	R
Inversion (variety)		T	R	R
Subordination			T	R
Rhetorical types				T
VOCABULARY				
Levels of usage (appropriateness)	T	R	R	R
Specificity	T	R	R	R
Figurative language	T	R	R	R
Vividness	T	R	R	R
Connotation-denotation	T	R	R	R

	K-3	4-6	7-8	9-12
COMPOSITION (Paragraph)				
Unity	T	R	R	R
Methods of development		T	R	R
Consistency			T	R
COMPOSITION (2 or more paragraphs)				
Outlining		T	R	R
Organization		T	R	R
Development		T	R	R
Unity		T	R	R
Explication			T	R
Consistency			T	R
Thesis statement				T
RESEARCH				
Note taking	T	R	R	R
Listing of resources	T	R	R	R
Outlining		T	R	R
Paraphrasing		T	R	R
Summarizing		T	R	R
Using references				T
Using proper research-paper forms				T

NOTE: As the listing above indicates, study skills are integrated with writing skills.

MANAGING TIME AND SELF

The number-one complaint of executives or administrators in any organization is the lack of time. School administrators invariably indicate that they would like to spend more time with people—talking with students, supervising teachers, understanding parents' points of view, etc. Somehow the clock and calendar keep moving and planned time to work with people disappears in a snowstorm of paper or a burst dam of crises.

Murphy's famous first law, "If something can go wrong, it will," is followed by a less famous, but extremely appropriate second law, "Everything takes longer than you think!"

One way to attack the problem of time is to contemplate what it is and what it means to us. Considering time in the abstract begins to give us handles for control. Once you control time, you control your life and, of course, your professional obligations.

Hold a workshop on time with fellow administrators or teachers, for we all need help in an area that is rarely confronted by educators.

Begin by answering the question "What is time?" in a sentence or two or in a short paragraph. Discuss each member's answer in a circle of five or six. Have the participants note the answer that each liked best. Then have those answers that received greatest approval listed on a large chart for everyone at the time-management workshop to examine.

You might wish to discuss the notion that writers, poets, artists, soldiers, philosophers, and people in all areas throughout history have been concerned with time. Here are a few of the more notable examples. They range from the poetic to the scientific; from the pragmatic to the ethereal:

What Is Time?

You can ask me for anything you like, except time—
Napoleon Bonaparte
1769-1821

Nae man can tether time or tide—
Robert Burns 1759-1796

. . . time was the most valuable thing that a man could spend—
Diogenes Laertius circa A.D.200

Nothing is so dear and precious as time—
Francois Rabelais 1495-1553

Remember that time is money—
Benjamin Franklin 1706-1790

Procrastination is the thief of time—
Edward Young 1683-1765

. . . this earth goes over to the squall of time!—
Archibald MacLeish
1892-

Time, you thief—
Leigh Hunt 1784-1859

And time, a maniac scattering dust—
Alfred, Lord Tennyson 1809-1892

If time be heavy on your hands—
Alfred, Lord Tennyson 1809-1892

Work is the scythe of time—
Napoleon Bonaparte 1769-1821

. . . on the bridge of time—
Sir Richard Francis Burton 1821-1890

. . . through the corridors of time—
Henry Wadsworth Longfellow 1807-1882

. . . in the tide of times—
William Shakespeare 1564-1616

Oft up the stream of time—
Samuel Rogers 1763-1855

Time is a . . . river of passing events—
Marcus Aurelius Antoninus
A.D.131-180

. . . time an endless song—
William Butler Yeats 1865-1939

. . . 'gainst the tooth of time—
William Shakespeare 1564-1616

Time, like an ever rolling stream—
Isaac Watts 1674-1748

Time travels in divers paces with divers persons . . . time ambles . . . trots . . . gallops . . . stands still—
William Shakespeare 1564-1616

Time is the image of eternity—
Diogenes Laertius circa 200 A.D.

Where time and eternity meet and blend—
Rollin John Wells 1848-1923

That's what it was to be alive. To move about in a cloud of ignorance; to go up and down trampling on the feelings of those about you. *To spend and waste time as though you had a million years.* To be always at the mercy of one self-centered passion, or another. Now you know—that's the happy existence you wanted to go back to.—(from *Our Town*)
Thornton Wilder 1897-1975

The system of those sequential relations that any event has to any other, as past, present, or future; indefinite and continuous duration regarded as that in which events succeed one another.—
The Random House Dictionary 1971

As a school executive, one cannot help but sympathize with Napoleon's prophetic statement that preceded Waterloo, when indeed time ran out as General Bleucher's Prussian troops arrived on the battlefield to reinforce Wellington less than an hour before French reinforcements, thus changing the course of history.

After contemplating the meaning of time in the abstract, list the general reasons for your wanting to find more time. Now fill out this chart:

Figure 4-3

Professional Task Preferences

As objectively and as honestly as you can, list the five things you like to do most and least in your job.

Five things I like to do *most*.	Rating (1 to 5)	Five things I like to do *least*.	Rating (1 to 5)
1. ______	☐	1. ______	☐
2. ______	☐	2. ______	☐
3. ______	☐	3. ______	☐
4. ______	☐	4. ______	☐
5. ______	☐	5. ______	☐

Now rate them in order of importance to you in the boxes to the right of each list.

Brainstorm with assistants or teachers what prevents you from doing the professional things you like to do and what keeps you doing the things in your job that you do not like doing. Keep this chart available as you complete the next self-training technique.

Self-administered Time Analysis Logs

Most time-management experts insist on a careful self-analysis of the way you use your time. Insights into why you are not doing the important things you like to do usually become readily apparent on these forms, or time logs. Keep one for two separate weeks during the fall and again in the spring. Hopefully you will have been able to change your behavior after analyzing your October-November time-utilization charts.

DAILY TIME LOG[3]

DAY OF WEEK________
DATE____________

TIME*	ACTION	PRIORITY 1=Important & Urgent 2=Important 3=Routine	DELEGATION 1=Ignore or Discontinue 2=Delegate to 3=Retain	DISPOSITION (Comment)
7:00				
7:30				
8:00				
8:30				
9:00				
9:30				
10:00				
10:30				
11:00				
11:30				
12:00				
12:30				
1:00				
1:30				
2:00				
2:30				
3:00				
3:30				
4:00				
4:30				
5:00				
5:30				
6:00				
6:30				
7:00				

*Many executives leave the time list blank until an interruption occurs or some new action is taken. They then note the beginning and ending times of each event.

Figure 4-4

Note that the log requires you to consider which items are delegated or retained and the degree of importance you attach to each task. The description of the action and its disposition also will aid you in assessing how you use your time.

The next chart (Figure 4-5) will assist you in analyzing the percentage of actual time devoted to each category of administrative action and requires consideration of daily goals (beyond survival).

WEEK OF________

TIME ANALYSIS[3]

I. DAILY GOALS (Important and Urgent)

	MON.	TUES.	WED.	THURS.	FRI.	SAT.
1.						
2.						
3.						
4.						
5.						

II. TIME ALLOCATION TO MAJOR CATEGORIES (Planning; Team; Secretary, etc.)

	CATEGORY	% of Time		CATEGORY	% of Time
1.			5.		
2.			6.		
3.			7.		
4.			8.		

III. ACTUAL TIME SPENT DAILY PER CATEGORY

	MON.	TUES.	WED.	THURS.	FRI.	SAT.
1.						
2.						
3.						
4.						
5.						
6.						
7.						
8.						

Figure 4-5

These time logs can be modified, of course, to suit your situation or position. You may add the origin of an item, the level of the initiator, and an exact elapsed-time column. It is difficult to discipline oneself to keep a faithful time log, therefore the simpler the format, the better. The results are eye-opening and are useful in building your resolve to use your time more effectively.

SETTING PRIORITIES

More insightful than Parkinson's first law, which insists that a task tends to fill up the time that is available, is his second law. School administrators (and all executives) should consider his proposition that we tend to devote time and effort to tasks in inverse proportion to their importance.

"Since the new flexible working hours began, Seymour, we haven't been able to locate yours."

Further, management experts, economists, and time-management consultants consistently find that very few actions tend to produce major results.[4] Conversely, many items on which an inestimable amount of time is spent often yield only a small fraction of the results that really affect our lives or professional efforts.

A simple representation of this concept, originally stated by a nineteenth-century Italian economist and sociologist, Vilfredo Pareto, indicates that 20% of all that we do produces 80% of our desired results, while 80% of our effort nets only 20% of the results.

Translating the Pareto principle to school life or situations implies that the time devoted to administrative tasks is disproportionate to the importance of those tasks, for example:

"A" Tasks: Most important, vital, necessary, urgent	10-20% of our time
"B" Tasks: Important, maintenance, ongoing	10-20% of our time
"C" Tasks: Least important, trivial, reporting items	60-80% of our time

"A" tasks would include meetings with students, planning curriculum changes, observing and aiding staff, meetings with parents, and the prevention of, or planning for, crises.

"B" tasks would include scheduling, discipline, testing programs, important statistical reports, general faculty meetings, and responding to crises.

"C" tasks would include attendance checks, meaningless and unused reports, nonproductive meetings, reading and signing bureaucratic memos, unnecessary phone calls, student insurance and photographs, lunchroom schedules, transportation checks, book and supply inventories, and talking to salespersons, etc.

Time logs will show you fairly accurately the disproportionate percentage of time spent on "C," or trivial, tasks.

A. B. C. TASKS:
TIME-RESULTS RELATIONSHIPS

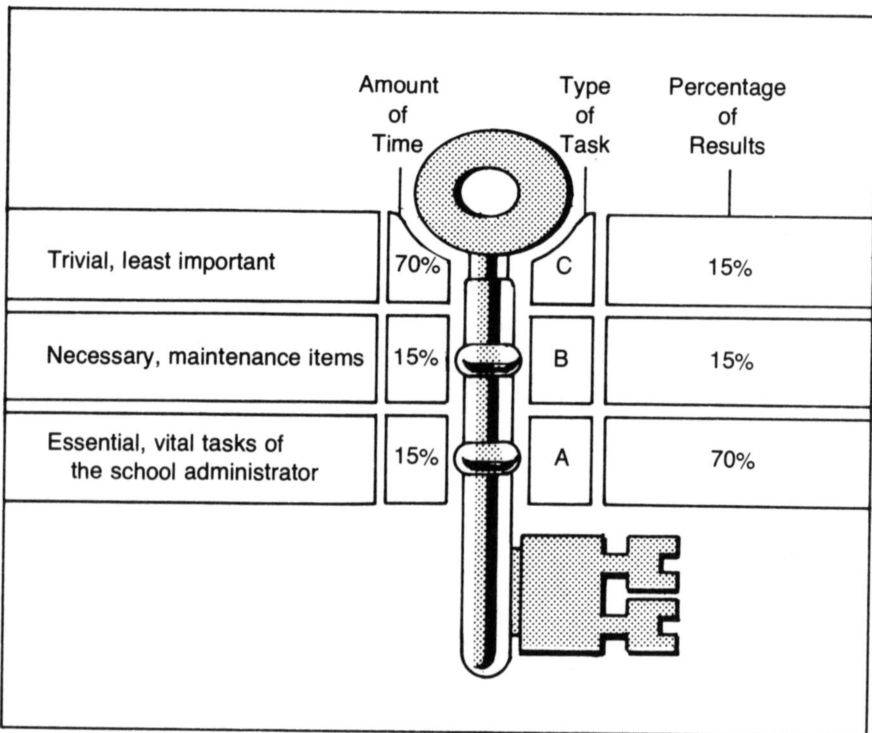

Amount of Time
Type of Task
Percentage of Results
Trivial, least important
70%
C
15%
Necessary, maintenance items
15%
B
15%
Essential, vital tasks of the school administrator
15%
A
70%

Figure 4-6

The implication of the A.B.C. Time-Results Relationships Chart (Figure 4-6) is that we devote a high proportion of our time to trivial tasks. Filling in meaningless statistical forms or reviewing lunchroom schedules often demands 70% of our time and produces only 15% of the results that really add to the quality of education or have impact on the objectives we set for students. Maintenance items such as testing programs or responding to crises take only 15% of our time but produce only 15% of the results. Finally, only 15% of our time is devoted to the important tasks of instructional leadership and management; yet this time results in 70% of the important results or objectives that are completed. Obviously we should improve this time allocation whenever we can.

An easy way to verify the general validity of this principle is to list all of the things you do every day for a week or a month and place them in "A," "B," and "C" columns according to your rating of their importance. You might do the same with your mail, the time log suggested earlier in this chapter, the last agenda for a faculty meeting, your phone calls for a week, etc. This is a mandatory procedure because you need to begin to find a way to identify "A" items and to complete them first. "B" items should be delegated and receive only part of your attention. "C" items should be eliminated or given to employees for whom they would represent more difficult tasks than those they are currently performing.

Establishing a Rationale to Set Priorities

It is easy to place items into three sections marked A, B, and C, but the choices may vary from one administrator to another and by the same school leader at different times or in the middle of a crisis. It is critical to set directions because, as most of us have learned, "If you don't know where you're going, any path will take you there."

To begin, classify all of the things you have to do today—phone calls, correspondence, reports, mail, observations, meetings, etc., into A, B, and C groupings. Place the A items on your desk and immediately *schedule* time to do them this morning! Delegate the "B" items and discard or delegate the "C" items. (You might delegate some of the "A" items to assistants, if appropriate.)

This approach may be used for daily tasks by a group or an individual to set the A, B, and C tasks for the day. A secretary and assistant might be good sounding boards and provide a consensus of those concerned with the final outcome.

Figure 4-7

PRIORITY GOALS GRID

(46 participants)

	First Place (3 points each)	Second Place (2 points each)	Third Place (1 point each)	Point Total
1. Writing Skills K-12	8	7	2	40
2. Provide Workshops for Individualized Instruction	8	5	3	37
3. Gifted Program	7	5	1	32
4. Learning Disabilities Program	5	5	6	31
5. Girls' Physical Education	4	6	3	27
6. Improved Homework Assignments	2	5	9	25
7. Report Card Revisions	2	5	3	19
8. Increase Time for Music Instruction	3	2	2	15
9. Increase Field Trips	3	1	4	15
10. Evaluate Outdoor Education Program	2	1	5	13
11. Increase Foreign Language Offerings		1	5	7
12. Released Time for Planning		1	3	5
13. Return to Ability Grouping		2		4
14. All-day Kindergarten	1			3
15. Provide School-owned Transportation	1			3

Arriving at Consensus—Priority Grid

Another approach to setting priorities, especially with your staff or at faculty meetings, is to agree to and list the potential priority items for all to see. Then allow all the participants to vote three times giving 3 points to each of their first choices, 2 to each of their second-place items, and 1 to each of their third-place choices.

An example of a priority grid to determine goals for the year might result in the type of tabulation shown in Figure 4-7.

Writing skills, workshops for individualized instruction, a program for gifted youngsters and one for those who are learning-disabled received the most votes and should, therefore, be given primary and immediate attention, whereas the second group of high-priority reforms concerned with girls' physical education, improving homework assignments, and report card revisions might be temporarily deferred. The lowest group (8-15) should be dropped from consideration at this time. The highest consensus scores should be rated against local criteria of importance, such as value to students, types and numbers of students affected, feasibility, likelihood of success, degree of projected community involvement and support, or long-range value to society.

OVERCOMING SELF-DEFEATING MECHANISMS

The counter-productive devices we sometimes use to prevent ourselves from achieving, completing, winning, deciding, enjoying, and self-fulfilling include procrastination, vacillation, and distraction. They are recognizable in the energy we expend rationalizing, acting negatively, and remaining disorganized.

PROCRASTINATION

Procrastination—putting off until later what can be done now—is a great thief of time. "A" items are placed on the bottom of the pile of a procrastinator's stacked desk, safely hidden for weeks or months.

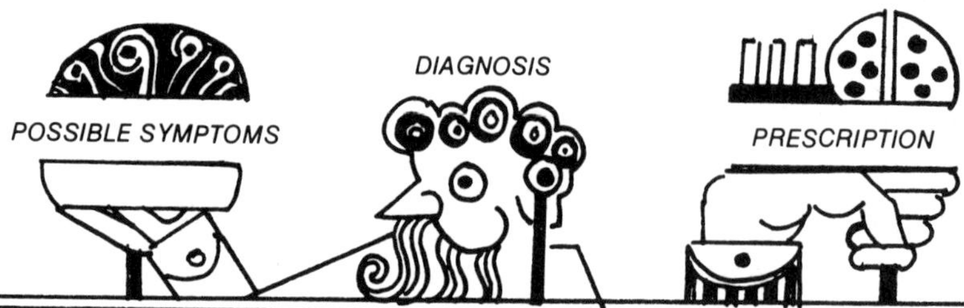

POSSIBLE SYMPTOMS	DIAGNOSIS	PRESCRIPTION
I'm feeling overwhelmed.	Stacked deskitis	Use A, B, C basket approach and secretary to clear work
I'll get to it when I feel up to it.	Slipped time disc	Self-examine time-wasters, eliminate interruptions
I just don't have the time.	Pressure fever	Organize into manageable pieces, delegate
I've got to get organized.	Disorganization depression	Use lists, priorities, time lines

VACILLATION

Vacillation—or indecision—can halt all A-type activities.

POSSIBLE SYMPTOMS	*DIAGNOSIS*	*PRESCRIPTION*
I can't make up my mind.	Indecisiveobia	Get the facts; use a sounding board
I'm really afraid of the consequences.	Action paralysis	Prepare, plan; try a small risk first
I have reasons for not doing it.	Rationalizationitis	Consider self-rewards; list the consequences of acting positively
I'll delay and it will go away.	Ostrich syndrome	List the consequences of not acting; share responsibility

Figure 4-8

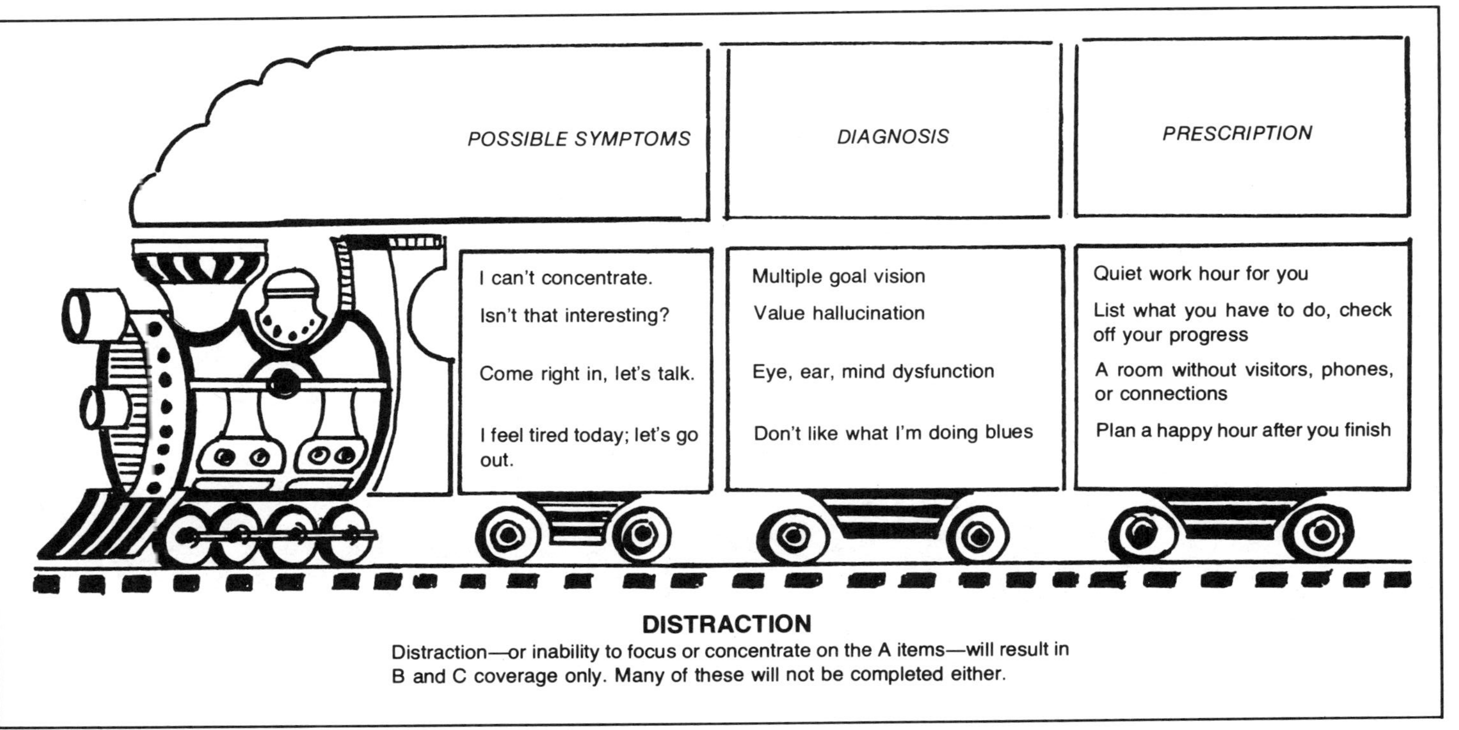

POSSIBLE SYMPTOMS
DIAGNOSIS
PRESCRIPTION
I can't concentrate.
Isn't that interesting?
Come right in, let's talk.
I feel tired today; let's go out.
Multiple goal vision
Value hallucination
Eye, ear, mind dysfunction
Don't like what I'm doing blues
Quiet work hour for you
List what you have to do, check off your progress
A room without visitors, phones, or connections
Plan a happy hour after you finish

DISTRACTION

Distraction—or inability to focus or concentrate on the A items—will result in B and C coverage only. Many of these will not be completed either.

Figure 4-9

Next, develop some key questions to brainstorm for the continuing answers to train yourself to manage time and life, as well as your job.

Here is a starter list:

1. How can I eliminate this task?
2. How can I reduce the time required for this job?
3. How can I lower the intensity of my negative feelings toward this?
4. How can I create opportunities to do the things I want to do?
5. How can I increase the time available for this creative experience?
6. What are the resources available to me?
7. What are some possible time lines for completion?
8. Which problems or obstacles can I avoid? How?
9. What are the advantages and disadvantages of this action?
10. What are the consequences likely to be?
11. What are my criteria or reasons for selecting this set of procedures? or making that decision?
12. Which things should I (can I) do first?
13. Who can (should) do this for me?

As another approach, several human relations and communications consultants suggest "self-role playing" to understand better the things we do or don't do and the feelings that motivate us into action or inaction. By "talking to yourself" as both questioner and respondent, insights into your own behavior may provide another managerial tool for action. This type of auditory analysis is described by James and Jongeward[5] and may reinforce or complement the visual-kinesthetic focus of brainstorming.

This method of overcoming self-deception, defense mechanisms, and hardened positions toward what seems to be the irrational behavior of others involves engaging in imaginary, multiple roles. For example, an irate parent may find it difficult to understand why her son must attend study hall under penalty of detention and/or suspension when he is an "A" student and his homework is always completed at home the night before it is due. Close your eyes and begin to examine the questions that will *support* your attitude, such as:

Why is she coming to see me?
Why doesn't she force her son to obey the rules?
Doesn't she know that I can't make exceptions?
Doesn't she realize that if I did excuse her son (let him "get away with it") that every youngster in the building would want to "cut" study hall?
How is she bringing up her son?
Doesn't she recognize that he will have no respect for authority?
Why can't this kid follow the rules?
Why is this mother such a troublemaker?
Why can't parents *and* their children conform to established school regulations?

How can I get her "off my back" quickly? (and spend my time more constructively on important matters)

Now assume the respondent's point of view and list as many alternative answers to each of the questions that you enumerated. For example:

QUESTIONS ABOUT THE PARENT	*ALTERNATIVE ANSWERS FROM THE PARENT*
Why is she coming to see me?	I am not a troublemaker. I am concerned about my son; he is very unhappy. You are the authority. You are the only one who is likely to help me. I have confidence in you. I believe that you will be fair. I don't want to waste your time; I know that you have many important things to do. This problem is important to us. This requirement should not apply to everybody. If it does, it is arbitrary and capricious. Why can't there be an alternative for some youngsters? What is the value of study hall? Why is study hall necessary?
Why doesn't she force her son to obey the rules?	These rules are not good ones (certainly not for everyone!) He can't *think* in study hall. He does all his work at home where it is very quiet. His homework is always done; why can't he do something more productive like going to the library or watching a film or using the art facilities? I can't make him obey. I am afraid of "turning him off" completely about his schoolwork. The rules are not applied uniformly; clever kids find a way to get out of it. He wants to be an attorney. This is a matter of principle to him. He will not give in even if it does mean suspension or expulsion.

As you place yourself in the role of the parent, try to respond through a successful bridging of the emotional and rational factors involved.

Possible Answers from the Administrator:

I understand how you feel, and I even sympathize with your position.
I am also concerned about __(her child's name)__.
There should be a way to work this problem out.
I am glad that you came in to discuss this problem with me directly.
Do you have any suggestions that stay within the rules and yet maintain __(student's name)__ principles?

Finally, what alternatives could you offer in response to the parent? *Is* this rule "arbitrary and capricious"? Can some flexibility be added? Is the rule worth applying without considering the human elements involved? Is there a way to change the schedule? Can there be an alternative to the study hall? What is the *purpose* of requiring study hall attendance? If the homework is consistently done at home, couldn't the student engage in other worthwhile educational practices during that time period? If the rule is based on administrative convenience (knowing where each student is at a given time), couldn't selected students "sign into" other positive educational activities instead of study hall? Shouldn't high school students be permitted some options? How will they be trained to cope with responsibility and decision-making requirements unless they are given opportunities in which to practice such skills? Should an advisory committee of parents, students, and teachers be established to study the problem and make recommendations?

By playing these roles and projecting potential questions, answers, and solutions, the administrator will have prepared properly to deal with difficult emotional confrontations and, at the same time, lay the groundwork for appropriate and positive administrative resolution of both short- and long-range problems. In this way much time will be saved and a climate of positive personal interaction will have been established.

Furthermore, once administrators and supervisors have mastered the techniques of managing time and themselves, it is recommended that they teach their faculties the same skills for personal use with students and parents for the improvement of teaching and learning.

NOTES FOR CHAPTER 4

1. R. Alec Mackenzie. *The Time Trap—Managing Your Way Out*. New York: Amacom (1972).
2. Robert N. Ford. *Motivation Through the Work Itself*. New York: American Management Association (1969): 24, 25. Also see chapter 3, "Increasing Faculty Motivation and Skill."

3. The time analysis charts (Figures 4-4 and 4-5) were developed by R. Alec Mackenzie. Figure 4-5 appears in *The Time Trap:* 22.
4. Joseph M. Juron. *Managerial Breakthrough.* New York: McGraw-Hill (1964).
5. Muriel James and Dorothy Jongeward. *Born to Win: Transactional Analysis with Gestalt Experiments.* Reading, Massachusetts: Addison-Wesley Publishing Company (1973): 15, 98, 155, 210.

Part II

Faculty Evaluation Programs

5

IMPROVING FACULTY EVALUATION:

Identifying Appropriate Criteria and Alerting Faculty

DISCARDING OUTMODED EVALUATION PROCEDURES

Administrators have been evaluating faculty for many years[1] in an effort to isolate those characteristics that produce effective instruction. Two weaknesses of previous attempts were due to difficulties in accurately identifying common positive characteristics of teacher personality and style, and objectively interpreting what was seen.

A third problem encountered by supervisors who sought to determine the comparative effectiveness of teachers centered on incorrect assumptions about what ought to be measured when observing classroom procedures.[2] For example, years ago it was considered appropriate for teachers to develop a lesson plan that included every subject to be taught and the amount of time anticipated for each topic. Supervisors expected to be able to visit a class at any given hour and observe the instructor teaching a specific lesson according to that plan. As part of the evaluation, teachers were chastised if they did not follow the schedule or if they were "not teaching" (a term used to describe anything other than the lecture, lecture-discussion, or "chalk-talk" method). Indeed, some supervisors continue to insist on whole-group lesson plans despite widespread acceptance of the reality of individual student differences.

As instructional methods improved, teachers continued to develop a class plan for each subject, but occasionally assigned different tasks to small groups of students dependent upon the "committee" members' ability to achieve. Since the assignments varied, the amount of time allotted for their completion varied, too. Supervisors anticipated that each student was learning something about the same topic, but to varying degrees. There were times, however, when teachers were admonished for not requiring everything of each student and were cautioned about lowering standards. After publication of the Rosenthal studies,[3] the reverse occurred and teachers were warned against predetermining student achievement on the basis of preconceived teacher attitudes.

With the increase of professional knowledge concerning the many differences among student learning styles,[4] class lesson plans are no longer appropriate, should not be required, and certainly should not be used as means of teacher evaluation. We now know that, although teachers need to develop a plan, it should be for *each* student (or for each similarly learning small group of students), and that youngsters should have significant control[5] over selected aspects of their own courses of study. If this procedure is implemented, most students should be permitted many choices and individual prescriptions should vary substantially from youngster to youngster. Indeed, Thomas observed that the lack of student options caused reduced participation in teacher-created learning centers.

When assessing, supervisors observing a modern instructional environment should recognize that each student involves himself in studies that may be different from his peers'. Unless each plan (or prescription) is analyzed, it is often impossible to determine the scope, time, or appropriateness of the design for the student who is using it. Thus, methods for evaluating teacher effectiveness no longer can rely solely on what the teacher intends to teach her charges; rather, *what* he or she does for *whom* and *why* and the extent to which each youngster progresses should be central to planning and evaluation.

A fourth difficulty with previous efforts to evaluate teacher effectiveness was caused by the use of instruments that were designed to measure other inappropriate aspects of the teaching-learning process—one example being the interaction that occurred between the teacher and the students when engaged in class discussions.[6] Given the research data that verifies that some students cannot learn well:

- through hearing or listening,
- from adults,
- among their peers,
- without silence,
- while seated,
- at specific times of day or night,
- without intake, etc.,

studies concerned with the monitoring of systems like interaction analysis appear to be oblivious to the need to (1) prediagnose a student's learning style and to then (2) determine whether the instructional method being used (lecture-discussion) complements that style. Even when an accurate record exists concerning the number of times a youngster is addressed and/or responds and the type of verbal interaction that occurred, without information concerning the youngster's sociological, physical, emotional, and environmental inclinations toward learning, there is no way of determining whether the strategy is even likely to succeed. Finally, the most effective way of measuring whether, in fact, the youngster learned what was intended would be to test his knowledge of the specified objectives *before* and *after* exposing him to the information.

CONSIDERING SUBJECTIVE APPRAISAL AND HUMAN FALLIBILITY

In addition to the problems caused by an incorrect measurement focus and the inappropriate instruments through which data were accumulated, supervisors expressed a very real concern about human reactions to assessment. Although observers may have been certain that a selected teacher was incompetent, they found it difficult to verify that their diagnosis was a result of objective analysis rather than personal bias. Furthermore, in many cases where teachers were willing to accept the accuracy of negative ratings, they were not always able to improve. This problem was then compounded by the cohesiveness generated among faculty when one of their group perceived himself as being in danger of being dismissed. Reaction to what can only be considered an "it can happen to me too" survival psychology caused many colleagues of the ineffective-and-not-able-to-change teacher to behave as if the criticism of one teacher was an assault on the ability of the entire staff. In addition, the divisiveness created by action to terminate a teacher can permeate an entire faculty and cause serious morale problems. Finally, once the tenure period has been completed, it is virtually impossible to dismiss a teacher, even when everyone (peers, parents, students, and administrators) acknowledges his or her relative ineffectiveness.

COPING WITH RENEWED PRESSURES FOR ACCOUNTABILITY

Although these problems have consistently faced administrators, they have recently been compounded by an entirely new set of contemporary societal pressures being exerted on the schools today: (1) Community and legislative demands for accountability are beginning to focus on the amount of academic progress a student achieves within a given time span as one way of judging how well he has been taught.[7] (2) The emerging evidence verifying the superiority of individualized instruction over traditional forms of teaching is incontrovertible.[8]

If teachers are to be held accountable by administrators and communities for the amount of academic progress evidenced by their pupils, and if it is necessary to vary the instruction for each youngster based on his special abilities, weaknesses, and learning style, then evaluation will be more important in the immediate future than it ever has been before.

One outgrowth of teacher assessments related to their ability to help children learn will be the assessment of administrators' abilities to recruit, supervise, and evaluate teaching faculties. Supervisors will find it increasingly difficult to protect the incompetent teacher or to concern themselves with staff morale as opposed to staff excellence.

Furthermore, if teachers must develop the skills of and ability to individualize instruction, administrators will be required to develop the skills of evaluating individualized instruction—an expertise that is very different from determining the strengths and/or weaknesses of traditional teaching.[9]

Thus, supervisors whose primary functions included observing, evaluating, and improving processes of both individual faculty members and programs will no longer be able to take shelter in outmoded evaluation principles they previously used. Evaluation must be undertaken as a full-time, interdependent function of teaching and learning. The results of individual student and teacher progress will receive greater and greater public attention, and demands for continuing improvement will undoubtedly increase.

DEVELOPING NEW TEACHING SKILLS PRIOR TO EVALUATION

Since youngsters learn in ways that are often vastly different from each other, it is futile to plan any instruction without first diagnosing *how* each individual does learn. This information can be obtained over a period of time through either observation or experimentation—that is, using baseline data and permitting choices of environmental, sociological, and physical options, and then comparing student progress after each effort. A faster method of determining learning style would be through administration of a learning style instrument.[10] It is not necessary for the teacher to administer and score the questionnaire to acquire the necessary information, for this is a task that can be performed by a trained parent or aide with the teacher confirming and interpreting the test results in order to develop appropriate prescriptions.

A profile for each student should be developed that includes information concerning how he learns, his achievement in each subject area on an objective-by-objective basis,[11] and any indication of special interests, talents, problems, or idiosyncracies. Much of this can be culled from previously developed testing and anecdotal data, though some of it may require the completion of a short interview or questionnaire form by the student and his parents. Again, this is not an assignment that, of necessity, must be assumed by a professional. The profile development for diagnostic purposes may be undertaken by a trained and competent parent or paraprofessional.

Although many literary references to the role of the teacher include diagnosis as one of the requisites of an effective instructional program,[12] the act of diagnosing need not necessarily be the responsibility of the teacher; rather, the *results* of diagnosis, neatly and accurately profiled, should be submitted to the professional teacher and then analyzed and interpreted by him/her for the purpose of developing a prescription that is uniquely based on the data included in each student's profile.

When a system cannot provide the professional with auxilliary assistance for obtaining individual diagnosis, that responsibility will have to be assumed by the teacher. It is unrealistic, however, to expect teachers to fulfill this diagnostic role requirement in addition to the many other remaining tasks that must be undertaken to produce effective instruction:

1. Individual student diagnosis is time consuming to the point where teachers (as the role is interpreted currently) are not able to conduct them and, in addition, perform their other teaching responsibilities.
2. Diagnosis requires skills that are different from those of prescription development, curriculum design, or the facilitation of learning; these skills are not easily developed in everyone and many teachers who are competent in one of the three areas are not necessarily able in the remaining two.
3. Currently available diagnostic instruments do not require professional expertise for their administration or scoring. The results of the testing can be profiled by paraprofessionals and submitted to a teacher for review, analysis, and use in prescription development. The costs of diagnosis would be sharply reduced by the employment of trained aides and computerized scoring. Thus, the professional teacher will be freed to analyze test results, develop prescriptions, and facilitate the learning process —functions that Herzberg suggests are more appropriate to the evolving role of intelligent or creative teachers than the "Mickey Mouse" functionary tasks they too often are asked to perform.[13]

The complexity of student individuality and the current diversity and variety of existing instructional resources require a revised operational definition of "teacher." The new teacher must become a curriculum specialist who is knowledgeable about and thoroughly immersed in the multitude of available learning resources. This evolving professional must be able to *analyze* and *interpret* a student's diagnostic profile to determine his/her appropriate objectives and the resources through which they may be achieved. What is suggested is a redesign of the instructional system to include:

a) efficient diagnosis of each student through selected instruments by computers or trained paraprofessionals who record test findings on a student profile form that is then submitted to the teacher,
b) analysis of each student's profile, including achievement in each curriculum area, potential for rate of learning (based on baseline data, I.Q., and teacher observations), learning style, and special interests or talents to be completed by either the teacher or a computer program,
c) recommendation (or assignment) of specified instructional objectives and their complementary and related curriculum resources, plus the addition of activities and appropriate paired and small-group techniques to form an individual prescription for each student *developed by the teacher*,
d) observation of and interaction with each student as learning is undertaken and pursued, *by the teacher*, and
e) evaluation of each student's achievement of prescription objectives through criterion-referenced assessments *developed by the teacher but administered by the paraprofessional*.

Relieved of the tedium and time-consuming responsibilities of diagnostic and posttesting procedures, teachers will be able to use the professional skills they have accumulated in ways that maximize learning. In addition, given accurate individual diagnoses, teachers will then be better able to develop appropriate student prescriptions and to guide youngsters through the instructional process. Redesigning the role responsibilities in this fashion will permit increased individualization of learning and enhanced professional growth of teachers.

ESTABLISHING CRITERIA FOR DETERMINING TEACHER EFFECTIVENESS

Years ago, certain educators suggested that the criteria for determining teacher effectiveness varied "from one job to another and tended to change over time,"[14] while others indicated that a teacher's personal characteristics influenced his/her performance.[15] Still others stated that the criteria for assessing one's ability to teach should be established in each situation by the pooled judgments of experts.[16] Each of these concepts is based on earlier rationales for teaching and learning that are now outdated.

The most recent literature stipulates that students achieve when:

- their learning style is considered in developing their prescriptions,[17]

- adequate diagnosis has been achieved and then used as a basis for developing individual prescriptions,[18]
- they are given selected options[19] in the learning environment, and then
- posttested through criterion-referenced instruments.[20]

Translated into what should become daily instructional practice, the research verifies that:

(1) Every student should be pretested to identify:
   a) those skills and knowledges that each student has not yet mastered.[21]
   b) each student's learning style[22] to determine the (1) environmental and sociological conditions under which he/she learns most easily, (2) the emotional factors that designate the kinds of options with which the student can cope, the length and structure suitable for the prescription (assignment, task, unit, work), the type of resources, and the pacing rate that can be reasonably expected.
   c) those curriculum materials that teach the objectives the student has not yet achieved *through* the multimedia that complement his/her learning style.

(2) As a result of the pretest data, a prescription should be developed for each student that includes (on a reading and comprehension level with which he is comfortable!) clearly described:
   a) objectives explaining what he is responsible for learning. The objectives should be written in behavioral terms so that he/she understands how he can verify that he *has* learned what is required; it is important, however, that the terminal behavior not be prescribed and that, here too, students are given choices of how they will demonstrate mastery of the objectives.

5-1

Photo 5-1. Teacher JoAnn Ezick recognized that while some students entered her home economics classes having borne the major responsibility for homemaking chores in their own households, others had never sewn or cooked. Because of the wide diversity of their individual abilities and experiences, she established a series of files that include directions for following patterns or recipes at many different levels. She explains how the system functions and then permits her students free rein in what they choose to make. (Photograph courtesy of Norwich Junior High School, Norwich, New York.)

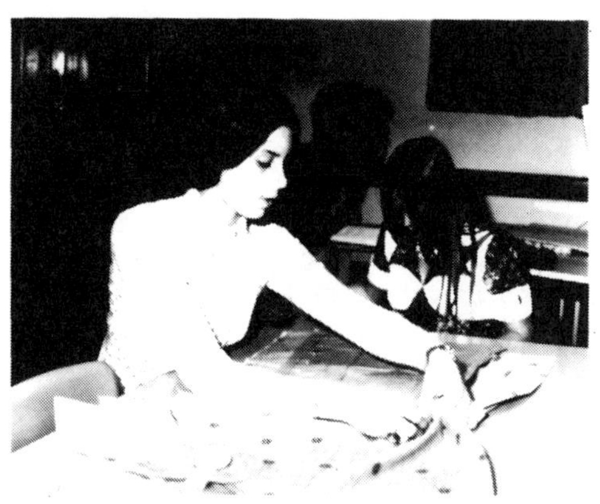

5-2

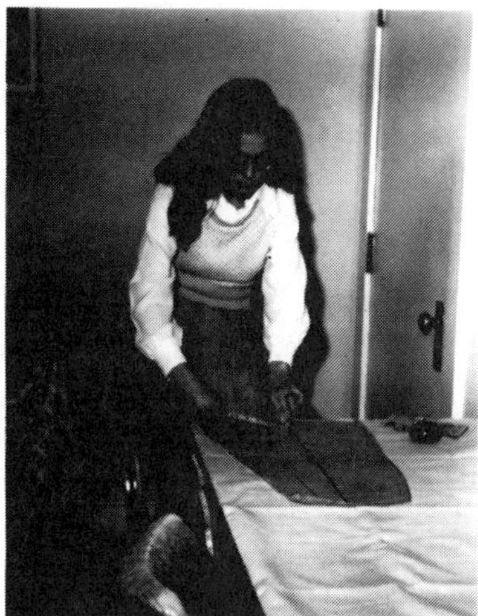

5-3

Photos 5-2, 5-3, and 5-4. Because students elect their own prescriptions based on their realization of their present skills and interests, they can be observed engaging in a variety of different creative activities simultaneously and are busily involved in learning, doing, and helping each other. (Photographs courtesy of Norwich Junior High School, Norwich, New York.)

5-4

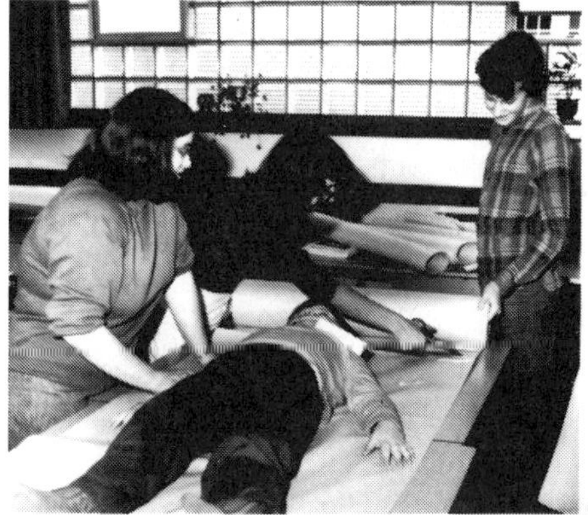

5-5

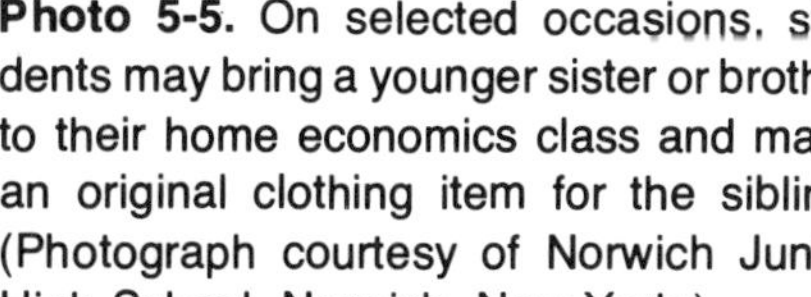

Photo 5-5. On selected occasions, students may bring a younger sister or brother to their home economics class and make an original clothing item for the sibling. (Photograph courtesy of Norwich Junior High School, Norwich, New York.)

5-6

Photo 5-6. Mrs. Ezick adapted a similar procedure for her foods classes. Rather than require uniform experiences, students are permitted to select a recipe that interests them and may follow those directions. On one occasion, students were observed baking cookies, donuts, different kinds of cakes, and miniature pizzas. (Photograph courtesy of Norwich Junior High School, Norwich, New York.)

5-7

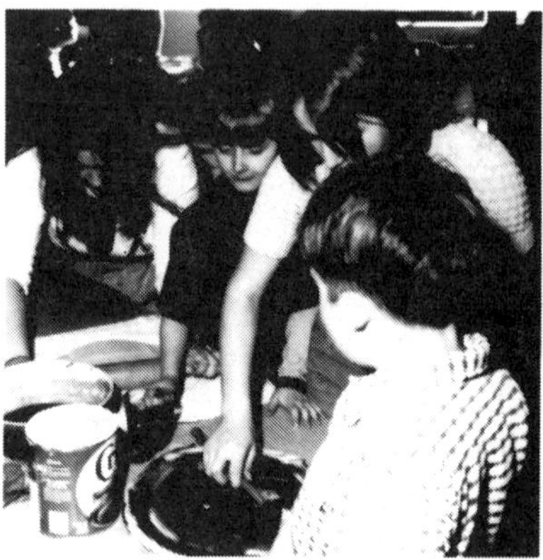

5-8

Photos 5-7 and 5-8. To help brothers and sisters understand one another and appreciate the influence the older teen may have on the younger sibling, and to provide a teaching experience for her students, Mrs. Ezick permits visiting privileges for siblings on predetermined special afternoons. In Photo 5-7 a big brother is tempting little sister with cookies they made together. Photo 5-8 shows a small group of interage youngsters observing baking techniques. (Photographs courtesy of Norwich Junior High School, Norwich, New York.)

b) resources through which he may learn (tapes, books, films, filmstrips, interviews, records, etc.).
c) activities through which he may reinforce the most difficult-to-achieve objectives.
d) group processes through which he may share the knowledges, skills, and/or attitudes that he has developed.
e) learning style inclinations of which he should be aware or any requirements that he must consider.

f) criterion-referenced questions so that he may test himself to determine what he has already mastered and what he still needs to learn. Such a self-assessment test may be used by the student at any time during his studies. He is responsible for self-correcting the answers and for learning those items that he did not respond to appropriately.

(3) Teachers should be available in the learning environment to facilitate student learning. Supervisors should be able to observe that:

a) teachers circulate while working with individuals and with groups and are questioning, teaching what appears to be causing difficulty, reassigning, controlling, observing, suggesting, and revising prescriptions if necessary, etc.

b) teachers work more closely with adult or authority-oriented students than they do with those who are self- or peer-oriented. They add resources as they are developed or become available. They conduct small-group teaching sessions, direct individuals and/or groups that do not appear to be pacing themselves appropriately, and suggest alternatives.

c) teachers develop prescriptions, resources, criterion-referenced tests, assist with the training for media use and creative activities, and generally help youngsters to achieve individually, in pairs, in teams, and/or in small groups (by selection or design).

d) teachers create an attractive learning environment by encouraging student creativity and achievement and by then using the results (outcomes) to decorate the area.

5-9

5-10

Photos 5-9 and 5-10. Since individuals learn through different perceptual strengths or modalities, one of the major advantages of providing multimedia resources is that youngsters who are able to learn by *listening* may choose to use records, cassettes, or tapes, whereas the visually oriented student may opt for filmstrips, films, pictures, books, study prints, and/or magazines. (Photographs courtesy of Norwich Junior High School, Norwich, New York.)

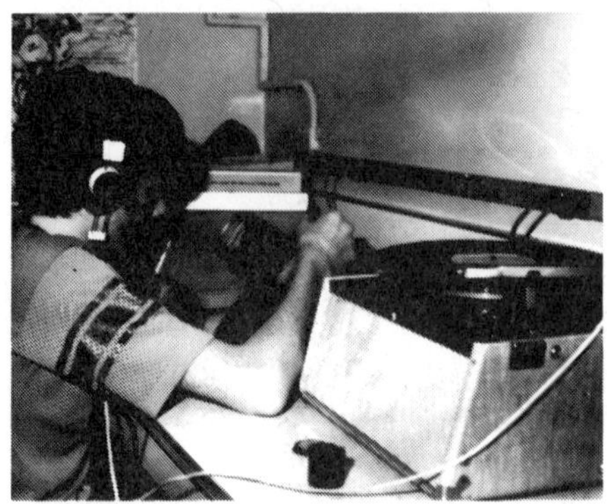

5-11

5-12

Photos 5-11 and 5-12. For youngsters who prefer *multisensory* resources (combined auditory and visual or visual and tactual, etc.), a single-concept filmstrip viewer and related record or a video cassette borrowed from the local BOCES Resource Center may be appropriate. (Photographs courtesy of Norwich Junior High School, Norwich, New York.)

5-13

5-14

5-15

Photos 5-13, 5-14, and 5-15. Expensive multisensory resources are often maintained in a school resource room or media center, but many professionals, convinced of the value of materials that respond to different learning senses, create games that require tactual (touching) or kinesthetic (whole body) activities. Diane Hill, teaching assistant, designed many games to teach and reinforce reading skills and uses them on a daily basis with youngsters who respond well to them. (Photographs courtesy of Norwich Junior High School, Norwich, New York.)

Photo 5-16. Corey Wolford, who teaches eighth- and ninth-grade mathematics, uses commercially produced games and puzzles to stimulate interest in that subject. (Photograph courtesy of Norwich Junior High School, Norwich, New York.)

5-16

(4) Teachers should create a humanistic environment by:

a) permitting each student to select at least some of the objectives incorporated into his prescription.

b) permitting less rapidly achieving students to work more slowly than more rapidly achieving students.

c) permitting more able learners to learn more than the average student and permitting less able learners to learn a little less than the average student; and not assigning negative labels to any children because they do learn less or more in a given amount of time.

d) permitting students to learn in ways that are comfortable for them *as long as they are not disturbing other learners*. This means that if selected youngsters are less threatened by working with a friend or two, they may do so. If some youngsters learn better (on some days or at some times, or usually) on the floor, near a heater, under a desk, in a den, or anywhere in the area, as long as they are not compromising the studies of their peers, they may do so. This example applies to every aspect of learning style. What is important is that teachers *support* learning through one's learning style, not merely give lip service to a concept or directive.

e) encouraging efforts toward achievement by recognition, praise, and/or reward.[23]

f) being firm in upholding rules for conducting oneself in the environment, but applying the rules kindly. One guideline should be that when someone is addressing the group, no one may converse; but that when the group is working individually or in small groups, students may interact quietly so that their words are not clearly discerned by their neighbors.

5-17

5-18

Photos 5-17 and 5-18. Teachers who permit those students who require mobility to move freely about the environment (as long as they continue working and do not disturb others) will find that behavior problems virtually disappear and that human tension is sharply reduced. Martha Farley, a veteran teacher, recognized that some youngsters need to work "behind, beyond, or beside" their peers and, therefore, constructed a cardboard partition to create a small, quiet media center apart from the remainder of the classroom. Here, students may use cassettes or filmstrips in privacy, away from the distractions of the movement or interaction of others. (Photographs courtesy of Norwich Junior High School, Norwich, New York.)

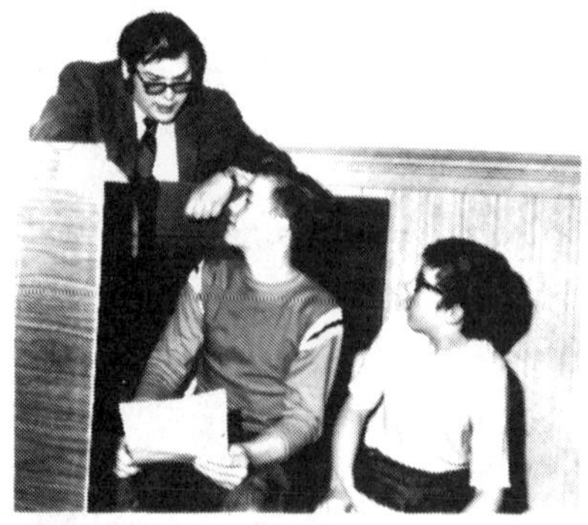

5-19

Photo 5-19. For youngsters who require even more separation from the larger group than dividers can provide, David Paul introduced a movable cardboard frame that his students may take into the adjacent hallway and use as a screen for private studying. Mr. Paul's assignments include a combination of some required and some optional objectives and, as long as his students complete their tasks and behave well, he permits them the freedom of working anywhere within his section of the building. (Photograph courtesy of Norwich Junior High School, Norwich, New York.)

5-20

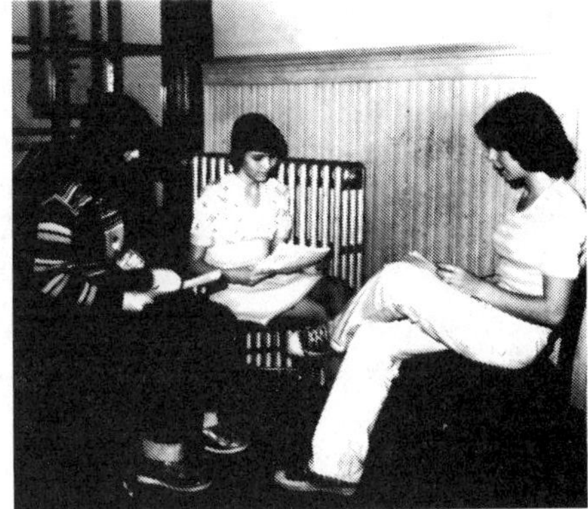

5-21

Photos 5-20 and 5-21. Norwich Junior High School is more than 75 years old and does not conform to the standards set for a modern building that is expected to meet the needs of today's teenagers. The principal and staff, however, have converted what could be a negative learning environment into one that is lively, activity-oriented, and responsive. In this positive setting, seventh, eighth, and ninth graders eagerly declare that "school is great!" and that they would ". . . rather be here than anywhere!" One of the simple structural changes that was made required the removal of heavy oak doors from hallway closets and cloakrooms. The insides were then painted, and student drawings and three-dimensional creations were placed on the walls as decorations. These and the halls are now used as study areas and instructional centers for students who require privacy or quiet when they concentrate. (Photographs courtesy of Norwich Junior High School, Norwich, New York.)

If teachers can be helped to fulfill these major roles, learning can be assured for the majority of our students. In fact, Benjamin Bloom of the University of Chicago has verified that through this type of instructional process, 80 percent of the students reach a level of achievement that only 20 percent previously attained without it (see footnote 8).

It has become increasingly evident that teaching effectiveness is neither dependent on personality characteristics[24] nor on the pooled judgment of experts.[25] Rather, teaching effectiveness can be determined by the quality of the performance of specific teaching tasks, namely (1) diagnosis, (2) prescription development, (3) guidance of students through the learning process (or the facilitating of learning), and (4) evaluation. When these tasks have been completed correctly, a student's baseline data should evidence academic growth that is favorably related to his previous progress records. When this type of growth is achieved, teachers may be considered effective in their instructional roles.

IDENTIFYING EFFECTIVE TEACHER AND STUDENT BEHAVIORS AND OUTCOMES

Before attempting to determine faculty effectiveness, it is only fair to acquaint teachers with what they should be *doing* (behaviors) if they hope to have a positive and genuine impact on how their students progress academically. Each teacher should be apprised of the specific knowledges and skills that facilitate learning for youngsters with vastly different abilities, achievement levels, and learning styles. Teachers should then be helped to translate the enumerated knowledges and skills into behaviors that they *use on an ongoing basis* in the educational environment, whether that environment is a classroom, a pod, a center, the community, or any other space. Finally, teachers need to be aware of how their knowledges, skills, and behaviors should affect student prescriptions, functioning, and progress.

REQUIRED TEACHER KNOWLEDGES AND SKILLS AND THEIR APPLICATION TO INDIVIDUAL STUDENT PRESCRIPTIONS

TEACHER KNOWLEDGES	*USE OF RELATED SKILLS*	*APPLICATION TO INDIVIDUAL STUDENT PRESCRIPTIONS*
1. The teacher recognizes that some students learn more quickly or more slowly than their peers. She therefore permits each student to progress academically at a comfortable pace.	The teacher observes each student to determine his approximate rate of learning in each subject area. She experiments with behavior modification (after mediation training),[26] token reinforcers, and other conditioning principles to increase each student's ability to learn within a given time interval.	Each student's prescription (assignment, contract, package, unit, program, etc.) may indicate a different required completion date or time interval ("between 8-10 days") than others.
2. The teacher recognizes that some entering students know more (or less) about a topic to be covered than their peers. She will therefore prescribe only those topic-related objectives that each individual has not mastered.	The teacher pretests each student to determine the extent of his knowledge of those objectives that she plans to prescribe for the topic.	Each student's prescription includes only those objectives that the pretest indicates he has not yet mastered.
3. The teacher recognizes that students learn through different perceptual preferences.	The teacher either diagnoses each student to determine the ways in which he is most likely to absorb and retain factual and conceptual information, or he or she permits students to self-select the resources (from among approved alternatives).	Each student's prescription lists alternative multisensory and multimedia learning resources.

5-22

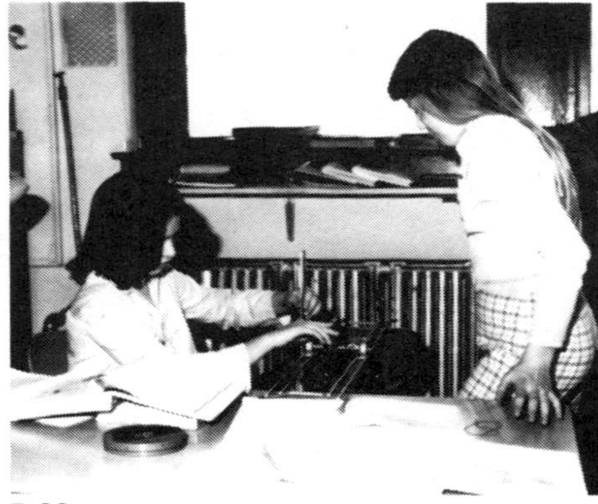

5-23

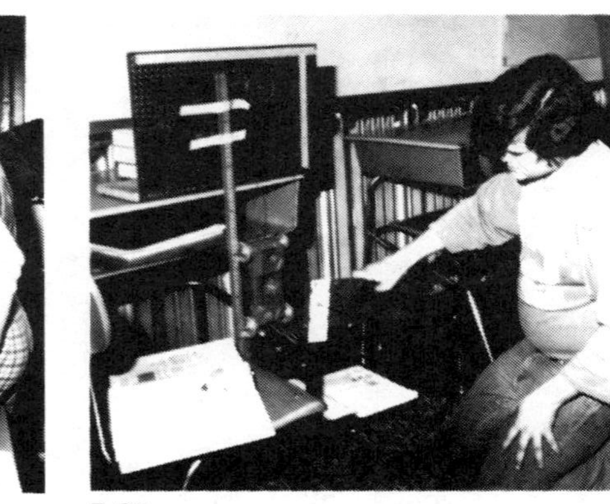

5-25

5-24

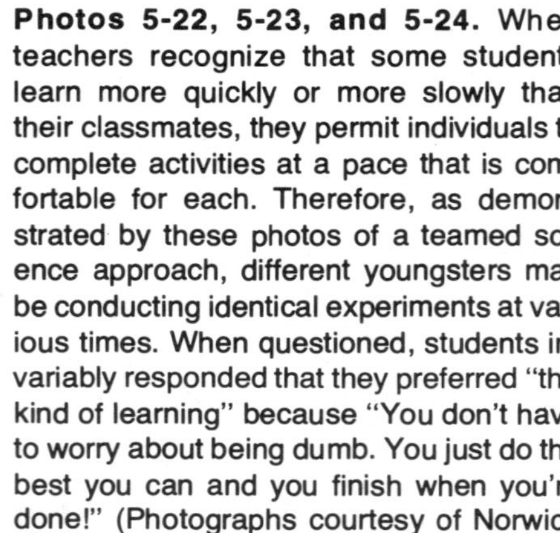

Photos 5-22, 5-23, and 5-24. When teachers recognize that some students learn more quickly or more slowly than their classmates, they permit individuals to complete activities at a pace that is comfortable for each. Therefore, as demonstrated by these photos of a teamed science approach, different youngsters may be conducting identical experiments at various times. When questioned, students invariably responded that they preferred "this kind of learning" because "You don't have to worry about being dumb. You just do the best you can and you finish when you're done!" (Photographs courtesy of Norwich Junior High School, Norwich, New York.)

Photo 5-25. Jim Law, a seventh-grade youngster, followed the directions for measuring the amount of work that it takes to pull a cart upwards. He experimented independently and was completely absorbed in the activity. He then repeated the procedures with care and noted the data. When questioned, he revealed that he was "responsible for checking" his answers before sharing them with his teacher. (Photograph courtesy of Norwich Junior High School, Norwich, New York.)

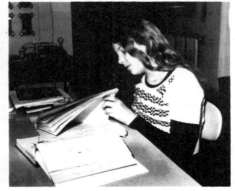

5-26

5-27

Photos 5-26 and 5-27. Milton McFee and one of his students are cooperatively reviewing the youngster's progress on a chart that delineates the various items that should be completed as well as each student's achievements. At the same time, another student is self-assessing her own learning prior to requesting an examination on that topic. (Photographs courtesy of Norwich Junior High School, Norwich, New York.)

TEACHER KNOWLEDGES	*USE OF RELATED SKILLS*	*APPLICATION TO INDIVIDUAL STUDENT PRESCRIPTIONS*
4. The teacher recognizes that each student internalizes information uniquely, dependent on comprehension and retention abilities and interests.	The teacher analyzes each student's achievement scores, apparent motivation and persistence, and interest in and/or facility with the subject.	Each student's prescription may include a different number of objectives from the numbers of those students who are identified as being receptive to learning or those who are recognized as being less able, less motivated, less persistent, and/or less interested.

TEACHER KNOWLEDGES	*USE OF RELATED SKILLS*	*APPLICATION TO INDIVIDUAL STUDENT PRESCRIPTIONS*
5. The teacher recognizes that students learn through different styles of study and practice.	The teacher either analyzes each student's learning style *or* permits youngsters to vary their environmental, sociological, and physical learning situations.	Each student's prescription will include environmental, sociological, and physical options *within approved alternatives*, except where the student does not appear to be progressing at near maximum efficiency. When this occurs, the teacher will require selected procedures or evidence of achievement.
6. The teacher recognizes that choices and options (a) increase motivation, (b) tend to produce increased achievement, and (c) provide opportunities for decision-making, problem-solving, and student self-assessment.	The teacher designs alternative options, resources, activities, small-group techniques, and test procedures in greater numbers than she intends to assign.	Each student's prescription includes opportunities for self-selected options.
7. The teacher recognizes that students respond to different teaching methods and that most students respond favorably to one or more of a variety of strategies.	The teacher designs alternative strategies for teaching the difficult aspects of a topic.	Each student's prescription may be accomplished through several self-selected learning strategies, including individual, peer, and/or small-group studies, contracts, packages, programmed learning, films, filmstrips, tapes, books, activity-oriented projects, etc.

8. The teacher recognizes that required curriculums are not necessarily appropriate for all students.

The teacher varies the curriculum requirements on the basis of individual diagnoses and often involves students in designing their own instructional prescriptions. On occasion, students may design a unique course of study with teacher input and approval.

Each student's prescription may evidence curriculum variations in subject matter, scope, depth, and due dates.

Doonesbury
by GB Trudeau

TEACHER KNOWLEDGES	*USE OF RELATED SKILLS*	*APPLICATION TO INDIVIDUAL STUDENT PRESCRIPTIONS*
9. The teacher recognizes that students need different amounts of structure and freedom.	The teacher diagnoses each student's learning style and, in conjunction with observations, determines how much structure should be provided for each.	Each student's prescription will clearly indicate those items that are (a) required and those that are (b) optional. The youngsters who require more structure will enjoy fewer options and will participate in more frequently supervised sessions.
10. The teacher recognizes that to facilitate learning for students who respond to different perceptual stimuli it is important to provide resources that are auditory, visual, tactile, and kinesthetic.	The teacher accumulates and/or develops tapes, filmstrips, films, pictures, transparencies, books, magazines, records, games and project activities related to the topic of study.	Each student's prescription enumerates available multisensory resources and guides individuals with specific perceptual needs toward resources that complement those needs.
11. The teacher recognizes that some youngsters need frequent opportunities in which to move, change their position, break away from their studies, interact with their peers, etc.	The teacher keeps large-group instruction to the absolute minimum and, during small-group interactions, permits those students who are not working directly with her to enjoy some mobility *providing* that, when permitted this freedom, they complete all their *requirements* without obstructing other students' progress.	Each student's prescription will include one or more required small-group and/or large-group interactions; the youngsters needing more mobility will be assigned more small-group tasks *provided* they can work well with one or more peers.

5-28

5-29

Photos 5-28 and 5-29. Some youngsters can learn through a basic "required curriculum"; others cannot apply themselves unless their studies are related directly to their interests or they are permitted options. Bernice Newcomb, a former engineer, responds to such motivational differences by teaching language, math, and science through various art forms. Students are permitted to become involved in drawing, painting, sculpture, film production, and many other creative activities—but all require "discipline" applications and all promote curriculum growth. Students who wish may schedule themselves into the art studios whenever they have available time, as long as they remain self-directed and quietly involved in their projects. (Photographs courtesy of Norwich Junior High School, Norwich, New York.)

5-30

5-31

5-32

Photos 5-30, 5-31, and 5-32. Tom Lloyd, who has been teaching for 27 years, changed his philosophy of how to educate children after exposure to the theories of William Glasser, Mark Roberts, Herbert Kohl, and Milo Stewart. He not only provides his social studies students with a choice of viable activities, learning strategies, and seating arrangements, but encourages them to spend their lunch and free time candle making and has helped them to develop a mini-business in which profits are spent on cooperatively determined ventures. Options aid in motivating most students. (Photographs courtesy of Norwich Junior High School, Norwich, New York.)

5-33

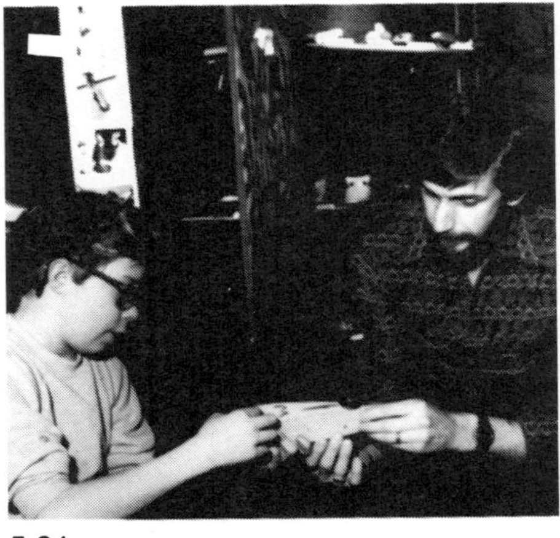

5-34

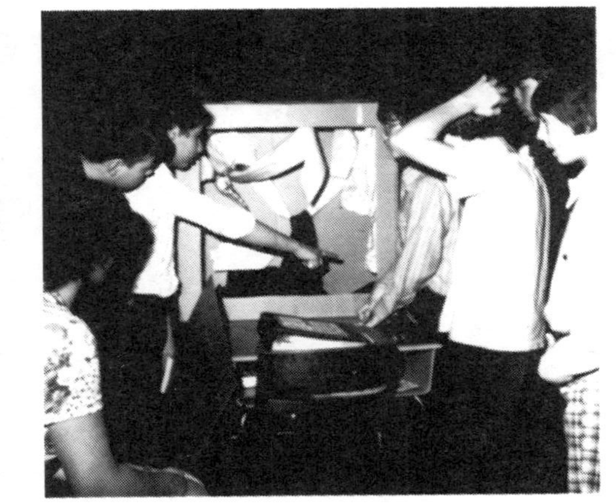

5-35

Photos 5-33 and 5-34. David Williams and David Doughty, who team-teach ninth-grade industrial arts, have developed self-instructional tapes and colored slide programs on the use of a belt-sander machine, the drill press, the pilot printing press, and oxyacetylene welding. Through this alternative, students may view each filmstrip and listen to the accompanying tape as often as necessary and may progress as rapidly as their developing skills permit. In Photo 5-34, Jim Manwarren displays his original derby car which was developed as part of an independent study program in which he studied the design of the racing course and the nature of propellants. In competition with many other ninth graders, Jim's car won on "Derby Day," a racing event conducted under the scrutiny of the teaching pair. (Photographs courtesy of Norwich Junior High School, Norwich, New York.)

Photo 5-35. In response to Earl Callahan's system of encouraging his students to select their reading matter from seven of 14 possible mini-themes and to then develop a creative activity to represent the focus of the material, Carmen Bucalo, a seventh grader, designed this three-dimensional, moving replica of *Fantastic Voyage,* which he is sharing with his classmates. (Photograph courtesy of Norwich Junior High School, Norwich, New York.)

Once teachers have identified the student differences that require varied prescriptions, they will need to know how their behaviors (what they actually *do* as a result of their knowledges and skills) will affect what students do.

TEACHER BEHAVIORS[27]	*RESULTANT OBSERVABLE STUDENT BEHAVIORS*
1. The teacher diagnoses each student and then prescribes on the basis of the results. When the teacher diagnoses the curriculum that will be incorporated into the prescription, he or she analyzes (a) what all students should learn, (b) what most students should learn, and (c) what some students should learn. She then assesses the abilities, interests, and motivation of each student and, using the same basic curriculum, prescribes varied numbers and kinds of objectives. When initially focusing on the curriculum, the teacher is using a "curriculum contract process" (see Figure 5-1).[28]	Students select their own (a) objectives, (b) resources, (c) activities, (d) assignments, (e) small-group techniques, (f) modes of learning, and/or (g) evaluation procedures from among approved alternatives.

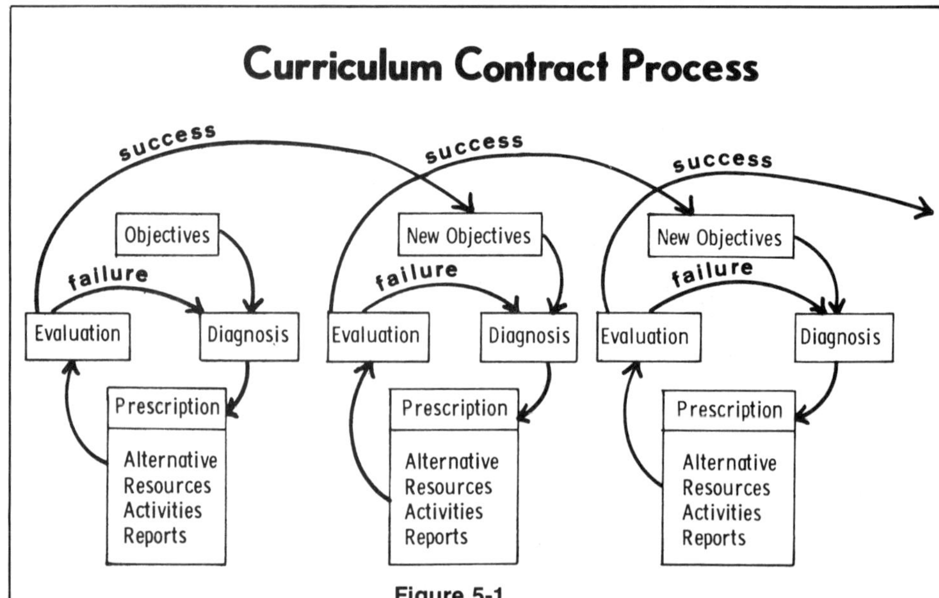

Figure 5-1

TEACHER BEHAVIORS	*RESULTANT OBSERVABLE STUDENT BEHAVIORS*
2. The teacher elicits student involvement in the development of individual prescriptions. When the teacher designs a prescription based on the student's identified interests and concerns, he or she is developing a curriculum for that specific student. The teacher analyzes the possible objectives within the topic and then determines the alternative resources, activities, and reporting techniques that might be appropriate for that curriculum. When initially focusing on the diagnosis of the student, the teacher is using an "independent contract process" (see Figure 5-2).[29]	Each student may be working toward the completion of varied and/or entirely different prescriptions from those of other students.

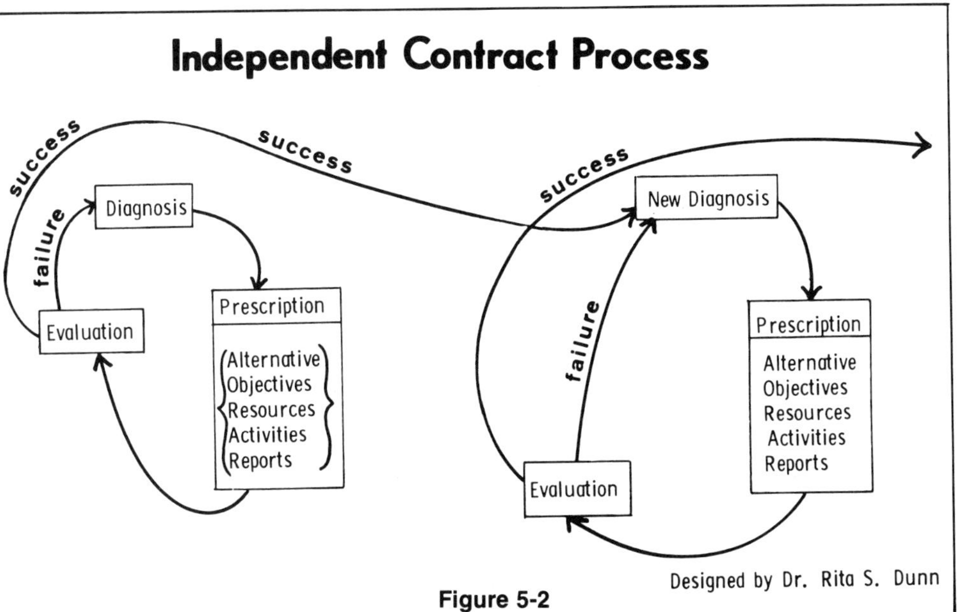

Figure 5-2

3. The teacher diagnoses on an ongoing basis and guides each student through the learning process.	The student is involved in individual and small-group teacher conferences (formal and/or informal) as he progresses through his prescription.

TEACHER BEHAVIORS	*RESULTANT OBSERVABLE STUDENT BEHAVIORS*
4. The teacher develops the student's independence and responsibility skills.[30]	The student uses a self-assessment instrument to continuously identify what he has already achieved and what he still must learn. He locates, uses, repairs, shares, and replaces resources and media. He finds assistance when necessary and assists others when he is able. He makes choices from among approved alternatives in objectives, resources, assignments, small-group techniques, modes of learning, evaluation procedures, and when and how he will pace himself. He learns to analyze his own progress and the achievements of his peers critically and to document his conclusions.
5. The teacher provides for a variety of small-group techniques to (a) prevent alienation in the learning environment, (b) provide for student discussion, (c) provide for reinforcement and retention of learning, and (d) build analytical skills.	The students engage in selected small-group interactions at varied intervals, e.g., team learning, group analysis, simulations, circles of knowledge, etc.
6. The teacher establishes and equips varied instructional areas to encourage diversity, mobility, variety, and options, e.g., interest centers, little theaters, game tables, reading corners, learning stations, magic carpet areas, media corners, etc.	Students move freely about the instructional environment and work alone, in pairs, or in teams as they determine. They maintain a relaxed atmosphere, work on interdisciplinary studies at times, achieve cooperative peer interactions, use varied instructional areas and resources, participate in planning some of the activities at the various areas, establish some of their own priorities, express their thoughts and feelings in acceptable terms, show initiative and, simultaneously, maintain a discussion level that permits those who need a conversational noise level to work.

5-36

5-37

5-38

5-39

Photos 5-36, 5-37, 5-38, and 5-39. By using anything that is movable in the classroom (such as bookcases and file cabinets) perpendicular to the wall, Patricia Carey, who teaches ninth-grade English, has been able to establish various instructional areas to permit students to work in ways they feel most comfortable—alone, with a friend or two, or in a small group. (Photographs courtesy of Norwich Junior High School, Norwich, New York.)

Photo 5-40. By using two bookcases at right angles to each other in a corner of the room and placing a large square of carpeting between, Mrs. Carey created an area that can be used for quiet reading or as a stage for dramatic presentations related to the readings her students select. Here, she observes three students interpreting a scene based on literature concerning the hazards of smoking. (Photograph courtesy of Norwich Junior High School, Norwich, New York.)

5-40

TEACHER BEHAVIORS	*RESULTANT OBSERVABLE STUDENT BEHAVIORS*
7. The teacher provides for a variety of learning experiences.	Students make selections from among many approved alternatives. They use materials and equipment available in and adjacent to the instructional setting and may also go beyond the indigenous environment for additional sources. Student studies may be nonschool centered at times and personnel resources may be used in and out of the educational facilities. Students may use contract activity packages, programmed learning, instructional packages, task cards, work-study plans, and/or community contribution programs at varied times when appropriate to their learning styles, tasks, prescriptions, and abilities. Students may experience brainstorming, independent study, case studies, group analysis, simulations, team tutoring, etc., at appropriate intervals.
8. The teacher provides for different learning rates and styles.	The students set their own pace within established or prescribed acceptable time intervals. They interact with adults and other students, as they prefer. They utilize their personal interests as one source of study focus. They involve themselves in creative activities allied with their personal talents and skills. They determine the order and extensiveness of their studies. They study in the environment they choose for time intervals with which they feel comfortable. They function within different amounts of structure and/or informality, dependent upon how they show their ability to progress independently.

5-41

5-42

Photos 5-41, 5-42, and 5-43. Some students lack the skills or confidence to work independently, but are able to progress academically when permitted to team with a friend or two. For such youngsters, short assignments (coupled with frequent teacher encouragement and praise) often generate sufficient motivation and persistence to provide for both personal and curriculum growth. (Photographs courtesy of Norwich Junior High School, Norwich, New York.)

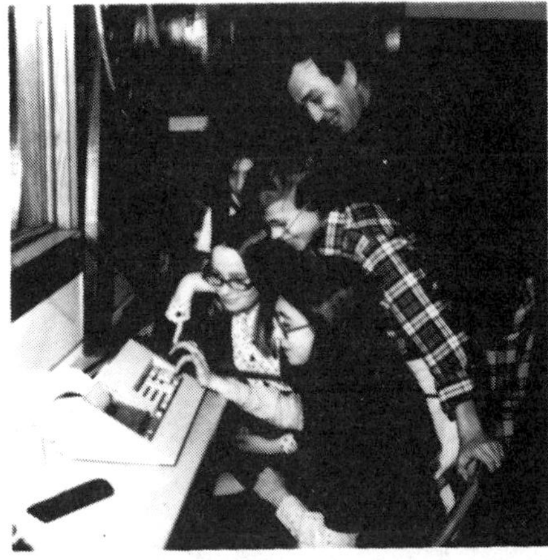
5-43

Photo 5-44. Sometimes parent volunteers are willing to guide students on a regular basis, providing academic assistance and adult encouragement to youngsters who need a little of both. (Photograph courtesy of Norwich Junior High School, Norwich, New York.)

5-44

TEACHER BEHAVIORS	*RESULTANT OBSERVABLE STUDENT BEHAVIORS*
9. The teacher provides for multilevel curriculum materials that transcend traditional, "graded" resources.	Students use multilevel resources to complete their prescriptions and select in accordance with their abilities and interests.
10. The teacher shares leadership with selected students as they mature and develop independent and group skills.	Students engage in paired, teamed, and small-group instruction when appropriate. They form cadres to assist others in locating, using, repairing, and replacing resources. They record their own progress. They establish some of their own priorities. They help plan their prescriptions. They add to approved alternatives in each area. They can identify their objectives and the criteria by which they will be evaluated. They participate in planning the evaluation instrument and in assessing their own progress. They share their learning with others through alternative reporting opportunities. They can eventually design and evaluate their own prescriptions.

5-45

Photo 5-45. Providing for curriculum studies and leadership experiences that transcend grade and age-level expectations often motivate students to produce beyond what would be considered "normal" achievement. An industrial arts exploration of how to make a lamp led youngsters to design and create original lamps that eventually became a class money-making venture. More valuable, perhaps, than the many knowledges and skills gained by the participants, was the love of learning and sense of achievement that they verbalized and demonstrated as they described their business, a "stock company" venture into the mass production of the lamp they designed. (Photograph courtesy of Norwich Junior High School, Norwich, New York.)

Prior to initiating a program for evaluation, it is necessary to alert teachers to the demands of contemporary professionalism which mandate the recognition of individual differences among students of any age. Once teachers acknowledge that learning occurs in widely diversified ways, they recognize the need for varied instructional strategies to respond to multiple individual differences. These differences in the ways in which people learn become obvious when professional teachers are trained in observing and recognizing various styles. Therefore, as a result, diagnostic and prescriptive skills become essential in determining how each student learns and what is required to develop a complementary framework within which he or she can function productively and enjoyably.

Once students are permitted to learn in ways with which they feel comfortable, they will begin to function differently from each other in the instructional environment. Because they may be concentrating on different objectives through different resources and methods, they will undoubtedly produce diversified outcomes. Thus, the student behaviors that may be observable at one time in a given environment probably will vary exten-

5-46

Photo 5-46. L. O. Anderson is a principal who walks among his students addressing each one by name, commenting on ". . . the fine project you completed . . ." or ". . . the nice work you did on that theme." He and his staff appear to have devoted their professional lives to exploring better ways to educate children. They established a library resource center, experimented with multitexts, provided multisensory resources, initiated independent study programs, advocated varied and optional activities, and designed learning packages and contracts—always keeping the best of each strategy and discarding the less-effective aspects. Willing to explore and evaluate new concepts, they changed an old, outdated building into a center of high interest, positive student and teacher attitudes, a variety of stimulating happenings, and an atmosphere of good feeling or, as Mr. Anderson describes it, "a place where kids want to be!" (Photograph courtesy of Norwich Junior High School, Norwich, New York.)

sively. Teachers will then need to respond to differing student behaviors through varied teaching strategies or behaviors of their own.

When teachers begin trying to educate their students through multiple optional methods based on individual diagnoses, they will need to assess their own effectiveness to continuously improve. It is at this point that teachers and supervisors will require objective instruments that reveal how well they are responding to the demands of effective teaching and which skills, if any, need to be improved.

Sample instruments and a discussion of their use are the focus of the next chapter.

NOTES FOR CHAPTER 5

1. D. Ryans. *Characteristics of Teachers: Their Description, Comparison, and Appraisal.* Washington, D.C.: American Council on Education (1960). Also see A. S. Barr. *Characteristic Differences in Teaching Performance of Good and Bad Teachers of the Social Studies.* Bloomington, Illinois: Public School Publishing Co. (1929) and *Evaluating Teacher Performance,* Educational Research Service. Washington, D.C.: American Association of School Administrators, Circular no. 3 (1969) and Circular no. 2 (1972).
2. Rita Dunn and Kenneth Dunn. *Educator's Self-Teaching Guide to Individualizing Instructional Programs.* West Nyack, New York: Parker Publishing Co., Inc. (1975): 218, 228-229.
3. Robert Rosenthal and Lenore Jacobson. *Pygmalion in the Classroom: Teacher Expectations and Pupils' Intellectual Development.* New York: Holt, Rinehart and Winston (1968). The authors contend that teachers may unintentionally motivate selected children by having a higher degree of expectation for them than for others.
4. *Educator's Self-Teaching Guide to Individualizing Instructional Programs:* chapter 3. Also, Rita Dunn and Kenneth Dunn. "Learning Style as a Criterion for Placement in Alternative Programs." *Phi Delta Kappan,* LVI, 4 (1975): 275-278. Another treatment of the subject can be found in Herbert M. Kliebard. "The Observation of Classroom Behavior: Some Recent Research" in *The Way Teaching Is,* C. Hitchcock (ed.). Washington, D.C.: Association for Supervision and Curriculum Development: Center for the Study of Instruction, the National Education Association (1966).
5. Robert F. Mager and J. McCann. *Learner-Controlled Instruction.* Palo Alto, California: Varian (1963). Research conducted by these two authors demonstrated the superiority of students who were permitted to control the instructional sequence of certain training tasks. It was also reported that learners' motivation increased with the amount of control they exercised over their own studies. John I. Thomas. *Learning Centers.* Boston: Holbrook Press (1975): 43.
6. Edmund J. Amidon and John B. Hough (eds.). *Interaction Analysis: Theory, Research and Application.* Reading, Mass: Addison-Wesley Publishing Co. (1967); William Morris Hill. "The Effects on Verbal Teaching Behavior of Learning Interaction Analysis as an Inservice Education Activity." *Dissertation Abstracts* 27A: 2084. Doctoral Thesis, Ohio State University, (1966); J. B. Hough and R. Ober. "The Effects of Training in

Interaction Analysis on the Verbal Behavior of Preservice Teachers.'' Paper presented at the annual meeting of the American Educational Research Association, Chicago, (1966); Donald M. Medley and Russel A. Hill. ''Dimensions of Classroom Behavior Measured by Two Systems of Interaction Analysis.'' *Educational Leadership* 27 (May 1960): 821-824.

7. For an interesting argument specifying the speciousness of holding teachers responsible for student achievement, see Robert W. Heath and Mark A. Nielson. ''The Research Basis for Performance-Based Teacher Education.'' Review of Educational Research 44, 4 (1974): 463-484. The authors present research contending that parental education and ''household items'' (socioeconomic standing) are the most salient determiners of student achievement in school, and they then conclude that teacher behaviors (instructional methodology) are so indirectly related to student achievement as to be virtually inconsequential.
8. James Block (ed.). *Schools, Society and Mastery Learning.* New York: Holt, Rinehart and Winston (1974). Benjamin Bloom of the University of Chicago verifies that the form of individualization with which he has experimented (''mastery learning'') helps ''80% of (the) students reach a level of achievement which only 20% attain'' without. He claims that this strategy, which is based on the development of objectives and units related to their achievement, including student-scored diagnostic tests and alternative resources, permits ''virtually all, rather than some, students . . . (to) learn most of what they are taught.'' Also see Robert M. Gagne (ed.). *Learning and Individual Differences: A Symposium of the Learning Research and Development Center.* University of Pittsburgh. Columbus, Ohio: Charles E. Merrill Books (1967). Chapter 2, ''How Can Instruction Be Adapted to Individual Differences?'' by Lee Cronbach and John B. Carroll's discussion which follows are especially pertinent. Also, Robert F. Peck. *Promoting Self-Disciplined Learning: A Researchable Revolution.* Washington, D.C.: U.S. Office of Education (1970); Kevin Ryan and James M. Cooper. *Those Who Can, Teach.* Boston: Houghton Mifflin Co. (1975): 366.
9. *Educator's Self-Teaching Guide to Individualizing Instructional Programs:* 228-229.
10. *Educator's Self-Teaching Guide to Individualizing Instructional Programs:* 94-110.
11. *Inside Education.* Albany, New York: State Education Department (December, 1974): 5.
12. John I. Goodlad. ''Diagnosis and Prescription in Educational Practice.'' *New Approaches to Individualizing Instruction.* Princeton, New Jersey: Educational Testing Service (1965): 27-37; Doris M. Lee. *Diagnostic Teaching.* Washington, D.C.: National Educational Association (1966); Madeline C. Hunter. ''When the Teacher Diagnoses Learning.'' *Educational Leadership* (1966): 545-549.
13. Frederick Herzberg, an interview. ''Managers or Animal Trainers?'' *Management Review* (July, 1971): 10-11.
14. Dale L. Bolton. *Selection and Evaluation of Teachers.* California: McCutchan Publication Corp. (1973): 103.
15. Claude T. Ware, Jr. ''Individual and Situational Variables Affecting Human Performance.'' *Human Factors* 6 (1964): 673-674; David G. Ryans. ''Assessment of Teacher Behavior and Instruction: Observation and Assessment of Teaching.'' *Review of Educational Research* 33 (1963): 423; H. Del Schalock. ''Issues in the Conceptualization and Measurement of Teaching Behavior.'' Paper presented at the American Educational Research Association annual conference, Chicago (1967); Smith B. Othaniel. ''Teach-

ing: Conditions of Its Evaluation.'' *The Evaluation of Teaching*. Washington, D.C.: Pi Lambda Theta (1967).

16. David G. Ryans. ''Notes on the Criterion Problems in Research, with Special Reference to the Study of Teacher Characteristics.'' *Journal of Genetic Psychology* 91 (1957): 33-61.
17. Beatrice J. Farr. ''Individual Differences in Learning: Predicting One's More Effective Learning Modality.'' Ph.D. dissertation, Catholic University of America (1971), University Microfilm, Ann Arbor, Michigan (July, 1971) 1332A. An experiment with 72 college students confirmed that individuals could accurately predict the modality in which they would demonstrate superior learning performance. The data also revealed that it is advantageous to learn and be tested in the same modality and that such an advantage is reduced when learning and testing are both conducted in an individual's nonpreferred modality. The most desirable conditions existed when learning and testing were both in the student's preferred modality. Also see George Domino. ''Interactive Effects of Achievement Orientation and Teaching Style on Academic Achievement.'' ACT Research Report, 39 (1970): 1-9. One hundred students were grouped in accordance with their perceptions of how they learned. Some of the groups were then taught in a manner consonant with their perceived learning style (''achievement orientation''), while others were taught in a manner dissonant with their orientation. The testing data revealed that the students who had been exposed to a teaching style consonant with the ways they believed they learned scored higher on tests, fact knowledge, teacher attitude and efficiency of work than those who had been taught in a manner dissonant with their orientation.
18. Norman E. Hankins. *Psychology for Contemporary Education*. Columbus, Ohio: Charles E. Merrill Publishing Co. (1973): 12, 16, 22, 335-362.
19. W. James Popham and Eva I. Baker. *Systematic Instruction*. Englewood Cliffs, New Jersey: Prentice-Hall, Inc. (1970); W. James Popham. ''Performance Tests of Teaching Proficiency: Rationale, Development and Validation.'' *American Educational Research Journal* 8, 1 (1971): 105-117. The authors demonstrated that teachers can be taught to define behavioral objectives, select learning alternatives, and assess learning outcomes, and that these three competencies resulted in increased student achievement.
20. L. J. Briggs. *Handbook of Procedures for the Design of Instruction*. Pittsburgh: American Institute for Research (1970).
21. B. S. Bloom, J. T. Hastings, and G. F. Madaus. ''Learning for Mastery.'' *Handbook of Formative and Summative Evaluation of Student Learning*. New York: McGraw-Hill (1971): 43-57.
22. Rita Dunn and Kenneth Dunn. ''Learning Style as a Criterion for Placement in Alternative Programs.'' *Phi Delta Kappan,* LVI, 4 (1974): 275-278.
23. *Psychology for Contemporary Education:* chapter 4. Also see C. A. Clark and J. J. Walberg. ''The Influence of Massive Rewards on Reading Achievement in Potential Urban School Drop-outs.'' *American Educational Research Journal* 5 (1968): 305-310; and C. A. Clark and H. J. Walberg. ''The Effects of Increased Rewards in Reading Achievement and School Attitudes of Potential Drop-outs.'' B. Feather and W. S. Olsen (eds.). *Children, Psychology, and the Schools*. Glenview, Ill.: Scott Foresman Co. (1969).
24. *Characteristics of Teachers*.
25. *Selection and Evaluation of Teachers:* 104.

26. R. O. Blackwood. "The Operant Conditioning of Verbally Mediated Self-Control in the Classroom." *Journal of School Psychology* 8 (1970): 251-258.
27. *Educator's Self-Teaching Guide to Individualizing Instructional Programs:* 254-260.
28. Rita Dunn and Kenneth Dunn. *Practical Approaches to Individualizing Instruction: Contracts and Other Effective Teaching Strategies.* West Nyack, New York: Parker Publishing Co., Inc. (1972): chapters 3 and 4.
29. *Practical Approaches to Individualizing Instruction: Contracts and Other Effective Teaching Strategies,* 124-145.
30. *Educator's Self-Teaching Guide to Individualizing Instructional Programs:* chapter 5.

6

DEVELOPING EVALUATION INSTRUMENTS:

Relating Objectives to Behaviors and Outcomes

EXAMINING SAMPLE EVALUATION FORMS

The purposes for evaluating faculty have traditionally included administrative desires to (1) stimulate the improvement of teaching performance, (2) decide on the reappointment of probationary teachers, (3) recommend probationary teachers for permanent status, (4) establish evidence where dismissal from service is an issue, (5) select teachers for promotion, (6) decide on reappointment of permanent teachers, (7) qualify regular teachers for salary increments, (8) qualify teachers for longevity pay increments, (9) qualify teachers for acceleration on a salary schedule, (10) establish qualifications for merit pay, (11) comply with state or district requirements, (12) determine a basis for writing references, and (13) identify inservice training requirements.[1]

Many widely used evaluation instruments include some criteria that are inappropriate for determining the quality of teaching performance or the improvement of the teaching-learning process and omit others that would be highly indicative of professional excellence. Examples of suggested deficiencies and omissions found in current checklists and observation instruments are included in the following categories.

Items That Only Tangentially Relate to Teaching Effectiveness

- personal characteristics, such as one's grooming, mode of attire, age, marital status, and number of children
- one's understanding of and adherence to policies, rules, and regulations established by the Board of Education
- attendance and regularity at assigned posts
- promptness in submitting records and reports and their accuracy

- cooperation with colleagues
- care of school property
- relationships with parents
- relationships with community agencies
- effectiveness in instructing, training, and developing subordinates
- care of the health of students

The inclusion of these essentially administrative, social, or extra-personnel responsibilities diminishes the professionalism of the teaching role and requires that it become so all-inclusive that attention is focused away from those characteristics that describe an effective *teacher*.

Items That Are Subjective and Dependent Upon the Evaluator's Interpretation

- knowledge of subject matter (Is the evaluator's knowledge of the subject matter equivalent to, superior to, or as recent as that of the teacher?)
- rapport with pupils (Is a student attitudinal instrument used to ascertain rapport or are the evaluator's perceptions the basis for decision-making?)
- control of classroom (Control is an item that is likely to be viewed or interpreted through one's personal philosophy of education.)
- efficient use of instructional time
- performance in the responsibilities concerned with the building
- initiative, resourcefulness, and industriousness
- cooperation with others
- courtesy, tact, self-control, and poise
- relationships with parents (Such information is frequently obtained through second-hand sources other than through personal observation.)
- ability to meet unusual or difficult situations
- quality of speech
- relationships with employers of students
- attitude toward students
- attitude toward teaching
- attitude toward parents and/or community
- observation of proper standards of conduct inside and out of school
- a sense of humor
- good attendance record
- recognition and use at all times of the proper channels of authority

That these items may contribute substantially to a person's value both as an instructor and as a colleague is not the issue. Rather, the substantive problem is the one that few can deny; we view these characteristics through very different perceptions and our conclusions are based upon our personal interpretations of what we see. In other words, these items are *not* bias-free and, like "facts," they do *not* "speak for themselves." They are at the mercy of those who choose to interpret them—as are the teachers who are judged on the basis of these criteria.

Items That Tend to Imply a Single Instructional Method

- evidence of lesson planning (This procedure is essentially associated with large- and, occasionally, small-group instruction.)
- use of good questioning techniques (There may be no need to question selected youngsters who have demonstrated the ability to progress independently and responsibly.)
- use of and adherence to district curricular guides; staying within course subject framework (Some youngsters cannot be motivated to achieve through subjects in district curricular guides or the structured course framework; the skillful teacher knows when the curriculum should be altered and how to do so for individual students.)
- daily preparation (Students may require long-term prescriptions and developing daily plans for them might be an inappropriate and self-defeating approach.)
- *use of* good homework assignments (Some students may not *need* home assignments and, thus, would not profit from homework.)

Our broadening knowledge of student differences requires evaluation criteria that demonstrate the teacher's awareness of and provision for individual variations in learning ability, potential, interests, and style. These items should be directly related to the teacher's ability to diagnose, prescribe for, and guide different types of students through the learning process, sometimes through different types of programs. The criteria should not be subjective in that they should yield essentially similar ratings from each member of a team of evaluators who is present during the entire visit. The evaluators, without discussing the observation, should rate the teacher on each of the itemized criteria in accordance with predetermined directions. After the observation it would be permissible and desirable for the team to meet with the teacher and openly discuss their individual ratings on each criterion. Should disagreement occur because of a misunderstood practice or procedure, the teacher would be encouraged to record his or her commentary concerning the item.

CLASSIFYING CRITERIA ACCORDING TO BEHAVIORS AND OUTCOMES OF BEHAVIORS

One means of determining the extent to which teachers are engaging in the kinds of behaviors that lead toward appropriate student progress is to watch them during class and actually observe what they are doing. What you see the teacher *doing* is called a "teacher behavior."

Similarly, when the teacher has diagnosed each youngster and prescribed an appropriate learning task or series of tasks for him, the student should be engaged in specific activities. These activities, what the student actually *does* in the learning environment, are called "student behaviors."

Sometimes teachers do what the literature describes as necessary for facilitating student progress, e.g., diagnose individuals to determine aptitude, knowledges, and/or skills. The evaluator may not, however, actually *see* the teacher diagnosing and may not be able to record that appropriate *teacher behaviors* either resulted from the diagnosis or were evident at all. It is possible, however, to observe the *results* of teacher diagnosis of the student by looking at the student's files where test scores, anecdotal records, performance notations, and completed materials may have been stored, commented upon, or noted by the teacher. Then, although the actual teacher *behavior* may not have been observed, the *results* of that behavior may be evident. The result or outcome of the teacher's and/or student's behavior(s) is called a "behavioral outcome."

When ratings are made with strict regard to both teacher and student behaviors and behavioral outcomes that are observable during a visit, the rating will tend to be objective. Verification of objectivity can be obtained by having a team of trained evaluators use a behavior-oriented instrument in the same classroom with all being present for the entire amount of time and then comparing results. It is possible that individuals may overlook a behavior or outcome or two, but comparison of the team's ratings (with an opportunity to discuss them with the teacher *after* they have been recorded) should yield essentially similar evaluations.

RELATING EVALUATIVE CRITERIA TO PROGRAM PROCEDURES

Very often evaluators begin the process of assessing the value and effectiveness of staff members by using instruments that have always been used in the district without examining, in depth, the specific items incorporated in them. It is important to note the many differences in instructional procedures that normally occur among (1) traditional, (2) transitional, and (3) individualized programs and to recognize that different types of criteria are required when endeavoring to assess the qualities of teachers functioning under varied philosophies; obviously, different sets of behaviors and behavioral outcomes can be anticipated.

Based on materials that compared classroom procedures formerly and currently used by teachers, administrators of Millburn Township, New

Jersey* designed the following scale to be used in conjunction with a behavior observation instrument to identify the characteristics of observed lessons. An overall review of the scale tends to classify the lesson as being either traditional, transitional, or individualized. It is suggested that a program could conceivably include elements of each which, when combined, might produce a distinctive hybrid, and that a program should not necessarily consist of only those characteristics listed under only one heading (see Figure 6-1).

*Theresa M. Weiss, Principal, and Gerald F. O'Malley, Assistant Superintendent

Figure 6-1

Code:

\+ *He/She does this.*
– *He/She does not do this.*
o *Does this procedure in combination with others.*

I. LESSON PLANS

____________________ *Subject*

TRADITIONAL Procedures	*TRANSITIONAL Procedures*	*INDIVIDUALIZED Procedures*
1. The teacher develops a class topic lesson plan with specific time allotments.	1. The teacher develops lesson plans for each topic, assigning a different number of objectives to each child dependent upon ability; uses varied time allotments.	1. The teacher develops a prescription plan for a child or group of children. [The students have significant control of their programs and vary them substantially.]
2. Uses lecture, lecture-discussion, chalk-talk approach.	2. Some chalk-talk lessons and/or direct teaching of small groups.	2. Mini-lessons given to individuals or small groups when need arises.
3. Specific lesson taught according to a predetermined schedule.	3. Specific lessons and direct teaching in a fairly flexible schedule.	3. Scope and time allotment varies from student to student.
4. Students are measured against group norms on graded materials. Same standards of achievement and grading for every child.	4. Standard of achievement dependent upon objective for each child and his ability.	4. Students evaluated through performance equivalents. Continuous diagnosis.
5. Teacher maintains class lesson plans.	5. Teacher maintains class lesson plans for selected studies and distributes individual prescriptions for others.	5. Each student follows an individual prescription, but participates in small-group lessons as needed. Individual prescription serves as a lesson plan. These are kept in individual pupil folders.
Comments	*Comments*	*Comments*
*1.*__________	*1.*__________	*1.*__________

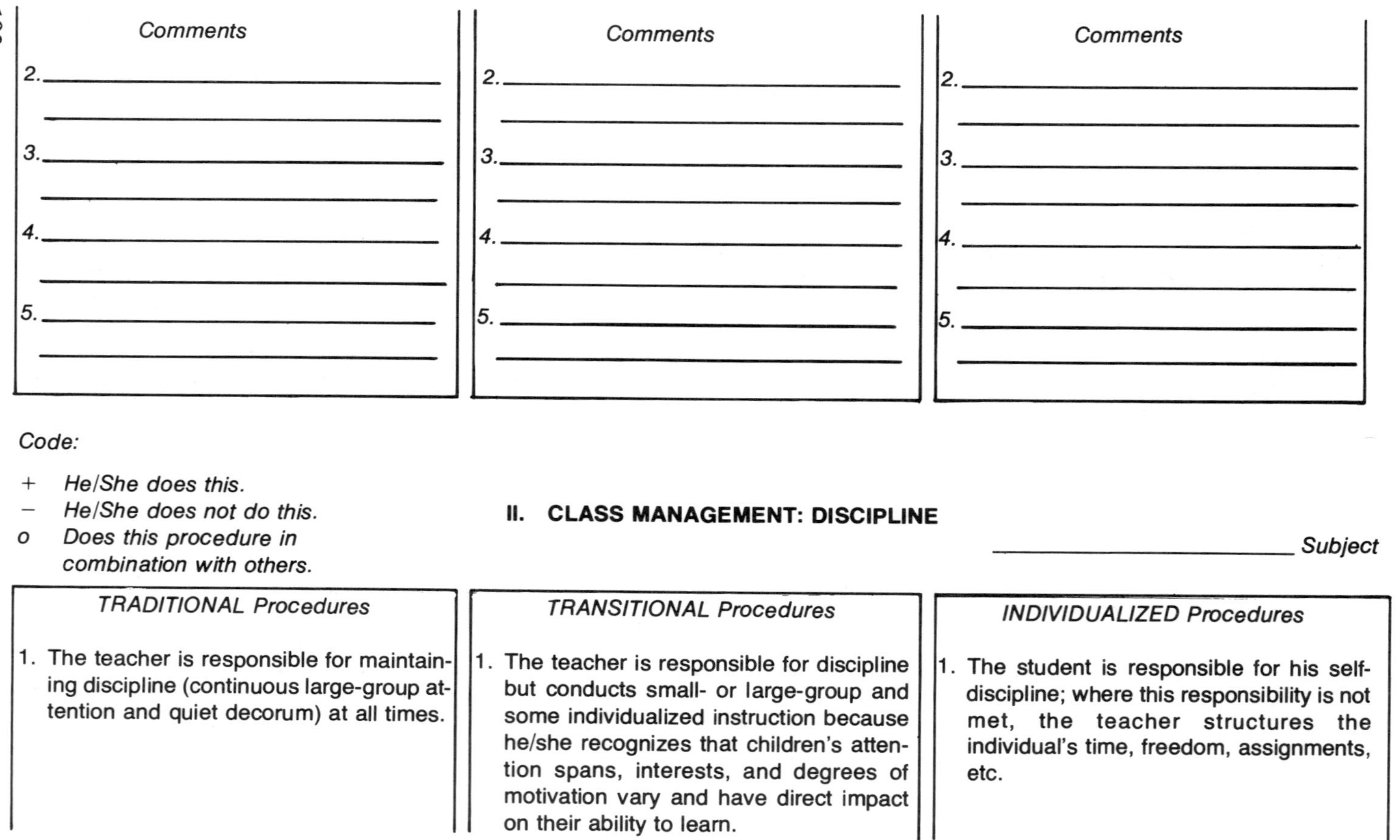

Comments	Comments	Comments
2.______	2.______	2.______
3.______	3.______	3.______
4.______	4.______	4.______
5.______	5.______	5.______

Code:

+ *He/She does this.*
− *He/She does not do this.*
o *Does this procedure in combination with others.*

II. CLASS MANAGEMENT: DISCIPLINE

____________ *Subject*

TRADITIONAL Procedures	*TRANSITIONAL Procedures*	*INDIVIDUALIZED Procedures*
1. The teacher is responsible for maintaining discipline (continuous large-group attention and quiet decorum) at all times.	1. The teacher is responsible for discipline but conducts small- or large-group and some individualized instruction because he/she recognizes that children's attention spans, interests, and degrees of motivation vary and have direct impact on their ability to learn.	1. The student is responsible for his self-discipline; where this responsibility is not met, the teacher structures the individual's time, freedom, assignments, etc.

2. Not paying attention is frowned upon by the teacher. 3. The teacher is expected to be aware and "strong" in handling the problems.	2. Students are expected to be quiet and attentive during group discussions, but may self-direct themselves at other times, as long as they progress academically.	2. Students may self-direct themselves at all times and elect to participate in small-group instruction at their discretion, or upon direction from the teacher, when needed. 3. In large groups, instruction is used merely to introduce new topics, concepts, or generalized studies; the students are expected to show continuous attention and quiet decorum. 4. In small-group instruction [3-8], paired, or individual work, decorum is a matter of working quietly so that others may learn without interference.
Comments 1. ________ 2. ________ 3. ________ 4. ________	*Comments* 1. ________ 2. ________ 3. ________ 4. ________	*Comments* 1. ________ 2. ________ 3. ________ 4. ________

Code:

\+ *He/She does this.*
– *He/She does not do this.*
o *Does this procedure in combination with others.*

III. ASSIGNMENTS

________________ *Subject*

TRADITIONAL Procedures	*TRANSITIONAL Procedures*	*INDIVIDUALIZED Procedures*
1. Students are assigned the same amount of study to be completed in an identical span of time. 2. Students move from one topic to the next when the time allocated to that *topic* has been exhausted. 3. Students complete most of their studies at their own desks. 4. Students are easily observed as working or doodling and daydreaming.	1. Students are given different assignments to be completed within varied amounts of time. 2. Students move to another topic when the time allocated to the *student* has been exhausted. 3. Students may be working at a variety of different instructional areas. 4. Students may be observed circulating among many instructional areas and appear to be actively involved in learning.	1. Students partially self-select their work and pace themselves within some limitations. 2. Students pace themselves in accordance with their interests and abilities. 3. Students may be learning in and out of the classroom. 4. The student is actively involved in learning and is aware of his own goals and next steps.
Comments *1.* ________ ________ *2.* ________ ________	*Comments* *1.* ________ ________ *2.* ________ ________	*Comments* *1.* ________ ________ *2.* ________ ________

Comments	*Comments*	*Comments*
3. ______	*3.* ______	*3.* ______
4. ______	*4.* ______	*4.* ______

Code:

- \+ *He/She does this.*
- − *He/She does not do this.*
- o *Does this procedure in combination with others.*

IV. INSTRUCTIONAL MATERIALS

______ *Subject*

TRADITIONAL Procedures	*TRANSITIONAL Procedures*	*INDIVIDUALIZED Procedures*
1. Students learn from teacher's lectures and books.	1. Students learn from teacher-led discussions, books, and multimedia resources.	1. Students learn through various resources of their own choice, such as research trips, multimedia, experimentation, discovery, inquiry, discussions, etc.
2. Texts are selected and assigned by teachers.	2. Both the teacher and the student select the materials.	2. Students assume responsibility for selecting study resources. The teacher serves as a guide and aid in the selection.

Comments	*Comments*	*Comments*
1. ______	1. ______	1. ______
2. ______	2. ______	2. ______

Code:

+ *He/She does this.*
– *He/She does not do this.*
o *Does this procedure in combination with others.*

V. STUDENT INVOLVEMENT AND BEHAVIORS

______ *Subject*

TRADITIONAL Procedures	*TRANSITIONAL Procedures*	*INDIVIDUALIZED Procedures*
1. Students gain recognition only by raising their hands.	1. Students observe the rules for gaining recognition during group instruction but interact freely and responsibly at all other times.	1. Students are treated like responsible adults and may interact with peers, teacher, and other adults.

2. Students are admonished for breaking teacher-made rules.	2. Students have delegated freedoms within a cooperatively developed framework. When necessary, they are admonished by the group and/or the teacher.	2. Individual students identify the ways in which they work best in accordance with their learning style and may operate independently within the confines of good manners and respect for the learning styles of others. When necessary, they are required to examine their own behaviors in cooperation with the teacher.
Comments *1.* ________ *2.* ________	*Comments* *1.* ________ *2.* ________	*Comments* *1.* ________ *2.* ________

Code:

+ *He/She does this.*
− *He/She does not do this.*
o *Does this procedure in combination with others.*

VI. STUDENT ASSESSMENT

________________ *Subject*

TRADITIONAL Procedures	*TRANSITIONAL Procedures*	*INDIVIDUALIZED Procedures*
1. Teacher administers his/her designed and/or commercially prepared tests when unit has been covered.	1. Teacher administers prepared criterion-referenced tests at different times to different students as individual work is completed.	1. There is a continuous diagnosis of the students that permits the teacher to curtail preparing and giving tests except on an individual basis as needed.
2. All students take the same test at the same time and are evaluated by the same criteria.	2. Teacher and student may determine when the time for assessment has arrived.	2. Students may use self-assessment instruments on a varied time schedule or as the need arises.
Comments	*Comments*	*Comments*
1. ________________	*1.* ________________	*1.* ________________
2. ________________	*2.* ________________	*2.* ________________

Further corroboration of recognized differences between individualized and nonindividualized procedures is manifested in Figure 6-2, an excerpt from materials developed by the Institute of Administrative Research at Teachers College, Columbia University. These items are in behavioral language and can be noted readily in terms of either their presence *or* absence.

Figure 6-2

POLAR CHARACTERISTICS DISTINGUISHING INDIVIDUALIZING FROM NONINDIVIDUALIZING TEACHING PRACTICES

	OBSERVED BEHAVIOR IN CLASSROOMS OF INDIVIDUALIZING TEACHERS	OBSERVED BEHAVIOR IN CLASSROOMS OF NONINDIVIDUALIZING TEACHERS
	TEACHER BEHAVIOR	
	Individualizing Pole	Nonindividualizing Pole
1T	*Objectives* The teacher pursues multiple objectives, each objective related to a specific pupil or a small group of pupils.	The teacher pursues a single preselected objective applying it without variation to all pupils in the class.
2T	*Planning and Preparation* The teacher's planning and preparation are in terms of individual students.	The teacher's planning and preparation are in terms of some single class norm. (This norm may be the average of the three or four "best" students.)
3T	*Communication-Direction* The teacher communicates with individuals in the class while other individuals of the class remain engaged in different activities.	The teacher communicates with all pupils in the entire class at one and the same time (i.e., "out loud"), even when addressing one youngster.
4T	*Communication-Message* The teacher uses feedback information from individual pupils as a basis for modifying the message being communicated.	The teacher's preselected communication is unmodified by circumstances other than his own objectives or by variations in its reception by individual pupils.
5T	*Function* The teacher's function is primarily observation of evidence of learning or the lack of it, and the motivation and guiding of students to independent learning activity.	The teacher functions primarily as a purveyor of information.

	Individualizing Pole	Nonindividualizing Pole
6T	*Evaluation* The teacher's evaluation of each pupil is based on the latter's individual growth and development.	The teacher evaluates the pupils en masse with a predetermined standard as the measure of success.

PUPIL BEHAVIOR

	Individualizing Pole	Nonindividualizing Pole
1P	*Objectives* The pupils pursue objectives that they themselves have established.	The pupils pursue objectives that the teacher has established.
2P	*Planning and Preparation* Each pupil's planning and preparation is unique; each is engaged in independent work, study, practice, or demonstration.	Planning and preparation is for the pupils en masse by the teacher's direction; all pupils are engaged in the same activity.
3P	*Communication-Direction* The pupils are engaged in small-group activity in which discussion is considered a function of learning.	The pupils' participation in class is restricted to asking or answering questions of the teacher.
4P	*Communication-Message* The pupils are encouraged to manifest originality, creative productivity, and purposeful divergence.	The pupils are restricted to recitation of predigested material and to conformity.
5P	*Function* The pupils are active participants in learning activities.	The pupils are passive recipients of knowledge.
6P	*Evaluation* The pupil evaluates his own growth and development.	The pupil makes no self-evaluation but accepts the teacher's opinion.

USING CRITERIA TO DETERMINE COMPARATIVE TEACHER RATINGS

Identifying those appropriate behaviors in which a teacher actually engages, the student behaviors that result because of the teacher behaviors, and the outcomes that are generated by both provides evaluators with precise information that may be used to help the professional person assess current strengths and areas for improvement. When used wisely, the data revealed about what actually occurs in a classroom setting are specific and clearly indicate what needs to be added, deleted, or altered.

Evaluation, then, should occur in terms of "... these are some of the behaviors that ought to be introduced ... these are some of the outcomes that you might consider changing. ..." Evaluation should *not* be an estimation of the teacher in comparison with his/her colleagues; it *should* be an evaluation of the teacher's own growth as evidenced by a comparison of previous and present ratings.

Some evaluation forms erroneously tend to compare teachers with each other in accordance with pre-established criteria (see Figure 6-3). The terms "superior," "above average," etc., can only be applied to an individual who is being compared with colleagues. In addition, such ratings do not indicate where improvement should be made and, as such, are insufficient tools for either self- or administrative assessment. However, should administrators elect to compare faculty as one means of acknowledging superior performance or as justification for maintaining some and/or dismissing others, a system may be developed to obtain a degree of objectivity. Establish a joint teacher-administrator committee. Agree on the number or percentage of appropriate predetermined teacher behaviors and outcomes that should be present to merit a "superior" or "above average" rating and then apply these criteria across the board to all teachers in terms of the specific actions or outcomes that are evidenced when classes are visited by teams of observers.

Figure 6-3

CITY PUBLIC SCHOOLS
DIVISION OF TEACHER PERSONNEL
ANNUAL EVALUATION FOR NONTENURED TEACHERS

Teacher ____________________ School ____________________

Subject or grade ____________________ Date ____________________

Directions: This report, one for each contract teacher not on tenure assigned to the building, is due in the office of the Assistant Superintendent, Personnel, by April 1. It is not to be used for teachers during their first two years of service in the (city) Public Schools when the Instrument for Evaluating Professional Growth and Teaching Service applies.

Indicate your estimate of the service rendered by this teacher by placing a check mark in front of the most appropriate paragraph. DO NOT CHECK MORE THAN ONE RATING. If you feel this does not adequately describe the teacher's service, the rating should be supplemented in the space below. Two copies are to be made—one for the principal and one for the Assistant Superintendent, Personnel.

☐ 1. The SUPERIOR teacher. This is a master teacher in the classroom. Exercises constructive influence and maintains cooperative professional relationship with parents, pupils, and administrators. Constantly strives in every way to be a superior teacher. Willingly accepts responsibilities beyond the requirements of his/her daily program.

☐ 2. The ABOVE-AVERAGE teacher: This is a strong and capable teacher. Does excellent work in the classroom, is responsible and reliable. Cooperates fully with school policies and administrative requests. Maintains harmonious relationship with pupils, parents, and co-workers.

☐ 3. The AVERAGE teacher: This is an acceptable teacher. This teacher is reliable, responsible, and shows promise. Participates to a reasonable degree in the activities of the school. A large majority of teachers fall within this category.

☐ 4. The BELOW-AVERAGE teacher: This is a weak teacher. This teacher has difficulty in adjusting to normal school situations. Continued effort and proper attitude may lead to improved performance.

☐ 5. The UNSATISFACTORY teacher: This is a teacher whose work indicates little or no aptitude for the teaching profession.

OTHER COMMENTS____

____

____

This is to certify that we have read and discussed the above report.

Principal______________________
Teacher_______________________

THIS COPY TO PRINCIPAL

IDENTIFYING GUIDELINES FOR THE USE OF TEACHER EVALUATION PROCEDURES

These guidelines for the use of teacher evaluation procedures are taken from a report, *Teacher Evaluation to Improve Learning*, published by the Ohio Commission on Public School Personnel Policies and contain concepts that are generally supported by most experts in this field.

1. Evaluation should be a continuous process.
2. No one technique or instrument is sufficient to do the total job of evaluation.
3. Each evaluation technique should be designed for a specific purpose.
4. By using a combination of techniques, a helpful data bank of a teacher's competencies can be accumulated.
5. Teachers need inservice training in the use of evaluation instruments that

they can use for self-assessment purposes. Adequate time should be provided for this training.

6. The evaluation of teachers needs to take place in light of specific teaching objectives.
7. A global approach to teacher evaluation is not effective. The teaching act must be broken down into specific skills [please see a listing in chapter 5] that can be evaluated, and an appropriate instrument and technique to measure each skill must be used.
8. An effective plan of evaluation requires sufficient personnel with adequate training and time to do the job.
9. All data collected on teachers by evaluators should be made available to the teachers so that improvement of instruction can be facilitated.
10. Teacher behavior should be evaluated in terms of the particular value system mutually agreed upon by the teacher and the evaluator.
11. In order to fully evaluate teaching, it is necessary to measure changes in student behavior.
12. Any evaluation program should have broad teacher involvement in its formulation and application.
13. The specific plan of evaluation for instructional improvement should be written into the negotiated agreement and/or board policy statements so that all have the same expectations regarding its use.

In light of the inadequacy of many of the forms that are being used in schools today, the authors would add several statements to the above list.

1. A team of evaluators should be used for each visit and analysis comparisons made among their observations and ratings.
2. Observation instruments should focus upon teacher and student behaviors (what is actually observed) and the outcomes of these behaviors rather than on items that lend themselves to bias or interpretation.
3. Teacher growth should be determined by comparing each evaluation with the previous one as a means of identifying areas of improvement. When growth has not been evidenced, it should be understood that it may be impossible for that teacher to improve in that particular area, and judgments should be made accordingly.
4. If teachers are to be compared with one another, ratings should be determined by computing the *number* of positive behaviors and outcomes that are manifested and the ranking of specific items should be agreed upon in advance.
5. When open-ended comments are solicited, sufficient space should be provided to permit meaningful statements. Small comment areas and closely printed lines tend to discourage an honest, full report.
6. When offering suggestions for needed improvement, evaluators should list sources for obtaining the specific information necessary, e.g., books, tapes, persons, etc. Evaluators frequently provide suggestions at the moment in which the evaluation is being discussed and many people

"block" under stress or anxiety. Give the teacher the *suggestions* in writing and provide him or her with alternative resources from which he or she can learn after overcoming the initial shock of criticism.

7. Incorporate into any evaluation form the question, "Is there any doubt in your mind about the future success of this teacher if made permanent?" Add, "If there is a doubt, what do you question?" Then leave sufficient space for the answer. This is one response that will be made carefully because the evaluator is being made accountable (in writing!) for predicting how well the teacher will do. His judgment is being placed "on the line" and, sometime in the future, he may be required to face the reality that he has made either a good or poor recommendation.
8. The *second* time that a teacher is rated as having demonstrated fewer than 90% of the desired positive characteristics on the scale that the evaluator(s) uses, notify the teacher that his/her contract will not be renewed.
9. Do not employ or dismiss individuals on the basis of how they are evaluated in previous systems. Many people who "make waves" are mistrusted by insecure or unknowledgeable peers, but may be exactly the kind of vibrant, innovative, bright person your building needs.
10. Do not judge a person by the degree to which he cooperates with his colleagues. Many outstanding (particularly innovative) people are scorned or ridiculed by their peers because they choose to do things differently, or work more, or achieve better results than they. Lend such a person your support and evaluate objectively what he/she is endeavoring to attempt.
11. Listen to the students (of any age) as they discuss or describe their teachers. Students often are the most objective and accurate evaluators of their teachers.

This report card has nothing to do with how well I am learning! It only shows how poorly my teacher is teaching!
REPORT

It is not true that they tend to downgrade teachers who give extensive work assignments; the contrary is true. Teachers tend to be respected by their students when they teach well. No teacher can satisfy or "win" every student, but the majority response will be revealing.

12. Recognize that individual teachers may be dismal failures with some students and brilliant, beloved favorites with others. Do not make across-the-board judgments. Match teachers with the students with whom they tend to be successful (see chapter 3).
13. Recognize the efforts of people who strive toward improvement, but do not equate their effort with success. Maintain high standards by upholding those criteria that have been established and justify these standards by reminding yourself of what you would have preferred in teaching excellence for your own children.
14. Evaluative comments are an indication of the quality of the evaluator.
15. Having individuals identify their own annual goals toward improvement may be fashionable at the moment but may be too general to be very productive. Few intelligent people will agree to assume the responsibility for achieving goals that they consider difficult or beyond their ability to master. As a result, to preserve the human relations situation, goal-setting sometimes becomes a charade. Administrative responsibility dictates that evaluators should assist teachers in identifying joint priorities and that these include those skills that are clearly absent or in need of improvement.
16. It is important for teachers to see themselves as others see them. Evaluation reports and the informal assessments of colleagues, students, and their students' parents should be available to them and generally maintained as a matter of record.
17. Teachers should be able to respond to any comments made by evaluators and to explain their perceptions to the reports. These rebuttals or reactions should also be made part of the record and maintained as part of the overall assessment design.

The largest part of any school budget is spent on faculty salaries. It is our belief that no community funds should be paid, beyond the first year of service in that system, to a single individual person who is not rated as "excellent" or "superior" in terms of identified criteria. Administrators often are loathe to indicate a teacher's weak points because of the resultant poor relationships that may develop between them, particularly when they will be required to work together during the remainder of the school year. Faculty morale deteriorates when honest but negative ratings are submitted and hostility often develops among faculty who are not involved in the establishment of the evaluation procedure. Many supervisors avoid such confrontations by soft-pedaling the areas of difficulty. Then too, administrators frequently avoid the problems and discomfort of dismissing teachers because of poor evaluations; overlooking poor ratings and rationalizing their potential to improve are supposedly easy ways out of an uncomfortable situation. Some administrators even develop a "Pygmalion" complex and believe they can improve anyone to a level of excellence. It is suggested therefore, that, if improvement is likely to occur for a person who apparently conveys the promise of growth, that person—after two ratings below 90%—should be dismissed, encouraged to seek employment elsewhere and permitted to grow in another school district, one that may perceive that teacher as being excellent in comparison with its staff. Very little will motivate extensive professional improvement as much as the knowledge that only excellent teachers will be retained by your school. Automatic retention and misdirected humanism adds to, and perhaps causes, apathy and/or complacency. In fact, these ineffective approaches appear to contribute to some people's lack of incentive toward excellence.

Sympathy should not be directed toward the "good" or "nice" teacher who faces dismissal because of his inability to achieve a ranking of "excellent" or "outstanding." Instead, consider the students who are not provided superior teachers to ensure their academic progress and personal growth, and consider the communities that pay excellent salaries for less-than-excellent performances.

Tenure laws, of course, prohibit the application of such standards of excellence to those teachers who are protected from scrutiny or dismissal, but it is not too late to apply these criteria to teachers who do not yet enjoy tenure. Tenure should be granted only to those faculty members who obtain "superior" ratings, and even these persons should be reassessed periodically. It is virtually impossible to dismiss a teacher after tenure has been awarded, which is reason enough to award it judiciously, infrequently, and only on the basis of demonstrated teaching effectiveness. Indeed, tenure itself should be called into question and three- to five-year contracts substituted.

UNDERSTANDING THE DIFFERENCES BETWEEN TEACHER PERFORMANCE AND EFFECTIVENESS WITH STUDENTS

The final section of this chapter provides a series of student and teacher behaviors and behavioral outcomes that may be selected by any faculty and administrative staff and incorporated into a complete or partial instrument through which the effectiveness of the teaching staff may be determined. On what basis, however, will individual or grouped criteria be chosen and how will they be applied? Should different teachers be assessed in relation to different criteria? Should the criteria be applied more stringently for some than for others? Must there be consensus among administrators and teachers concerning which items will be included and which will be omitted?

It should be noted that if the behaviors of the teacher are measured in some way, e.g., by observations made by administrators, peers, students, or parents, then the teacher's *performance* is being evaluated. However, if the incremental knowledges, skills, or attitudes gained by the students as a consequence of the contact with a particular teacher, his/her methods or materials is measured, then the teacher's *effectiveness* is being evaluated. Thus, observations to identify what the teacher is *doing* in the classroom, what the student is *doing as a result of what the teacher did,* and the outcomes of either or both are merely *preliminary* (although they are necessary and directly related) to evaluating the teacher's effectiveness. They constitute the first step.[2]

The second step should be measurement of the incremental knowledges, skills and/attitudes gained by students as a consequence of having been taught by that teacher. Whether or not pupil achievement is truly an index of teacher performance has been a contradictory issue because of the recognized differences among students. Teaching better students (or the elimination of poorer students) tends to make a teacher appear to be more effective[3] than those who teach less able children.

More and more, however, research studies are beginning to demonstrate that teacher performance can be measured reliably in terms of pupil achievement. Justiz,[4] McNeil,[5] Moffett,[6] Cohen and Brawer,[7] and Popham[8] each conducted field-based research, the data of which appears to verify that it is possible to provide evidence of the relationship between teacher-stated objectives and their achievement by students.

Faculties may cooperatively or individually examine the following list of performances to determine whether they wish to incorporate all, most, many, or some of the items into an instrument that will reveal which of the stated desirable behaviors are, in fact, present in individual classroom situations. Once a majority of the teacher behaviors are observable on a daily basis, the student behaviors should become equally as apparent. The outcomes may be present almost as soon as both sets of behaviors are adopted.

All teachers will not be able to adopt specific behaviors with equal ease and it may be that choices should be permitted based on pre-established or cooperatively determined priorities. Since experienced teachers do not necessarily tend to achieve higher evaluations than do younger teachers, the criteria should be applied with equal consistency—unless teachers are willing to admit that some are not as able as others. Once they do, there is justification for merit pay and differentiated staffing based on teaching effectiveness.

One final caution before you begin to examine the suggested criteria for inclusion into what may become your personalized evaluation design: Three important conditions should be present to evidence that a rating scheme for teacher evaluation does, in fact, measure anything of value. These three requirements are:

1) more than one rater and, preferably, a team should conduct the evaluation,
2) the raters should closely agree in their ratings, and
3) the ratings should indicate differences among teachers.[9]

EXAMINING SELECTED INSTRUMENTS THAT ARE CONCERNED WITH TEACHER AND STUDENT BEHAVIORS AND/OR OUTCOMES

During the past few years educators have recognized that previously designed devices to measure teacher and/or program effectiveness are inappropriate for assessing either teacher performance or the quality of that performance. Most of the newer instruments that have been designed and field tested are based on the criteria that are emerging as indicators of individualized programs—criteria that coincide with a belief in the need for individual diagnoses, prescriptions, and choices.

The following instruments each incorporate selected aspects of observable teacher and student behaviors and/or outcomes of those behaviors. Items that require supervisors to make judgments and are not answerable through direct observation only are noted by the asterisk (*) placed before them.

THE INDIVIDUALIZED INSTRUCTION SCALE

Project Individualized Instruction, a former ESEA Title III program, developed a structured observation-interview procedure to gather data on programs of individualization. This instrument was the end product of a three-year developmental effort that included (1) extensive discussion with practitioners, (2) field testing, (3) appraisals by educators on Long Island, New York and by an external evaluation consultant.[10]

The project participants and area experts decided that the instrument should assess individualization in terms of a formally stated definition of that term and should differentiate the degree of individualization among programs that claimed to be individualized. Thus, instead of determining the presence *or* absence of certain features in a program, the observer was asked to rate the degree to which each feature was present.

Project Definition of Individualized Instruction

As defined by the project participants, individualized instruction meant the adaption of instructional practices to the requirements of each learner. This procedure provides a learning environment in which a student can be taught according to his needs, at a pace that is appropriate for him, and in a way that efficiently uses the available resources as he proceeds toward the competency goals of his program.

This definition assumes that selected goals and objectives need not be common to all learners because uniform goals and objectives may not apply equally well to every student. It further assumes that some latitude exists for individuals at all levels to provide some input into decisions concerning selected instructional objectives. Moreover, in a limited number of cases the individual may be free to make some or many decisions for himself.

This framework of individualized instruction assumes that objectives are selected for or by individuals in light of substantial learner diagnosis, which determines the way the teacher guides and extends student learning. To select objectives, or to move toward their attainment, complete, continuous monitoring of the learner's status is of paramount importance. Information obtained through monitoring is comprised of data not only concerned with the learner's academic achievement, ability, and attitude, but also is concerned with his emotional, physical, sociological, and environmental needs, interests, expectations, maturity, and other relevant data.

Since it is not always possible to predetermine which specific resources and instructional strategies may be best suited to each learner, alternatives should be available for achieving each individual's objectives.

Description of the Individualized Instruction Scale

Literature concerned with the Individualized Instruction Scale (I.I. Scale) suggests that it was designed to assess the degree to which a particular program is individualized. Since the criteria generally associated with individualization are reflective of effective educational procedures, it is appropriate to include this scale as one example of an instrument that may yield data that provide insights into positive and/or negative classroom procedures that are observable during a specific time interval. The scale yields a score that reflects the extent to which classroom practices agree with the definition of individualization developed by the project. Users of the scale should find the results helpful in determining the extent to which the observed classroom is individualized and the extent to which specific teacher and student behaviors are evident in that situation.

General Instructions for Administration

Before administering the scale, review each item in all three sections of the scale and determine how it is scored. Notice the row of numbers (1,2,3,4,5) to the left of each item. To evaluate each item, circle the appropriate number as described in the next step of these general instructions. Respond to each item to the extent that it reflects the program you are observing.

Each item should be scored on a continuum that ranges from 1 to 5. In deciding on your response, keep the following guidelines in mind:

- A rating of 5 indicates that the item is an *excellent* description of the program and is entirely accurate.
- A rating of 1 indicates that the item *barely* describes the program.
- A rating of 2 through 4 indicates various points that lie between the two extremes. Descriptors are provided at the top of each column for your guidance.

Examples of Rating Procedures

Item 1 in the Observation section is, "Students work without direct supervision." As you observe in the classroom, if you *see* that all of the students are being directly supervised by the teacher and that no students appear to be working totally independently under their own supervision, then your response is 1 and you would circle 1 to the left of the item. However, if, as you continue to observe, you note that the teacher becomes involved with a small group or an individual and that, generally speaking, students actually do supervise themselves part of the time, you might choose to circle either 3 (moderately) or 4 (considerably), dependent upon the amount of direct supervision you note in that situation. If you noted that students in a given situation appeared to be working with an absolute minimum of direct supervision, you would circle the 5 to the left of that item, indicating that, as you observed, you saw little or no direct supervision of students.

Although some items may be difficult to respond to, the recorder is requested to make every effort to score every item. Only if an item is *totally* inappropriate and cannot be rated should it be omitted.

This scale may be administered by someone in the program (such as the teacher or a student) or by an outside evaluator (administrator or colleague, etc.). If it is to be self-administered, follow "Instructions for Self-Administration." If it is to be administered by someone who is not actually involved with the program, follow the instructions titled "Instructions for Outside Evaluator."

Instructions for Self-Administration

Section 1

For the Observation section of this scale (1), select a 45-minute time period that you consider to be representative of the program. Familiarize yourself with the items before you attempt to record what is seen. Several trial attempts prior to official usage will be helpful in terms of both personal comfort with the instrument and accuracy of the recorded data.

Make a judgment on each item in accordance with the "General Instructions" previously explained.

Section 2

For the section referring to student responses, try to imagine how your students will answer a visitor who may ask these questions. For example, how do you believe your students would respond to an outsider who asked, "Do you feel free to voice your feelings to the teacher(s)?" (Item 26)[11], or "Do you decide with whom you will work?" (Item 35)? The closer you come to predicting actual student responses, the more often your own rating will tend to agree with an outside evaluator's score.

Section 3

This section is designed to elicit information from the teacher. Since, presumably, the teacher or someone directly concerned with the program will be responding to the items, rate them in the same manner as in the previous sections.

Instructions for Outside Evaluator

Section 1

For the Observation section of the scale, ask the teacher to select a 45-minute time period that he believes is representative of the program. While in the room, make a judgment on each item in accordance with the "General Instructions" previously explained. Base your responses on what you actually *observe* during the time period and *not* on what you believe might occur. Divide the observation period into two parts. Move around the room and observe the program in operation before responding to any of the items. Then select a quiet place in the room and answer as many items as you can. Continue the observation, again moving about the room as needed in order to respond to the remaining items that have not, as yet, been scored.

Section 2

This section on student responses is designed to elicit information about the program that may not be readily observable. Walk about the room while sampling several students' responses to each of the items numbered 23-40. Directions in the User's Guide that accompanies the I.I. Scale suggest that the evaluator paraphrase the items ". . . to make the questioning relaxed and in language appropriate to the maturity of the students."[12] It may be necessary to paraphrase the items included in the scale, but extreme caution should be taken to avoid biasing the questions or asking them in ways that might conceivably alter (even slightly) their original meaning.

Each student to whom you speak should be asked several questions. The responses of the various interviewed youngsters should be compared with each other before any one item is rated. Minimally, at least three students' responses should be elicited prior to reaching a decision concerning any item. The items may be responded to in any sequence that appears to be most efficient for you.

Section 3

This section is designed to elicit information that is available only from the teacher. Here, too, it is suggested that the questions may be paraphrased or grouped to make the most efficient use of time.[13]

Suggested Time Limits

The following time guidelines for administration of the I.I. Scale are suggested by the guide that accompanies it:

1. Observation: 30 to 45 minutes.
2. Student Responses: 20 to 30 minutes (more or less, as needed).
3. Teacher Responses: 20 to 30 minutes (more or less, as needed).

Scoring Procedures

No separate key is necessary to score this scale. Complete directions for scoring are printed on the front cover of the instrument. With the exception of items 3, 8, 16, 17, 29, 45, and 50, scores are obtained simply by summing the circled responses. For those items just indicated, it is first necessary to convert the circled score to a weighted score. These items are negatively keyed and thus a high score on these seven items would not be reflective of an individualized situation. The table below will aid you in converting the circled scores for these items:

Item	Circled Rating				
	1	2	3	4	5
3	5	4	3	2	1
8	5	4	3	2	1
16	5	4	3	2	1
17	5	4	3	2	1
29	5	4	3	2	1
45	5	4	3	2	1
50	5	4	3	2	1

Interpretation of Test Results

The purpose of the I.I. Scale is to rate the degree of individualization present in a program, not to rate the quality or goodness of it. The scores on items relate to specific characteristics that are features of individualization. While in some ways they may also be indicators of overall quality, the observations and ratings are made only in reference to individualization. A low score, therefore, does not mean a program is educationally unsound, but rather that when compared to the project's definition, there is a low degree of individualization. A low rating on any item indicates that the program is low on that specific feature.

Thus the final score, when obtained, reflects the extent to which instructional practices have been adapted to the needs of individual learners by providing a learning environment in which:

1. each learner has some personalized objectives that he may help define,
2. learning experiences are adjusted to the unique needs, interests, and capabilities of the learner,
3. the learner's rate of progress is adjusted with consideration for his level of development, and
4. the learner's advancement is evaluated in light of defined objectives.

Limitations of the Scale

One important fact should be kept in mind when interpreting these results: The scores obtained are, at best, estimates. No single scale affords an infallible and unalterable measure of a universe. I.I. Scale scores, therefore, must be regarded as approximations and should never constitute the sole basis for making important educational decisions.

Qualifications Required to Administer the Scale

The User's Guide for the I.I. Scale indicates that it was designed to be used with a minimum of training. It is recommended, however, that prior to actual administration, users thoroughly familiarize themselves with all of the items and how each is to be scored. It may also be helpful if a practice run is made with a co-worker. After exploratory usage, each item and the rationale for specific ratings can be discussed.

Figure 6-4

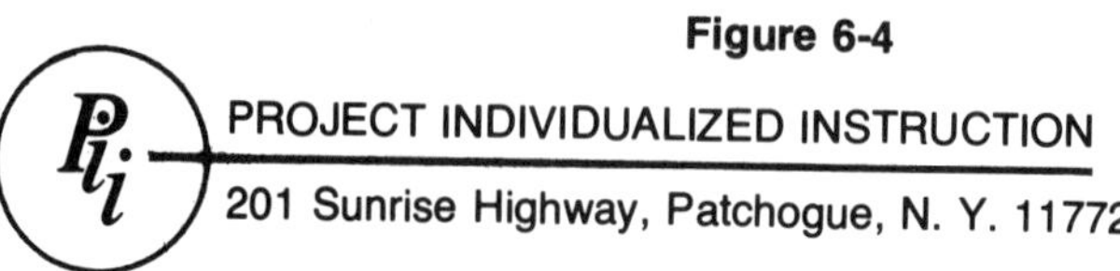

PROJECT INDIVIDUALIZED INSTRUCTION
201 Sunrise Highway, Patchogue, N. Y. 11772

INDIVIDUALIZED INSTRUCTION SCALE
FINAL REVISION

Scale administered by:____________________ Date:__________

School and Program Name:______________________________

District:____________________ Teacher(s):________________

How to score:

1) Scan the 50 responses to make certain that there are no omitted items. If an item has been omitted, draw a line through all the numbers for that item so that no credit will be allowed for the item scoring.

2) Count the number of items that have been answered, omitting any item through which a line has been drawn. Place the number of items answered in the two boxes labeled "B" below. (If all the items have been answered, enter "50" in these boxes.)

3) Before beginning this step, read the instructions on page 5 of the Guide. Next, find the sums of the circled and weighted scores on each page. Enter the sum in the appropriate space at the bottom of the page.

4) To find the ITEM SUMS, add the totals for the two pages and enter in box "A."

5) Perform the following computations to obtain a CORRECTED RAW SCORE (C) and a SCALE POTENTIAL (D).

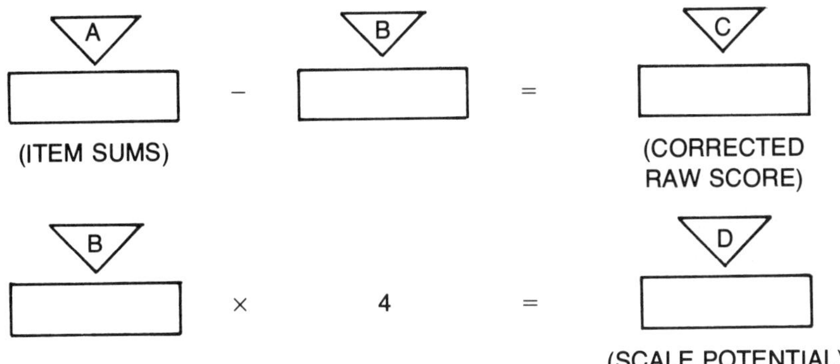

6) To obtain the PROGRAM SCORE, divide Corrected Raw Score (C) by the Scale Potential (D), round to two decimal places, then multiply by 100. Enter below and in the appropriate space.

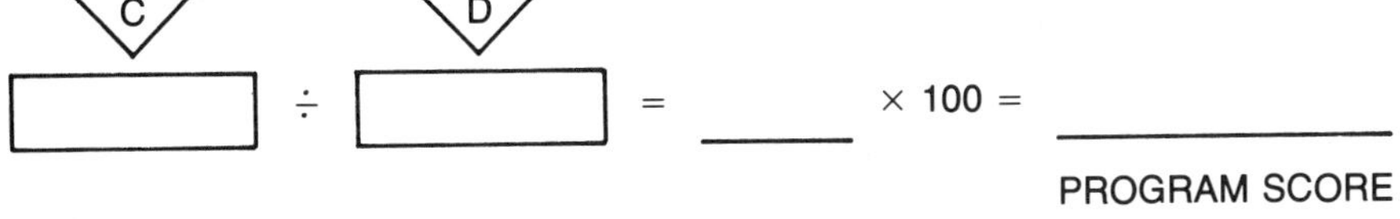

OBSERVATION

Respond to items 1-22 to the extent they describe the program at the time of observation.

barely	somewhat	moderately	considerably	completely		
1	2	3	4	5	1.	Students work without direct supervision.
1	2	3	4	5	2.	Students locate sources of information without asking teacher(s).
1	2	3	4	5	3.	Student behavior is nonproductive or disruptive.
1	2	3	4	5	4.	Students gather necessary materials for a given task.
1	2	3	4	5	5.	Students have free access to materials and equipment.
1	2	3	4	5	6.	There is a wide selection of equipment (A-V, or any special items appropriate to the subject) in the classroom.
1	2	3	4	5	7.	Different materials are in use simultaneously.
1	2	3	4	5	8.	Teacher initiates most tasks.
1	2	3	4	5	9.	Students work on different tasks.
1	2	3	4	5	10.	Different instructional strategies (e.g., reading, discussion, writing, etc.) are in use simultaneously.

barely	somewhat	moderately	considerably	completely		
1	2	3	4	5	11.	Materials and equipment are arranged in interest areas by subject or special topic.
1	2	3	4	5	12.	Informal student groups are observed.
1	2	3	4	5	13.	Skills groups are formed as needed.
1	2	3	4	5	14.	There is peer teaching in the classroom.
1	2	3	4	5	15.	Students move around the room freely.
1	2	3	4	5	16.*	Students may not talk while they are working.
1	2	3	4	5	17.	Students' desks are arranged in rows.
1	2	3	4	5	18.	The available instructional materials are appropriate for a wide range of abilities.
1	2	3	4	5	19.	Teachers interact with individual students while they are working.
1	2	3	4	5	20.	Instructional time is primarily devoted to working with individuals and small groups.
1	2	3	4	5	21.	A wide variety of instructional materials is available.
1	2	3	4	5	22.	There are teacher-made materials, devices, etc. in the room.

Page Total ______

STUDENT RESPONSES

Interview several students before recording your responses to items 23-40. Paraphrase the items when necessary.

barely	somewhat	moderately	considerably	completely		
1	2	3	4	5	23.	Students move through the subject matter at different rates.
1	2	3	4	5	24.	Student conferences are held to plan future instructional activities.
1	2	3	4	5	25.	Students schedule their activities for the day.
1	2	3	4	5	26.*	Students feel free to voice their feelings to the teacher(s).
1	2	3	4	5	27.	Students operate the available equipment themselves.
1	2	3	4	5	28.	Students score their own work.

barely	somewhat	moderately	considerably	completely		
1	2	3	4	5	29.*	Students are allowed to leave class only as a supervised group.
1	2	3	4	5	30.*	Students may change their seats whenever they wish.
1	2	3	4	5	31.*	Students are free to rearrange the room furniture.
1	2	3	4	5	32.	Each student has an individual contract, work agreement, or prescription sheet.
1	2	3	4	5	33.*	Students may go to the school library at any time.
1	2	3	4	5	34.	Students have latitude in the selection of tasks to satisfy required work.
1	2	3	4	5	35.	Students decide with whom they will work.
1	2	3	4	5	36.	Students can tell what they will study next in a given subject.
1	2	3	4	5	37.	Students maintain, or have access to, records of their own progress.
1	2	3	4	5	38.	Students are tested when they are ready.
1	2	3	4	5	39.	The results of tests are interpreted to students individually.
1	2	3	4	5	40.	Teachers discuss nonacademic concerns with students.

Page Total ______

TEACHER RESPONSES

Discuss items 41-50 with the teacher.
Respond to each item as it describes teacher practices.

barely	somewhat	moderately	considerably	completely		
1	2	3	4	5	41.	There are written objectives for each student.
1	2	3	4	5	42.	Different objectives are identified for individual students.
1	2	3	4	5	43.	Objectives for each student are reviewed and revised regularly.
1	2	3	4	5	44.	For students with similar needs, several alternative activities are available.
1	2	3	4	5	45.	The decision to assign new work is based upon progress of the class as a whole.

barely	somewhat	moderately	considerably	completely		
1	2	3	4	5	46.	There are different passing "grades" for different students.
1	2	3	4	5	47.*	There are additional personal contacts with children's parents aside from those scheduled by the school.
1	2	3	4	5	48.	Teacher's records include detailed information on student interests, needs, background, etc.
1	2	3	4	5	49.	Samples of each student's work are kept on file.
1	2	3	4	5	50.	Most students take the same test.

Page Total______

*Items on the I.I. Scale that are preceded by an asterisk (*) are those that do not permit rating solely through observation. For these, questioning is necessary before an accurate response may be recorded. For example, it is necessary to ask students whether or not they may change their seats whenever they wish. During a given observation period students may not actually change their seats, but they may, at all times, be permitted to do so (Item 30). Students may be "allowed" to leave class "only as a supervised group" (Item 29), but they may leave individually despite the rules (which may not be enforced during a visitation).

For the most part, the Individualized Instruction Scale tends to elicit classroom information based on observable student and teacher behaviors and the outcomes of those behaviors. For example, for Item 32, if an observer actually saw a teacher designing or assigning a contract, work agreement, or prescription sheet to a student, that would be recorded as a "teacher behavior." If the student were *observed* using such a prescription, it would be recorded as a "student behavior." But, assuming that students are engaged in many kinds of instructional activities during the observation period but were not actually *observed* using contracts, how could the evaluator rate this item? He might look at a file of "Student Prescriptions" and notice that each student had actually had a contract assigned to him (whether cooperatively designed or not.) He might not see the contract being used, but the fact that the contracts did exist is verification that "Each student has an individual contract. . . ." The contracts in and of themselves verify that the teacher actually did develop one for the student. Therefore, the contract is an outcome of the teacher's behavior—or, a "behavioral outcome.'' The evaluator did not actually see the behavior, but he did see the *results* of it.

THE REMSEN INDIVIDUALIZATION INDEX

Behavioral outcomes are dependent on the teacher's translation of his/her knowledge and skills into observable actions or results that are readily apparent in the instructional environment. One instrument that appraises the degree to which important outcomes are evidenced in classes or schools is known as the ''Remsen Individualization Index.''[14] The first section of the Index is solely concerned with specific characteristics that cannot be *observed* but must be obtained through questioning. These items would all be listed as ''outcomes.'' Section 2 essentially relates to teacher and student behaviors, although most of the items may be recorded as outcomes if the *results* of the behaviors are seen when the behaviors themselves are not in evidence while the teacher is being observed.

Each of the characteristics listed in the Index is checked by either an observer or an observation team. In Section I, check the items that most closely resemble the situation that exists in the classroom. This section, entitled ''Decision-making Locus,'' may be completed through interview and verified by observation.

The weight ascribed to each of the six items in Section I increases for each category as shown on the printed index: The first description receives one point; the second, two; and so forth. Thus, each individualization refinement receives an additional point. The overall range, therefore, is 6 to 31.

In Section II, the ''Implementation Locus,'' ''Teacher Behaviors'' scoring is as follows:

Items 1-4	A—Always	= 4
	B—Often	= 3
	C—Occasionally	= 2
	D—Seldom	= 1
	E—Never	= 0
		Possible Range: 0-16
Items 5 & 6	Yes = 1	
	No = 0	
		Possible Range: 0-12

(Part A of Section II is an interview guide)

In Section II, the "Observation Guide," scoring is as follows:

Part 1:	Teacher Behaviors	Items 1-7 #5 has subitems	yes = 1 no = 0 Possible Range: 0-10
Part 2:	Student Behaviors	Items 1-8	yes = 1 no = 0 Possible Range: 0-8

Summary

		Range
Section I	"Decision-making Locus" interview + observation	6-31
Section II	"Implementation Locus"	
	Teacher Behaviors—interview items 1-4	0-16
	Items 5 & 6	0-12
	Observation Guide	
	A. Teacher Behaviors—observation	0-10
	B. Student Behaviors—observation	0- 8
	Total range:	6-77

After adding, the total score indicates the degree to which individualization techniques are being used in the class, school, or district. In Section I: 12 points or below, very little implementation; between 13 and 18 points, individualization is beginning to appear in the instructional program; 19 to 25 points, the program appears to emphasize heavy student involvement and is routinely individualized; 26 to 31 points, a well-individualized program with comprehensive reference to objectives, resources, pacing, diagnoses, curriculum, activities, and leveling.

In the second section, a score of 17 points or below, very little implementation; between 18 and 27, individualization is beginning to appear; 28 to 37 the program is routinely individualized; and 39 to 46, a well-individualized program.

For the total, a score below 29 indicates that assistance is necessary if the program is to progress toward effective individualization; between 29 and 45 suggests that an individualized program is under early development; a score between 46 and 61 indicates that the program is moving toward individualization; and 62 through 77 represents highly developed programs.

Supervisors are encouraged to use this instrument as an initial means of appraising the instructional process. It should be noted, however, that like the Individualized Instruction Scale, this instrument indicates only the degree to which the individualization process has been introduced; it is not a measure of quality.

REMSEN INDIVIDUALIZATION INDEX

NAME: ______________________ DATE: ______________________

SCHOOL: ______________________ GRADE/LEVEL ______________________

YEARS TEACHING: ______ YEARS TEACHING IN THIS SCHOOL: __________

SECTION I: DECISION-MAKING LOCUS
STRUCTURED INTERVIEW GUIDE FOR TEACHER RESPONSES

Directions: For the six areas of this section, read each of the options and select the *one* option that best describes your situation. Also, feel free to make additional comments.

Directions: For the 5 subitems below, read each of the options and select the *one* option that best describes your situation. Also, feel free to make additional comments.

1. *Determination of Curriculum Objectives*	*Weight*
a. Are the curriculum objectives for any grade level determined *mainly* by the administration and/or its officers based on the average ability and/or achievement of that grade level?	1
b. Are the curriculum objectives for a particular class determined *mainly* by the classroom teacher based on the average ability and/or achievement of that grade level?	2
c. Are the curriculum objectives for a particular class determined *mainly* by the classroom teacher and students in that class based on the average ability and/or achievement of that grade level?	3
d. Are the curriculum objectives for a particular class determined *mainly* by the classroom teacher and students based on results of diagnosis and needs of students in that class?	4
e. Are the curriculum objectives for a particular class determined *mainly* by the classroom teacher and student in that class based on the results of diagnosis and needs of that student?	5
Additional Comments:	

Directions: For the 4 subitems below, read each of the options and select the *one* option that best describes your situation. Also, feel free to make additional comments.

2. *Selection of Instructional Resources*	*Weight*
a. Are the instructional resources for any grade level determined *mainly* by the administration and/or its officers based on what could be made available for the whole class?	1
b. Are the instructional resources for a particular class determined *mainly* by the classroom teacher based on what has been made available for the whole class?	2
c. Are the instructional resources determined *mainly* by the classroom teacher and the student in that class based on the results of diagnosis of, and the needs of, that student?	3
d. Are the instructional resources determined *mainly* by the student based on his own selection from among approved alternatives?	4
Additional Comments:	

Directions: For the 7 subitems below, read each of the options and select the *one* option that best describes your situation. Also, feel free to make additional comments.

3. *Determination of Level of Instruction*	*Weight*
a. Is the level of instruction for a class based *mainly* on *class* results on standardized tests?	1
b. Is the level of instruction for a class based *mainly* on *class* results on criterion-referenced* tests? *A criterion-referenced test evaluates a student's mastery or nonmastery of each objective, usually stated in behavioral terms.	2
c. Is the level of instruction for an individual based *mainly* on *individual* results on standardized tests?	3
d. Is the level of instruction for an individual based *mainly* on *individual* results on criterion-referenced tests?	4

e. Is the level of instruction for an individual based *mainly* on evaluation by the teacher on informal performance criteria?	5
f. Is the level of instruction for an individual based *mainly* on evaluation by the teacher and student on informal performance criteria?	6
g. Is the level of instruction for an individual based *mainly* on evaluation by the student on informal performance criteria?	7
Additional Comments:	

Directions: For the 7 subitems below, read each of the options and select the *one* option that best describes your situation. Also, feel free to make additional comments.

4. *Determination of Pacing*	*Weight*
a. Is the pacing of instruction in *any one* curriculum area determined *mainly* by deadlines imposed by the set curriculum for that area?	1
b. Is the pacing of instruction in *any one* curriculum area determined *mainly* by the teacher on the basis of individual diagnosis?	2
c. Is the pacing of instruction in *all* curriculum areas determined *mainly* by the teacher on the basis of individual diagnosis?	3
d. Is the pacing of instruction in *any one* curriculum area determined *mainly* by the teacher and student on the basis of individual diagnosis?	4
e. Is the pacing of instruction in *all* curriculum areas determined *mainly* by the teacher and student on the basis of individual diagnosis?	5
f. Is the pacing of instruction in *any one* curriculum area determined *mainly* by the student on the basis of individual diagnosis?	6
g. Is the pacing of instruction in *all* curriculum areas determined *mainly* by the student on the basis of his own diagnosis?	7
Additional Comments:	

Directions: For the 4 subitems below, read each of the options and select the *one* option that best describes your situation. Also, feel free to make additional comments.

5. *Determination of Evaluation of Objectives*	*Weight*
a. Is the method of evaluation based *mainly* on interpretation of standardized test results?	1
b. Is the method of evaluation based *mainly* on interpretation of criterion-referenced tests?	2
c. Is the method of evaluation based *mainly* on interpretation of performance criteria prescribed by the teacher?	3
d. Is the method of evaluation based *mainly* on the student's interpretation of his own performance criteria?	4
Additional Comments:	

Directions: For the 4 subitems below, read each of the options and select the one option that best describes your situation. Also, feel free to make additional comments.

6. *Determination of Learning Activities*	*Weight*
a. Are the learning activities determined *mainly* by the teacher on the basis of grade-level requirements?	1
b. Are the learning activities determined *mainly* by the teacher on the basis of individual diagnosis?	2
c. Are the learning activities determined *mainly* by the teacher and student on the basis of individual diagnosis?	3
d. Are the learning activities determined *mainly* by the student selected from approved alternatives?	4
Additional Comments:	

	Minimum	*Maximum*
Subtotal Section 1	6	31

SECTION II: IMPLEMENTATION LOCUS

A. *Teacher Behaviors* (Interview or Self-response)

Directions for Items 1-8

For items 1-8 of this section, answer the question posed with one of the following options: (A) Always, (B) Often, (C) Occasionally, (D) Seldom or (E) Never.

Select the option that best fits your situation using the following response option guide:

A—Always: at least once every day
B—Often: at least once each week
C—Occasionally: at least once each month
D—Seldom: several times a year
E—Never: not at all

	Weight				
	A	B	C	D	E
1. To what extent do you prescribe learning activities for individual students based on their specific needs?	4	3	2	1	0
2. To what extent do you make provision for students to form groups based upon special interests?	4	3	2	1	0
3. To what extent do you differentiate assignments based on the individual student's abilities?	4	3	2	1	0
4. To what extent do you consider student input in planning for activities off school grounds (field trips, etc.)?	4	3	2	1	0

	Minimum	*Maximum*
Subtotal Section IIA 1-4	0	16

Directions: For each of the subitems under #5 and #6 respond with either "yes" or "no." Select the option that best fits your situation. In addition, feel free to comment.

5. Do you employ the following group instructional strategies?

	Weight Yes	No	Additional Comments
a. Brainstorming* *A leader poses a problem that has multiple possible answers. Each member is encouraged to call out his thoughts on the specific problem. All ideas are recorded and reviewed in total when finished. No analysis, editing, or criticism is permitted during the procedure.	1	0	
b. Team Learning* *Students form groups and members cooperatively attempt to teach themselves required concepts that are common to each member's prescription. The group is provided with material that incorporates the objectives to be mastered.	1	0	
c. Circles of Knowledge* *Students form small groups in order to review material. The teacher distributes questions to each group; questions must have multiple possible answers. A member is designated to begin, and then each member in turn (clockwise or counterclockwise) provides one possible answer. Members make corrections when necessary. No one may skip his turn and each must wait his turn. The recorder notes answers of each participant.	1	0	
d. Case Study* *Students form small groups. Problems in short-story form are distributed to members. A single problem is focused upon, studied, and discussed. A recorder is appointed to record responses.	1	0	

	Weight Yes	No	Additional Comments
e. Role Playing* *A technique useful for demonstrating perceptions of persons or situations. Students assume roles. No solutions are sought.	1	0	
f. Simulations* *Hypothetical situations are presented to the students. These situations may occur within their lives. Participants demonstrate how they might behave in the projected situation. The objective is to develop alternative solutions to given problems.	1	0	
6. Do you provide for the following instructional areas, such as: a. Learning Stations* *Small areas or tables that house specific materials related to a given curriculum, such as math or reading.	1	0	
b. Interest Centers* *Small areas or tables that house interdisciplinary material connected with a selected theme, such as pollution, transportation, etc.	1	0	
c. Little Theaters* *Small areas set aside in which children can make props, costumes, scenery, books, scrapbooks, slides, transparencies, etc., and participate in theatrical productions.	1	0	

	Weight Yes	No	Additional Comments
d. Game Tables* *Small areas or tables that house a repertory of games.	1	0	
e. Media Areas* *Small areas that house multimedia for student use, such as overhead projectors, 8mm cartridges, viewers, etc.	1	0	
f. Magic Carpets* *Small areas defined by remnants of carpet where students are permitted to go to study or to read.	1	0	

g. Other (Please describe briefly)

	Minimum	*Maximum*
Subtotal Section IIA 5 & 6	0	12

SECTION III: OBSERVATION GUIDE

Directions: For each of the 7 questions below answer "yes" or "no" and feel free to comment.

A. *Teacher Behaviors*	*Weight* Yes	No	Additional Comments
1. Is there evidence of the teacher's fluid movement among individuals and groups during the instruction?	1	0	

	Weight Yes	No	Additional Comments
2. Is there evidence of varied instructional strategies taking place *simultaneously* in the classroom?	1	0	
3. Is there evidence of the implementation of the various instructional resources?	1	0	
4. Is there evidence that the teacher keeps collections of the students' work for use in his/her evaluation of their progress?	1	0	
5. Is there evidence that the teacher permits students to function on the basis of their own individual learning styles? For example: 5a. Environmental Style* *Does the teacher permit the student to function in a posture that the student finds most comfortable? and/or to engage in an area the student finds conducive to learning, such as near or away from light or heat, etc?	1	0	
5b. Emotional Style* *Does the teacher permit the student to select from among a variety of situations those that may respond to his personal characteristics?	1	0	
5c. Sociological Style* *Does the teacher permit the student to function independently, in dyads, in small groups, in large groups, as the student chooses?	1	0	

	Weight Yes	Weight No	Additional Comments
5d. Physical Style* *Does the teacher permit the student multisensory resources, intake, mobility, and/or time options, if necessary?	1	0	
6. Is there evidence that the teacher incorporates flexible small-group *instruction** into instructional methods? *Instruction in which small groups of various sizes are formed, disbanded, and re-formed with different members based upon student needs.	1	0	
7. Is there evidence that the teacher provides *multilevel instructional resources?** *A variety of resources made available to provide for the needs of children of varied ability levels.	1	0	

	Minimum	*Maximum*
Subtotal Section II Observation Guide A	0	10

Directions: For each of the 8 questions below answer "yes" or "no" and feel free to comment.

B. *Student Behaviors*	Weight Yes	Weight No	Additional Comments
Students *usually:* 1. Work constructively in small groups without the teacher's immediate presence and/or guidance.	1	0	

	Weight Yes	No	Additional Comments
2. Work constructively in the various instructional areas without the teacher's immediate presence and/or guidance.	1	0	
3. Demonstrate comprehension of the results of the teacher's diagnosis of their work.	1	0	
4. Participate in self-diagnosis.	1	0	
5. Participate in the development of their own learning prescriptions (objectives, resources, and evaluations).	1	0	
6. Locate independently learning resources whenever needed.	1	0	
7. Use learning resources independently.	1	0	
8. Record progress independently.	1	0	

	Minimum	*Maximum*
Subtotal Section II Observation Guide B	0	8

Summary Score

Section I	Decision-making Locus		☐
Section II	Implementation Locus		
	Teacher Behaviors	Items 1 - 4	☐
		Items 5 & 6	☐
	Observation Guide:		
	Teacher Behaviors		☐
	Student Behaviors		☐
	Total		☐

THE COMPAIN KEY

The Compain Key is one instrument that devotes itself explicitly to recording quantitatively (a) what the teacher does and (b) what the student does when they are in the instructional environment. The items included in the Key, again, focus on diagnosis, prescription, and guidance through instructional tasks as the basis for effective teaching. When the results of the Compain Key are paired with the baseline data for individual students, both teacher effectiveness and student academic success become apparent. To ensure fair interpretations of the combined data, it should be noted that individual teachers may be extremely effective with certain students and relatively ineffective with others. The authors do not believe that *any* one teacher can reach *all* youngsters. We strongly believe, however, that teachers should be permitted to teach only those youngsters who evidence excellent academic progress while under their tutelage and who, simultaneously, enjoy being part of the environment established by that teacher.

Obviously, as indicated in several previous chapters, the authors believe that student learning styles and teacher teaching styles should be matched, unless the teacher evidences the ability to respond to varied student learning styles; this ability to cope with different kinds of learners in one instructional setting can *only* be manifested through individualization skills.

The observer using the Compain Key is directed to consider each of the items in two ways: (1) how many of the students can be observed doing what is described (all? most? some? or none?) and (2) how much of the time do the students who do what is described actually engage in the practice (always? most of the time? sometimes? or not at all?).

Recorders are urged to use the following indices to categorize the number of students referred to and the amount of time indicated:

Proportion Code		Translation
All of the Students	=	90% or more of those present
Most of the Students	=	between 51% and 89% of those present
Some of the Students	=	less than 50% of those present
None of the Students	=	literally zero students present

Time Code		Translation
All of the Time	=	90% or more of the time while observing
Most of the Time	=	between 51% and 89% of the time while observing
Some of the Time	=	less than 50% of the time present while observing
None of the Time	=	literally no time at all while observing

When using the Compain Key, circle two items in each category—the number of students involved in the selected behavior, and the amount of time devoted to the practice.

Example: An observer using the Compain Key enters a classroom where he remains for a 45-minute interval. During that period he notices that most of the students work on tasks by themselves, but often move from the area in which they are studying to others where peers are similarly involved. Students interact with other students for what appears to be curriculum discussions and then return to where they were conducting their work. At other times, students seek assistance from the teacher and then, similarly, return to their studies either alone or with a classmate or two.

For item 1 of the Compain Key, the observer might circle 2 (most of the students) and 2 (most of the time) to provide the information that most of the students work independently most of the time.

For item 8, the observer might circle 3 (all of the students) and 2 (most of the time) to indicate that all the students appear to be mobile most of the time.

COMPAIN KEY

By Rita Compain, C.W. Post College, 1972*

Teacher________________ Time of observation ____________

School ________________ Date of observation ____________

Form completed by____________ Subject ______ Section ______

Section A: *Observed Student Behaviors*

Proportion Code	Time Code
3 All of the Students	3 All of the Time
2 Most of the Students	2 Most of the Time
1 Some of the Students	1 Some of the Time
0 None of the Students	0 None of the Time

	Proportion	*Time*	*Comments*
1. Work independently	______	___	______
2. Are self-directed	______	___	______
3. Self-select learning resources	______	___	______
4. Use multilevel curriculum resources	______	___	______
5. Engage in creative work at times	______	___	______
6. Work in small groups at times	______	___	______
7. Are involved in self-paced learning	______	___	______

		Proportion	*Time*	*Comments*
8.	Move freely and purposefully about the area	____	____	____
9.	Follow an individual prescription	____	____	____
10.	Use varied instructional areas	____	____	____
11.	Interact with peers	____	____	____
12.	Interact with teacher	____	____	____
13.	Interact with other adults at times	____	____	____
14.*	Are aware of own goals	____	____	____
15.	Use a self-assessment instrument	____	____	____
16.	Appear to be actively involved in learning	____	____	____
	Totals	____	____	

Section B: *Observed Teacher Behaviors*

Time Code 3 All of the Time 1 Some of the Time
2 Most of the Time 0 None of the Time

		Proportion	*Time*	*Comments*
1.	Plans on an individual basis	____	____	____
2.	Plans collaboratively at times	____	____	____
3.	Organizes selected activities	____	____	____
4.	Directs selected activities	____	____	____
5.	Establishes varied instructional centers	____	____	____
6.	Interacts with individual children and small groups	____	____	____
7.	Encourages student decision-making	____	____	____
8.	Diagnoses individuals	____	____	____
9.	Prescribes for individuals	____	____	____
10.	Guides individuals and small groups	____	____	____
11.	Evaluates on an individual basis	____	____	____
12.	Responds in varied ways to individuals	____	____	____
13.*	Maintains workable noise level	____	____	____
14.	Provides structure for those who need it	____	____	____
15.	Provides flexibility for those who need it	____	____	____
16.	Moves freely about the room	____	____	____
17.	Instructs children in use and care of multimedia	____	____	____
18.	Asks multilevel questions	____	____	____
19.*	Establishes an interactive atmosphere	____	____	____
20.	Employs small-group techniques	____	____	____
21.	Works in different curriculum areas	____	____	____
22.	Makes options available to students	____	____	____
	Total	____	____	

*Items on the Compain Key that are preceded by an asterisk (*) are those that do not permit rating solely through observation but, rather, require a subjective opinion, e.g., whether or not a noise level is "workable" (Item B-13) or whether an atmosphere is "interactive" (Item B-19) depends upon one's individual tolerance (or lack of tolerance) for sound and one's own ability to function among people in a given environment.

SELECTING CRITERIA FOR A PERSONALIZED EVALUATION INSTRUMENT

Because most evaluation instruments reflect the philosophy and objectives of the persons who design them, it certainly would be appropriate in this age of rapid instructional transition for administrators and teachers earnestly to discuss and determine their beliefs concerning the ingredients that constitute effective teaching. The final design or form should reflect the best of their cooperative thinking. Adapting someone else's inventory is acceptable only when one's goals coincide directly with the designer's.

Most faculties include members whose instructional methodology ranges along a wide continuum from what might be described as die-hard traditional to the very informal, less-structured systems that include open classroom,[16] open campus,[17] and open university.[18] Conformity of support for one particular pattern is not mandatory, but wide diversity often causes confusion and friction among the professional staff, parents, and students.

It might be wise for faculties to read and then discuss the various programs as described in chapter 3 in Figures 3-8 through 3-11 and then to identify specific objectives toward which individuals might care to work.

Below is a listing of teacher behaviors that appear to be consistent with current trends toward diagnosing each student and then developing a course of study (or "prescription") based on the findings. These behaviors would constitute some excellent preliminary objectives for selected faculty members.

Observable Teacher Behaviors as Faculty Objectives

Teachers:

1. Diagnose each student for current knowledge, aptitude, and learning style.
2. Prescribe on the basis of the individual diagnosis.
3. Guide each student through the learning process based on an ongoing diagnosis and flexible prescription.
4. Work with individuals, small groups, and/or whole groups.
5. Use a variety of small-group techniques (role playing, team learning, circle of knowledge, etc.) for reinforcement and for those who sociologically learn well with their peers.[19]
6. Work on different levels with different students.
7. Guide students toward independence and self-direction.[20]
8. Establish and equip a variety of instructional areas.[21]
9. Provide for a variety of alternative learning experiences.
10. Develop a wide variety of multimedia and multisensory resources.

11. Prescribe objectives, resources, and activities in cooperation with students.
12. Continue an ongoing assessment of student work.
13. Use flexible room arrangements.[22]
14. Provide access to materials within room, in adjacent areas, and/or at out-of-school sites.
15. Provide for different learning rates.
16. Provide for different learning styles.
17. Design programs to provide for student interaction in a variety of positive ways.
18. Provide multiple curriculum and instructional options for students.[23]
19. Involve students in group decision-making.
20. Provide opportunities for independent decision-making.
21. Instruct students in care, use, and repair of media.
22. Move from student to student and from group to group.
23. Identify and provide for the learning strengths and interests of individual students.
24. Provide leadership opportunities for selected students.
25. Provide opportunities for creative thinking and activities.

One outgrowth of working toward some of the above enumerated teacher behaviors as objectives on which faculty growth might be focused would be the gradual development of observable student behaviors—another form of objectives against which to measure instructional performance.

Observable Student Behaviors as Faculty Objectives

Students:

1. Establish some of their own objectives.
2. Use varied alternative media and resources.
3. Use varied small-group techniques (team learning, circles of knowledge, etc.).
4. Use flexible seating arrangements.
5. Work alone (independently), in pairs, and/or in teams at times.
6. Move freely about the instructional environment.
*7. Maintain a conversational noise level.
8. Create materials and resources.
9. Make choices and select from among options and alternatives.
10. Interact with adults and other students.
11. Work on different levels.

---

*To eliminate the element of bias, define a "conversational noise level" as one where no one is disturbed by the conversation of another person or group. If this definition does not appeal to you, develop one of your own.

Photo 6-1. To provide for effective instruction, students should be diagnosed to identify the extent of their current knowledge, the ways in which they are most likely to achieve new knowledge (their learning styles), and the number and kind of objectives with which each is likely to be successful. Photo 6-1 represents a positive *teacher behavior*, for teacher Martha Lewis can be observed diagnosing an individual student. If the student's records indicated the date(s) and results of diagnosis, the record would be a *behavioral outcome*. (Photo courtesy of P.S. #220 Queens, New York City.)

6-1

Photo 6-2. After diagnosis, individual prescriptions are developed for each youngster so that there is no confusion about (a) what needs to be learned, (b) the resources that may be used to learn, (c) the required and optional activities, and (d) the way(s) in which the youngster may demonstrate that the objectives have been achieved. Here, teacher Carol Ries is explaining the prescription designed for this youngster. The *act* of designing a prescription for a student is a *teacher behavior*. The prescription itself is a *behavioral outcome*. (Photo courtesy of P.S. #220 Queens, New York City.)

6-2

Photo 6-3. Marcia Knoll, principal, visits every classroom and examines each student's prescription. Here she is demonstrating a positive adult *behavior*, for she can be *observed* discussing this youngster's prescription and offering suggestions for self-evaluation: If she noted on the student's prescription the date and comments she made, those written statements would be an *outcome* of her guiding behaviors, or a *behavioral outcome*. (Photo courtesy of P.S. #220 Queens, New York City.)

6-3

6-4

Photo 6-4. While teacher Thalia Cassuto is working with six youngsters on a specific learning task, the remaining students in her class are involved in different small-group instructional techniques (such as circle of knowledge, team learning, or role playing) so that they may progress toward the completion of objectives with peers who have been trained to work without constant teacher or adult supervision. Students engaged in the small-group techniques are demonstrating *student behaviors. The materials* used in the techniques are the *results* of the teacher's behavior of having developed them; they are, therefore, *behavioral outcomes*. (Photo courtesy of P.S. #220 Queens, New York City.)

6-5

6-6

Photos 6-5 and 6-6. Teacher Carol Ries is guiding this student toward gradual self-direction and eventual independence. She has listed a series of required and alternative activities on the chalkboard and is explaining which must be completed and which may be selected as choices. Her guidance of the student is a positive *teacher behavior*; the *activities* are *outcomes* of her behavior—providing choices. (Photos courtesy of P.S. #220 Queens, New York City.)

Photo 6-7. This is an 840-square-foot classroom in which the teacher has placed bookcases, orange crates, and tables perpendicular to each other and the wall to establish different instructional areas for varied curriculum activities. The diversity of these separated sections permits organization of available resources, varied strategies to be used simultaneously without interference with each other, and control of student discipline. The redesign of this classroom is an *outcome* of the teacher's *behavior*. (Photo courtesy of P.S. #220 Queens, New York City.)

6-7

6-8

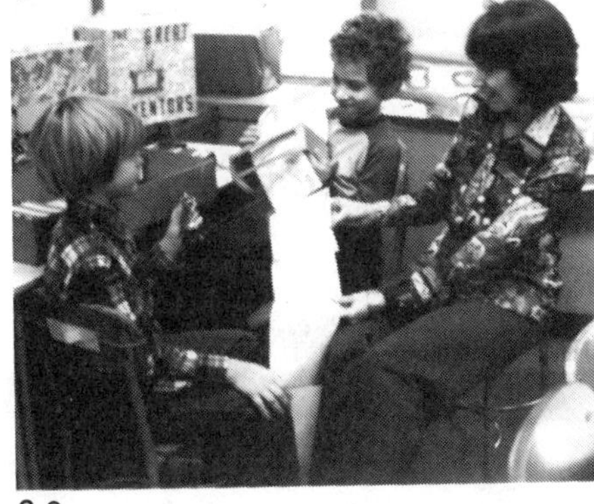

6-9

Photos 6-8 and 6-9. Since individuals learn through different senses, an effective instructional program should provide multimedia through which students may achieve. In Photo 6-8, a student teacher is observing children operate a filmstrip viewer independently as the principal simultaneously supervises the student teacher. In Photo 6-9, teacher Maxine Lindfors is evaluating the efforts of two of her students who used the multisensory instructional packages that Mrs. Lindfors created. The development of the instructional packages (multiple activities that teach a single concept through four different senses) is a *teacher behavior*; the packages themselves are *outcomes*. (Photos courtesy of P.S. #220 Queens, New York City.)

6-10

6-11

Photos 6-10 and 6-11. While training youngsters to work independently with their prescriptions, the teacher may determine what the student should learn and how he may demonstrate that he has achieved what has been assigned to him. As quickly as is reasonable and appropriate for each, however, students should become involved in determining some of their objectives, most of their resources and activities, and all of their learning style preferences. This teacher is showing her student the different resources he may use to complete a specific objective; he will decide which one he will use. Developing prescriptions cooperatively are positive *teacher and student behaviors*. (Photos courtesy of P.S. #220 Queens, New York City.)

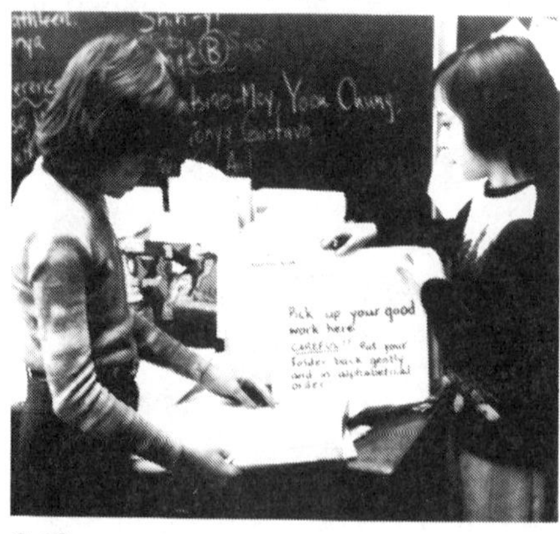

6-12

Photo 6-12. Ongoing assessment of a student's work and progress provides positive reinforcement, increases motivation, and develops the ability to self-assess. These students are locating their own folders in an accessible box on which the teacher has printed: "Pick up your good work here. CAREFUL!! Put your folder back gently and in alphabetical order!" This box of individual folders provides direct and ongoing evaluation and is a positive *behavioral outcome*. (Photo courtesy of P.S. #220 Queens, New York City.)

6-13

Photo 6-13. When students form a small group, either by choice or assignment, they should be permitted opportunities to engage in some group decision-making. When this occurs, it is a positive *student behavior*. Individuals should not be required to conform to group decisions on a continuing basis. (Photo courtesy of P.S. #220 Queens, New York City.)

6-14

Photo 6-14. Encouraging students to establish some of their own objectives increases motivation and persistence. This youngster has decided what she would like to learn about a particular topic, has listed the objectives related to her interest, and is depositing them into a special envelope that her teacher has posted for that purpose. The envelope says, "Social Studies Plans: Put your choice of objectives in this envelope." When students determine objectives for their prescriptions, they demonstrate positive *student behaviors*. (Photo courtesy of P.S. #220 Queens, New York City.)

12. Self-assess their work and progress.
13. Can explain what they are doing and why.
14. Work on interdisciplinary studies at times.
15. Tutor each other at times.
16. Achieve cooperative and positive peer interactions most of the time.
17. Assume responsibility for the location, care, repair, and return of materials and resources.
18. Use varied instructional areas.
19. Confer with individuals, small groups, and the teacher.
20. Select some of their own activities.
21. Use some form of programmed learning, contracts, task cards, out-of-building studies, and/or instructional packages.

22. Set their own pace within approximate time intervals.
23. Participate in planning some individual activities.
24. Set up and use media independently.
25. Record their own progress.
26. Establish some of their own priorities.
27. Involve themselves in creative art activities (music, dance, dramatics) to capitalize on their talents and/or interests.

A third area on which to focus might be the observation of behavioral outcomes—the results of behaviors. Although teachers may not actually be observed doing some things, the fact that they did could be evident through the presence of the specific items listed on page 244.

6-15

6-16

Photos 6-15 and 6-16. When students are able to work independently or with a peer or two (by choice), obtain assistance when necessary, and also function cooperatively in small groups at times, they are evidencing positive *student behaviors*. (Photos courtesy of P.S. #220 Queens, New York City.)

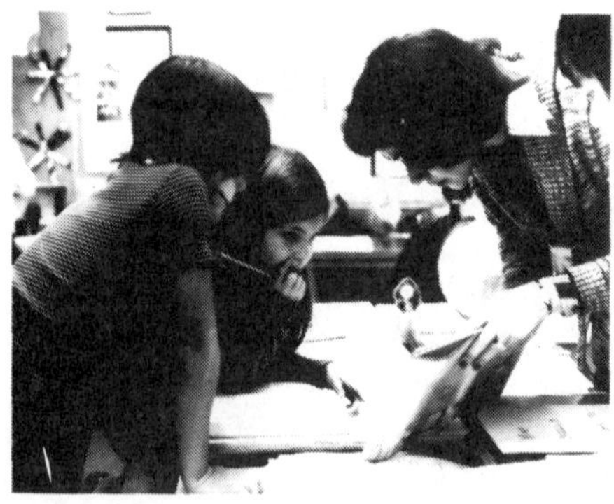

6-17

Photo 6-17. Some youngsters tend to learn most efficiently when in direct contact with an adult. For these, a gradual weaning from sole reliance on an authority figure toward peer and, eventually, increased independent achievement would constitute positive *student behaviors* for that learner. (Photo courtesy of P.S. #220 Queens, New York City.)

Photo 6-18. Students involved in achieving identical objectives should be able to use varied levels of resources and activities to accomplish what they should learn. This youngster's teacher has established charts that clearly indicate the alternative levels and routes that may be selected based on a youngster's ability, preference, and/or learning style. These charts and the varied choices made available to students are outgrowths of the teacher's behavior. You do not see the teacher actually designing the prescriptions, but you do see the *results* of her efforts. The charts and varied choices are, therefore, *behavioral outcomes*. (Photo courtesy of P.S. #220 Queens, New York City.)

6-18

Photo 6-19. When problems arise, it is necessary that a system exist wherein a student can obtain assistance as quickly as possible. This youngster is signing up for a conference with her teacher. That she uses the established procedures to request guidance is a positive *student behavior*. The sign-up sheet verifying that the process for gaining assistance has been established and explained sufficiently to the students (so that they are able to use it) is a positive *behavioral outcome*. (Photo courtesy of P.S. #220 Queens, New York City.)

6-19

Photo 6-20. This youngster's teacher has mounted a chart that reads, "I have a quick question" on one side and "I would like a conference" on the other. This permits students to indicate that they require assistance and the approximate amount of time that it might take. This chart is a positive *behavioral outcome*. (Photo courtesy of P.S. #220 Queens, New York City.)

6-20

Observable Behavioral Outcomes as Faculty Objectives

The results of teacher and/or student behaviors might include the presence of:

1. Individual student records that contain diagnostic data.
2. Individual student prescriptions that include objectives, resources, activities, and/or self-assessment tests that often differ from those prescribed for other students in the same group.
3. Listed options or evidenced activities that are so varied that options must have been provided.
4. Varied resources, preferably of a multisensory nature.
5. Varied instructional areas, such as learning stations, interest centers, etc. When students are using these areas constructively and knowledgeably, an observer could consider the teacher's training of the students as being the behavior that caused the positive outcome.
6. Different types of seating arrangements that suggest a response to student needs for either formal or informal designs.
7. Different activities occurring simultaneously.
8. Students using varied small-group instructional techniques correctly, suggesting an outgrowth of teacher training.
9. Correct usage of media and resources, suggesting an outgrowth of teacher training.
10. Prescriptions that evidence some student-designed or selected objectives, resources, activities, or assessment alternatives.
11. Students using varied-level resources, suggesting teacher preparation of the resources.
12. Students using contracts, programmed learning, task cards, out-of-building studies, or instructional packages, suggesting teacher preparation.

6-21

Photo 6-21. Whereas students should not be *required* to tutor each other, some youngsters (of all ages) tend to learn better from their peers than they do from adults or authority figures. That one youngster in this photo is assisting the other is a positive *student behavior*. Since some people do *not* like to learn from their classmates or colleagues, this behavior is not a requisite for every learner. (Photo courtesy of P.S. #220 Queens, New York City.)

6-22

Photo 6-22. The ability to move and speak quietly when others are engaged in learning is a positive *student behavior*. (Photo courtesy of P.S. #220 Queens, New York City.)

6-23

Photo 6-23. Students need to assume responsibility for the location, care, repair, and return of materials and media resources. That these youngsters are doing so is a positive *student behavior*. Their ability to do so is an outgrowth of their teacher's training and is, therefore, a *behavioral outcome* too. (Photo courtesy of P.S. #220 Queens, New York City.)

6-24

Photo 6-24. Students should be able to select some of their own activities. These youngsters are able to sign up for the ones of their choice on the chart that their teacher has posted. That they make such choices is a positive *student behavior*. The chart and the options it provides are *behavioral outcomes* (of the teacher's positive actions). (Photo courtesy of P.S. #220 Queens, New York City.)

6-25

Photo 6-25. Because students learn through different kinds of instructional methods and resources, programmed learning, contracts, learning activity packages, task cards, instructional packages, multimedia and/or educational games should be observable and in use. When any of these varied approaches can be *seen*, they are recorded as positive *behavioral outcomes*. (Photo courtesy of P.S. #220 Queens, New York City.)

6-26

Photo 6-26. Students should be taught how to record their own academic progress. When they are seen making appropriate notations, it is a *student behavior.* If they are not observed recording, but if the records are visible, the records themselves are considered to be *behavioral outcomes*. (Photo courtesy of P.S. #220 Queens, New York City.)

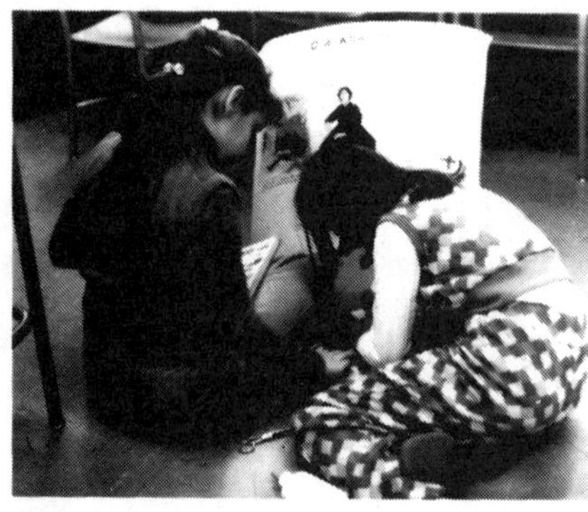

6-27

Photo 6-27. Since students have different interests, talents, and skills, they should be permitted to establish some of their own priorities to capitalize on their special characteristics, to make school meaningful, and to increase their motivation. When students are given options and some free time to pursue their interests, it is viewed as a positive *behavioral outcome* of the teacher's professional planning. (Photo courtesy of P.S. #220 Queens, New York City.)

After considering these three lists of what could easily become initial faculty growth objectives, you may use them in any of the following ways:

- Assign selected objectives to all teachers and permit the choice of any additional number of objectives that appears to make sense.

-or-

- Suggest that each faculty member select a given number of objectives from among the three lists to work toward this semester, quarter, year, etc. (your choice).

-or-

- Suggest that each faculty member select at least three (any number that appears reasonable) objectives from each of the three lists to complete within a given amount of time.

-or-

- Require specific objectives of some (based on your previous evaluations) and different objectives for others, to be completed in a given amount of time.

-or-

- Any combination thereof.

The objectives toward which individual faculty members will work should then be written clearly on a sheet of paper together with the approximate time intervals during which they may be measured. Flexibility will be necessary during the first and/or second attempts because it is difficult to estimate how long it will take to achieve given objectives without having had prior experience working with specific goals. Copies of the listed individual objectives should be maintained (a) by the teacher, (b) by the supervisor, (c) in a central file, and (d) in the teacher's file. Any evaluation team that eventually observes the teacher should use these stated objectives as their basis for future assessments.

6-28

6-29

Photos 6-28 and 6-29. Marcia Knoll, principal of P.S. #220 Queens, meets with each teacher to examine the diagnostic data recorded for individual students and to offer suggestions for translating the findings into appropriate prescriptions. Here, a fifth-grade teacher is describing the resources that are available to complement one youngster's objectives. (Photo courtesy of P.S. #220 Queens, New York City.)

6-30

Photo 6-30. When different types of seating arrangements are available, suggesting the teacher's awareness of students who need either a formal or an informal environment in which to concentrate, the options are considered to be *behavioral outcomes*, or outcomes of the teacher's preparations. (Photo courtesy of P.S. #220 Queens, New York City.)

6-31

Photo 6-31. Since students learn through different perceptual strengths (visual, auditory, tactual, and/or kinesthetic), the presence of multisensory resources is recorded as a *behavioral outcome* of the teacher's planning. (Photo courtesy of P.S. #220 Queens, New York City.)

Teachers should have access to materials that will enable them to reach the objectives they either have had assigned to them or agreed to work toward. They should be able to self-assess themselves by observing their own class in operation while simultaneously looking for evidence of those behaviors or outcomes for which they are responsible. It is also possible to have colleagues visit and attempt to see the various behaviors or outcomes for which the teacher has contracted or been assigned.

Once the initial hurdle has been overcome and some of the behaviors and outcomes are apparent in classrooms, you might wish to develop a more sophisticated instrument that better reveals the extent to which the various objectives are being met. It is possible to adapt the Compain Key, described in this chapter, to whatever objectives are being focused upon in each classroom. Merely add the categories of "children" and "amount of time" at the top of your own instrument, and check the characteristic phrases that seem to be most appropriate. The combination of selected (or assigned) personalized objectives, when matched against the number of students involved with them and/or the amount of time in which those behaviors or outcomes are observable, will yield sufficient information to indicate whether your teaching faculty is, indeed, moving toward increased instructional effectiveness.

One final reminder: The results of this instrument should be combined with information concerning student academic progress (preferably baseline data) to yield accurate results concerning teaching effectiveness. However, even on an ongoing basis, the information provided will be more accurate and revealing than that usually made available through many current and widely used evaluation forms.

NOTES FOR CHAPTER 6

1. "Evaluating Teaching Performance." Washington, D.C.: Educational Research Service, American Association of School Administrators and Research Division, National Education Association (1972): 1-2.
2. John W. Menne. "Teacher Evaluation: Performance or Effectiveness?" *National Council on Measurement in Education News,* 17, 2 (1974): 11-12.
3. "Teacher Evaluation: Performance or Effectiveness?"
4. Thomas B. Justiz. "A Method for Identifying the Effective Teacher." Unpublished doctoral dissertation, University of California, Los Angeles, 1968.
5. John D. McNeil. *Toward Accountable Teachers.* New York: Holt, Rinehart and Winston, Inc. (1971).
6. George McHatton Moffett. "Use of Instructional Objectives in the Supervision of Student Teachers." Unpublished doctoral dissertation, University of California, Los Angeles (1966).

7. Arthur M. Cohen and Florence B. Brawer. *Measuring Faculty Performance.* Washington, D.C.: American Association of Junior Colleges (1969).
8. W. James Popham. "Performance Tests of Teaching Proficiency: Rationale, Development, and Validation." *American Educational Research Journal* 8, 1 (1971): 105-117.
9. "Teacher Evaluation: Performance or Effectiveness?"
10. The work presented here was developed pursuant to an ESEA Title III grant, NYSED #24185. Contractors undertaking such projects under government sponsorship are encouraged to express freely their professional judgment in the conduct of the project. Points of view or opinions stated do not, therefore, necessarily represent official position or policy of the USOE, or the New York State Education Department, or the four Nassau-Suffolk, New York Boards of Cooperative Educational Services sponsoring this project.
11. This particular item will be responded to differently by individual students in any given class, dependent upon their unique personalities and relationships with the teacher and/or observer(s). It is *not* usually observable and would *not* be suggested for inclusion on any scale that purports to be bias-free.
12. *Individualized Instruction Scale and User's Guide:* Final Revision, Prepared by Project Individualized Instruction under an ESEA Title III Project, sponsored by the four Long Island, New York Boards of Cooperative Educational Services (1975): 4.
13. *Individualized Instruction Scale and User's Guide:* 5.
14. Ann T. Remsen. "Relationship Between Teachers' Perceptions of Principals' Leadership Behavior and Individualization of the Teaching-Learning Process as Implemented in the Elementary Schools." Ed.D. dissertation, New York University (1974): Appendix B.
15. Rita Dunn and Kenneth Dunn. *Educator's Self-Teaching Guide to Individualizing Instructional Programs.* West Nyack, New York: Parker Publishing Co., Inc. (1975): 261-266.
16. Many variations exist of the instructional program labeled "open classroom," but, basically, its philosophy centers about the concept that children are permitted to select their own curriculum, resources, schedule, and pacing. Children may remain with a topic as long as it interests them and may study alone, with a friend or two, or in a small group. Since children learn in individual ways, the teacher is responsible for providing an environment rich in multimedia resources and for encouraging student involvement with the materials. Objectives, if used, are determined by the child and may vary from student to student and on a continuously changing basis. Grades are not given, but evaluations are made in terms of the child's demonstrated growth. A positive and happy attitude is considered very important for student progress.
17. In a unanimous decision, the Massachusetts State Board of Education approved a recommendation by (then) State Education Commissioner Neil V. Sullivan, permitting them to operate "open high school programs in which all students need not be present at all times." The statewide program, which was unique in the nation in 1970, permitted students to be scheduled in programs of less than 5.5 hours of formal instruction or in programs where student learning was partially self-directed within or outside a high school. Participating schools were still required to provide the regular 5.5 hour program for those who wanted it. The decision was based on the success of three pilot programs in Brookline, Winchester, and Falmouth, as reported in *Education, U.S.A.*, Fall (1970): 80.
18. Many institutions of higher education have been experimenting with nontraditional programs that tend to focus on consultations with advisors, listed objectives, resources,

activities, etc., such as a contract approach, no attendance requirements, and demonstrated competencies to verify mastery of required subjects. In the "external degree" programs, academic credit is often permitted for work and experiences completed off campus, and in most "open university" programs, students may study and complete requirements away from the university, indicating when they are ready to be tested or evaluated, as reported in *Inside Education*. New York: State Education Department, June (1974).

19. For specific examples of how to design and use many techniques such as team learning, circle of knowledge, brainstorming, role playing, simulations, and group analysis, see Rita Dunn and Kenneth Dunn. *Practical Approaches to Individualizing Instruction: Contracts and Other Effective Teaching Strategies.* West Nyack, New York: Parker Publishing Company, Inc. (1972): chapters 5, 6, and 7.
20. For explicit methods for developing student independence and self-direction, see *Educator's Self-Teaching Guide to Individualizing Instructional Programs:* chapter 5.
21. For directions concerning how to establish learning stations, interest centers, magic carpet areas, media centers, little theaters, and game tables, see *Practical Approaches to Individualizing Instruction:* 68-75.
22. For illustrations and directions for redesigning an ordinary classroom (without much cost) to accommodate varied learning styles, see *Educator's Self-Teaching Guide to Individualizing Instructional Programs:* chapter 4.
23. For directions for developing a curriculum based on student interests, see *Practical Approaches to Individualizing Instruction:* chapter 8.

7

DESIGNING NEW AND MORE EFFECTIVE APPROACHES TO EVALUATION

BUILDING RECEPTIVITY AND AVOIDING ANXIETY

"Working with people is both the high and low point of a school principal's job," according to a survey conducted by the Wisconsin Association of School Boards in 40 randomly selected Wisconsin school districts. The study gathered statistical as well as subjective information concerned with the major likes and dislikes of principals. Most respondents stated that they liked working with teachers, students, and "positive thinking" parents, but disliked "tons of trivia" such as paperwork and "Mickey Mouse" duties. They also were disturbed by trying to "remake substandard or marginal" teachers, their lack of involvement in decisions made by superintendents and school boards, the adversary relationships created by teacher unions, and discipline problems caused by "students who do not want to be in school."

The authors posed the following two questions in brainstorming sessions with administrators and teachers: "Which five things do you like to do *most* on your job?" and "Which five things do you like to do *least* on your job?" Responses were remarkably similar to the results in the Wisconsin survey. These are the composite rank order results obtained during a series of sessions with approximately 150 principals and other administrators.

What I Like to Do Most on the Job

1. Working with teachers, students, and parents
2. Planning and implementing new and better programs

What I Like to Do Least On the Job

1. Administrivia
2. Attending nonproductive meetings
3. Writing meaningless reports to which there is little feedback

What I Like to Do Most on the Job

3. Developing practical curriculum with staff
4. Helping teachers to do a better job
5. Improving myself; achieving my objectives

What I Like to Do Least On the Job

4. Evaluating and dismissing incompetent teachers
5. Dealing with grievances
6. Dealing with very difficult students and parents.

A consensus of more than 300 teachers from urban, suburban, public, and nonpublic schools paralleled the likes and dislikes expressed by administrators:

What I Like Most About My Job

1. Working with students
2. Creating a new teaching strategy that works
3. Reaching the unreachable youngster
4. Working and developing social relationships with other teachers
5. "Growing," achieving self-improvement as a professional

What I Like Least About My Job

1. Impossible discipline problems
2. Writing reports, paper work, non-teaching assignments
3. School and community politics often related to evaluation by "untrustworthy" or "incompetent" administrators
4. Attending boring, interminable meetings
5. Lack of money, poor working conditions

Given the kinds of things that administrators and teachers like about their jobs, it would seem that effective evaluation and counseling programs should be relatively easy to implement, maintain, and improve when necessary. Unfortunately, too many evaluation plans become entangled with human relations problems and manifestations of personality, such as rapport with other staff members, mode of dress, or cooperation with the department or the administration. A teacher's personality becomes relevant only when it affects his own or someone else's teaching performance.

It is useful, therefore, to compare the obstacles to evaluation and counseling from the principal's or supervisor's point of view with the perspective of the teacher in order to overcome anxiety and to build receptivity and understanding.

Obstacles to Evaluation and Counseling From:

Principal's Point of View

Is reluctant to criticize

Believes that criticisms or suggestions are necessary to justify observation and follow-up meeting

Is uncertain of how to (a) project plans for teacher growth and (b) make them appear acceptable and realistic

Feels inadequate about his lack of knowledge of teacher or department goals

Is concerned about the pressures of work that require postponement of follow-up meetings or lack of preparation to give advice

Is aware of poor physical facilities, schedule, or working conditions

Is concerned about the tendency for the teacher's personality to become a major issue

Is aware of the special problems in teacher-school relationships, i.e., long, worthy service, on tenure but now below standard

Recognizes that he cannot know enough about the teacher's day-to-day performance

Is not convinced of the validity or benefits of the evaluation program

Is aware of the implications of a too casual and/or hurried judgment of what is observed

Is fearful of becoming involved in something he may not be able to finish

Is bogged down with evaluation forms or procedures

Is concerned about his ability to put fragmented events into proper perspective

Teacher's Point of View

Is concerned about the principal's or supervisor's sincerity; believes appraisal is merely an administrative chore

Is concerned about being criticized —does not understand objectives of the program

Has received little value from past observations and appraisals

Is not given an opportunity to prepare for the lesson or the follow-up meeting

Does not respect principal's competence to evaluate

Believes that the principal must find something wrong

Believes that the granting of tenure must be tied to observations to make them important and worthwhile

Believes that the administrator may have no real understanding of teaching-learning requirements and standards of teaching performance

Suspects that past mistakes will never be forgotten

Perceives that the administrator lacks understanding of evaluation and does not know how to supervise

Has fears of being reprimanded for speaking his thoughts; is afraid of his supervisor

Believes that the appraisal categories are not related to teaching performance

Is concerned about the implications of the personal relationship between himself and the supervisor, i.e., personal friendship

Is wary because no specific action has been taken to help him improve

Principal's Point of View

Tries to communicate many items of performance in a single observation

Is occasionally aware of personal bias or prejudice, i.e., teacher makes as much or more money

Has a tendency to concentrate on negative characteristics

Is required to observe a set number of times during the year regardless of teacher's ability

Has difficulty finding time to cope with crises and still meet observation and meeting schedules

Teacher's Point of View

Dislikes comparisons of himself with others

Is disconcerted because the evaluation has interrupted important work

Does not realize opportunities that are available for growth through evaluation

Is unable to feel at ease in a somewhat artificial situation, especially with a principal with whom open discussion is difficult

Is unable to express himself due to the formality of the follow-up meeting

Is fearful of prejudice or of personality becoming the issue

Is apprehensive during the time between observations and meetings

Is unwilling to try to see himself as others do; seeks fortification from colleagues

Has personal problems and is unwilling to reveal them

ENCOURAGING SELF-EVALUATION THROUGH JOINT OBJECTIVES

It is suggested that principals and supervisors meet with teachers to seek the means to overcome these obstacles and to work productively toward their mutual goal—the improved instruction of children. There are several steps that are recommended:

1. Consider together the things that are desired by teachers and administrators in your efforts to work together. A beginning list that could be enlarged and modified through brainstorming and analysis sessions might include these items:

What Administrators Want

- To identify, develop, and retain excellent teachers
- To improve teaching and learning for each and every individual student

What Teachers Want

- To know what is expected of them and (with varying degree) to participate in decisions that affect them

What Administrators Want

- To maintain and improve services to children through the acquisition of adequate budgets and community support
- To maintain a congenial cohesive staff that works together on important school objectives

What Teachers Want

- To be made aware of their ratings in the perception of the principal or administrator
- To be appraised objectively rather than subjectively
- To be made aware of their specific strengths and weaknesses
- To be told specific ways in which they can improve their teaching performance
- To be directed toward what they can do to develop themselves for advancement, improvement, or diversified contribution

2. Establish performance goals together. The goals should be:

- Agreed upon mutually
- Reasonable
- Attainable but beyond the teacher's present level
- Measurable (quantified if possible)
- Personalized for the teacher; designed to consider the employee's desires, ability, and stage of development
- Aimed at increasing the teacher's responsibility
- Designed to help the teacher to develop special skills
- Constructed to gain commitment from both the teacher and the administrator

3. Obtain agreement from:

The administrator to consider the:

- Specific performance to be improved
- Problems in quantifying improvement
- Developmental needs of teachers
- Means of evaluating the results

The teacher to:

- Modify his teaching or experiment with selected methods
- Seek self-improvement
- Achieve observable improvement in specific areas or techniques
- Improve by certain dates

4. Begin the self-evaluation program by:

- Setting goals with the teacher

- Emphasizing results, not measurements
- Allowing the teacher to establish the steps for reaching the goals
- Agreeing on standards of performance in advance

5. Monitor and review progress at regular intervals by:

- Recording changes in direction, deletions, additions, improved emphasis, growth
- Reviewing progress at the initiation of either the teacher or administrator
- Encouraging the teacher to demonstrate and share improvements

6. Have both the teacher and administrator keep a log of the results by:

- Listing descriptions and degrees of growth
- Describing obstacles that are overcome or those that are still problematic
- Assessing the level of achievement against previous, joint agreements on standards of performance
- Recording additional significant accomplishments
- Seeking or supplying assistance when unusual difficulties are encountered

7. Measure progress toward goals together. Summarize strengths, gains, and areas of continued, needed improvement, if applicable.

8. Repeat this cycle every year.

The likelihood of success in the self- or joint evaluation process will increase if some basic tenets are followed. These include:

- Firm joint agreement and commitment to goals
- Frequent communication and exchange of views of progress
- Recognition and matching of different teaching and learning styles
- The use of self-competition instead of absolute or competitive rating scales such as 1 - 2 - 3 - 4 - 5 (excellent down to unsatisfactory)
- Moderate and appropriate changes in teaching goals and plans as the need is evidenced
- Clear directions and explanations from expectations through growth and assessment

DESIGNING PEER EVALUATION PROGRAMS

Another approach gaining conceptual acceptance and attracting interest by some teachers and administrators is peer evaluation. Typically, a group of teachers meet with the principal and department or grade-level chairman and agree to visit each other's classrooms, grade each other's papers, compare consistency of grading scores, and observe teacher and student behaviors for the specific purpose of offering positive and constructive criticism based on previously established goals. Peer evaluation teams consisting of five to eight teachers usually reduce anxiety and increase cohesive action toward self- and team improvement.

It is essential to follow a plan that builds acceptance and positive interaction.

1. Setting the stage or pre-agreement negotiation:

> In any evaluation situation, fear of the unknown and anxiety about performance in front of professional colleagues (or even the usual one-supervisor-at-a-time visitation) should be reduced or eliminated. Discussion about objectives, informal and frequent exchanges, multiple observations without the principal or supervisor, predetermined schedules, etc., will tend to calm the participants and build receptivity, indeed, enthusiasm for the idea.
>
> The notion that fellow experts in a specialized discipline or grade level will understand each other's problems and will not place written evaluations into one's file should be well received and reduce anxiety.
>
> Further, the argument against the artificial, one-shot lesson disappears as the peer team plans continuing discussion, multiple visits of varying length, and meetings to analyze strategies, individuals and groups of students, continuing goals, etc.

2. Agreement on appraisal or the rules of the game:

> Each member of the team should participate and agree to the procedures and evaluation techniques to be used. For example, several dry runs or informal visits should be planned and concurrence reached concerning the end of the informal evaluation period and the methods used thereafter.

3. Implementing and assessing the program itself:

> Self- and peer growth should be assessed on a continuing basis. The process should be modified if participants do not meet objectives or growth is blocked.
>
> Motivation is undoubtedly increased as peers strive to do well in front of their colleagues. Grading or rating is improved, too, as teachers realize that their peers will be judging their evaluations of students.

An additional benefit of improved consistency is likely to result as the appraisal of student work is analyzed and debated. Whether individualized objectives or the more traditional grading patterns are used, the subsequent peer observations will modify assessment toward increasingly consistent rating procedures.

One example of improved consistency among raters of English compositions involved a team of three teachers, a journalist, a technical writer, and an English professor.[2] After analyzing several studies of composition rating techniques, the grading team entered into a self-training program to gain consistency among themselves. They were able to reduce the variance of grades by more than 60% and the total grade range on a given composition from A through F to B through D with a strong cluster at the true, or arithmetical, mean.

Figure 7-1 demonstrates that a specific composition graded by a substantial number of raters was given the mean mark of C or Fair. If the individual rater, however, used the TEC Rating Scale, he marked the composition with its true, or arithmetical, mean mark of C, not 41% but 66% of the time.

COMPOSITION SCORES BASED ON SINGLE AND TEC SCALES

GRADE	SINGLE-SCALE PERCENTAGES	TEC 8-COMPONENT SCALE PERCENTAGES
A	5	a
B	24	17
C	41	66
D	24	17
F	5	a
Totals:	99	100

a Total = .2 percent (the other figures in the column are rounded off).

Figure 7-1

The results shown in Figure 7-1 can be expressed in another way: If 1,000 raters were given this C composition to grade using their usual rating system, only 410 of them would give it the true grade; if 1,000 raters graded it on the TEC scale, 660 would give it the true mark. The eight-component scale, then, is more consistent than varied grading procedures generally employed by English teachers.[3]

This team of peers and other writing professionals had developed a rating scale[4] based on criteria that proved reliable in assigning grades on an eight-component scale (see Figure 7-2).

Figure 7-2
RATING SCALE FOR STUDENT COMPOSITIONS*

Student† ______________________ Teacher ______________________

Composition Title ______________________ Grade ______________

Directions: For each quality listed below, encircle the number that most nearly describes the position of this paper on the following scale:

5 (A)	4 (B)	3 (C)	2 (D)	1 (F)	0 (U)
90-100	80-89	70-79	65-69	54-65	
Excellent	Good	Fair	Passing	Failing	Unacceptable

1. General Merit
   - 1.1 Quality of Ideas 5 4 3 2 1 0
   - 1.2 Development of Ideas 5 4 3 2 1 0
   - 1.3 Organization, Relevance, Movement 5 4 3 2 1 0
   - 1.4 Style, Flavor, Individuality 5 4 3 2 1 0
   - 1.5 Wording (Choice of Words) 5 4 3 2 1 0

   Total General Merit Score: ______________

2. Mechanics
   - 2.1 Grammar, Sentence Structure 5 4 3 2 1 0
   - 2.2 Punctuation and Capitalization 5 4 3 2 1 0
   - 2.3 Spelling 5 4 3 2 1 0

   Total Mechanics Score: ______________

   Grand Total: ______________

SUGGESTED SCALE FOR GRAND TOTAL:

5 (A)	4 (B)	3 (C)	2 (D)	1 (F)	0 (U)
40-100	33-89	26-79	19-69	15-63	Below 54
39-98	32-88	25-77	18-68	14-62	
38-97	31-86	24-76	17-66	13-60	
37-95	30-85	23-74	16-65	12-59	
36-94	29-83	22-73		11-57	
35-92	28-82	21-71		10-56	
34-91	27-80	20-70		9-54	

3. Handwriting and Neatness 5 4 3 2 1 0

November 1963; revised January 1964; revised February 1964; revised March 1965.

---

*This revised form is based on the rating scale developed by Dr. Benjamin Rosner and Dr. Paul Diederich for the New York State Education Department's Project on Improving Competence in English Expression.

†Code numbers are used instead of names in the study.

Figure 7-3

RATING SCALE CRITERIA FOR STUDENT COMPOSITIONS*

1. *GENERAL MERIT*

1.1 *Quality of Ideas*

5 This paper says something a bit fresh and original or puts an old thought in a new light within the limits of student knowledge and experience.

3 The paper has familiar and conventional thoughts.

1 The ideas are primitive or are based on uncontrolled emotion.

1.2 *Development of Ideas*

5 The treatment develops the points the student wants to make; there are no obvious gaps and there is no padding. Each main point is developed; it is treated at sufficient length to make it clear, convincing, or appealing. The details chosen are specific and concrete.

3 The development of ideas is occasionally sketchy or superficial. There may be an error or two in logic. The paper may be padded.

1 There is little development of ideas. The arguments, if any, frequently do not support the point they are intended to make and contain inconsistencies and fallacies. Often the paper will repeat one point endlessly. In a narrative, many of the details seem pointless.

1.3 *Organization, Relevance, Movement*

5 The paper starts at a good point, moves in a straight line, gets somewhere, and stops at a good point. There is nothing in it that obviously does not belong, and nothing is left out without explanation if it is essential to the point the writer is trying to make. The paper follows a plan that is apparent to the discerning reader. The topic is broken up into reasonable parts, and the connection of one part with another is clear. There is a feeling of *movement* toward a predestined conclusion. One is never at a loss as to where one is or where one is going.

3 The organization tends to be correct but monotonous. The steps are there, but the transitions are either overmechanical (the list without any sense of climax) or nonexistent. A more adroit writer can suggest the divisions of the paper with clarity and smoothness.

1 The paper seems to have no plan; it merely rambles. It starts anywhere and never gets anywhere. There is usually some attempt at an ending, but it is not natural and inevitable; it is stuck on. At many points one asks, "Where is this heading?" The results of any guess one makes are generally not validated.

1.4 *Style, Flavor, Individuality*

5 The writer expresses his ideas clearly, economically, and interestingly. His sentences indicate the proper relationships between ideas by adept subordination or parallelism, and they display rhythm, grace, and euphony. There is a fitting variety of sentence type and length and a fitting use of simile, imagery, or rhetorical device.

*These definitions are based on those originally developed for the New York State Project on Improving Competence in English Expression by Prof. Benjamin Rosner of Brooklyn College and Dr. Paul Diederich of Educational Testing Service. November 1963; revised January 1964; revised February 1964; revised March 1965.

Figure 7-3 (cont.)

3 The writer is correct but pedestrian, or awkward. Most of his sentences are commonplace and often wordy. They may show a heavy reliance on a stock device like the rhetorical question. He is seldom wrong but never interesting. At times he may be unclear.

1 The writer seldom gets beyond the simple declarative sentence and the primer style. His writing is at best immature, at worst incoherent.

1.5 *Wording* (Choice of Words)

5 The writer uses a sprinkling of uncommon words or of familiar words in uncommon contexts that reveal a fresh perception of their meaning. He is aware of connotation and nuances of denotation. Most of his choices, of course, are correct and some are felicitous.

3 The writer who most obviously belongs in the middle category is the cliché expert, the one whose choice of words is conventional. One may also put here the student who often uses words inappropriately, or who uses too many pretentious or jargon words.

1 The writer uses words carelessly and inexactly and gets too many of them wrong. A paper written entirely in a childish vocabulary may also get a low rating, even if no word is demonstrably wrong.

2. *MECHANICS*

2.1 *Grammar, Sentence Structure*

5 Rare, minor errors in grammar or usage despite varied and complicated sentence structure.

4 Errors only in fine points of grammar or usage although sentence structure is not noticeably varied or complicated.

3 Few serious errors in grammar or usage; some faults in sentence structure, parallelism, subordination, etc.

2 Several serious errors in grammar or usage; some basic structural errors such as fragments or run-on sentences.

1 Too many serious errors in grammar, usage, and sentence structure.

2.2 *Punctuation and Capitalization*

5 Sophisticated use of punctuation in a varied and complicated sentence structure.

4 Errors only in difficult points of fairly complicated constructions.

3 Several errors in complicated constructions or correct punctuation of simple constructions.

2 Careless and inconsistent punctuation with frequent errors.

1 Basic punctuation omitted or haphazard.

2.3 *Spelling*

5 The paper contains no misspelled words and gives further evidence of the writer's excellence in spelling by the sophistication of its language.

4 The paper contains a few errors in the spelling of unusual or difficult words but still gives evidence of overall competence.

3 The paper gives evidence of the general competence of the writer in the spelling of words in the basic vocabulary but contains a few errors.

2 The paper contains several errors but is not notably deficient.

1 The paper contains many serious errors, but they do not interfere with the reader's comprehension of the subject matter or the writer's intent.

NOTE: Consider the use of the apostrophe as part of spelling.

3. *HANDWRITING AND NEATNESS*

5 Clear, attractive, well-spaced, correct manuscript form.

4 Clear but not attractive, or pretty but rather hard to read.

3 Average in legibility and attractiveness. Some violations of manuscript form.

2 Hard to read. Messy.

1 Almost impossible to read.

Similar peer evaluation programs would serve other academic or special-area disciplines equally well.

OBTAINING STUDENT EVALUATIONS

"A quiet change is taking place on college campuses: Faculty are being held accountable, as never before, in how well they serve students and there is a marked shift in the way faculty are being evaluated. What counts more and more is teaching, student advising, committee activities. . . ."[5]

This impact on college campuses has begun to make itself felt at the high school level, as well. Indeed, indirectly, student opinions of teachers have caused community pressure on tenure or rehiring practices across all school levels and, in turn, has influenced many board decisions.

Whatever the objections to the use of student evaluators because of their nonprofessional, untrained, and/or biased status, etc., the trend has been established and many teachers and administrators have seized the opportunity to use student input constructively.

As in the case of peer evaluation, student informational feedback may influence teacher behavior more effectively than supervisory feedback.[6]

Anonymous feedback writeups given to the teacher for his own use are not very threatening to most teachers. It is suggested that planning sessions be held with students to examine the forms cooperatively prior to use. Follow-up discussions with students would aid teachers and administrators in prescribing behavior changes to improve teaching performance.

However, just as with the teacher evaluation instruments discussed in chapters 5 and 6, forms designed to elicit student perceptions of the teacher should incorporate only those items that may be observed and similarly identified by several members of a coordinated visiting team. Student reactions, of course, are based on ongoing, continuous immersion in the learning process that is essentially created by the selected teacher and, as such, are more likely to provide an accurate picture of the gestalt of the instructional environment than can periodic visitations.

It is acceptable to ask students to identify their personal reactions to the learning environment being evaluated. It is equally acceptable to solicit individual student perceptions of their teachers. What must be emphasized, however, is that each human being brings to an instructional situation his or her own uniqueness and a learning style that often differs drastically from that of other people. Few teachers can respond with equal effectiveness to all students because teachers, too, are unique. The teacher's teaching style may complement many (the majority of) students and may not be able to reach some.

Samples of checklists, Figures 7-4, 7-6, 7-8, and comment forms, Figures 7-5, and 7-7, follow. It should be noted that the examples included herein represent actual student evaluation lists currently being used, but do *not* exemplify objective, bias-free types of questions. Indeed, these forms represent appropriate beginnings toward student evaluation but fall prey to the same types of subjective distortions found in forms generally used by supervisors to evaluate teachers. Therefore, several significant factors should be considered when weighing student feedback:

1. When anything other than observational items are analyzed, student responses may be reflective of the student's emotional, physical, and/or sociological weaknesses (and/or strengths) rather than an accurate perception of the teacher.
2. A 10%-20% negative reaction to teachers on subjective questions may be indicative of an incorrect matching of teaching and learning styles.
3. Negative reactions may be caused by teacher imposition of a modus operandi or curriculum demand on the basis of diagnostic testing but not particularly appreciated by the student.
4. Specific demands may have been placed upon the teacher that were not consistent with either his or her philosophy or natural teaching style, such as a traditional administrator requiring that every student complete grade-level studies within specific time spans or that each student remain seated. A teacher may not be a free agent in that classroom.
5. Questions that elicit personal reactions respond to emotional biases; each student may not interpret such questions in the same way. Thus, responses to an item such as, "Does the teacher have any irritating habits?" will be of varying significance without any means of determining their relative importance. For example, one student, intent on her work, may not have noticed whether or not the teacher, in fact, does have any irritating habits. A second student, having the same habit himself, might not be aware of the existence of that mannerism. A third student may be annoyed by something, but may be unable to identify the source of the irritation; he may not be a visually oriented person who sees mannerisms. A fourth student may be acutely aware of a mannerism, while a fifth, because of his personal orientation, might consider that mannerism cute or attractive. Finally, if the teacher is serving in an appropriate role, the mannerism (if it exists at all) may not intrude on the instructional process, for the student may be functioning either independently or with selected peers with little teacher interaction. Therefore, the mannerism may be something with which there is little contact and, thus, is relatively unimportant.

It is recommended therefore, that student evaluation forms be designed so that they respond to what the teacher does, what the student does, and the outcomes of both behaviors, rather than include essentially subjective questions. The following forms are provided, however, so that you may examine what other systems have been using. Certainly, local forms should be developed based on the teaching styles that are considered desirable by cooperative faculty-administrator analysis and those styles that are actually being employed by the teacher being observed or evaluated. For example, items pertaining to "lectures" and "whole-class discussions" would be appropriate only when being applied to teachers who function in traditional ways. An alternate question form is supplied to increase the objectivity of contemplated student evaluations (Figure 7-9).

A. Rolling Hills Local School District, Byesville, Ohio

A.1

SAMPLE STUDENT CHECKLIST

Mark "yes" or "no" before each statement as it applies to your teacher:

_______ Is interested in you as a person.
_______ Encourages students.
_______ Has a good sense of humor.
_______ Doesn't talk about students behind their backs to other students.
_______ Is friendly and understanding.
_______ Knows his/her subject and sticks to the subject in class.
_______ Has a good reason for giving punishment to students.
_______ Explains the subject and tries to help the students.
_______ Is patient with students.
_______ Has any irritating personal habits.

Figure 7-4

A.2

SAMPLE

Comment on these characteristics as they apply to your teacher:

Is clean and neat in appearance and is clean minded.
Is liberal—not picky at every little thing.
Gives the proper kind of punishment and punishes all students the same for the same wrong.
Treats all students and all classes alike—has no pets.
Uses modern teaching methods and makes the subject interesting.
Treats students according to their ages.
Speaks clearly and writes clearly so all students can see what has been written.
Gives a reasonable amount of homework.

Figure 7-5

The following questionnaires (B and C) are additional examples of forms currently being used in school systems to elicit students' perceptions of their teachers and their learning environments. Only Form D is suggested by the authors as being inclusive of essentially objective questions aimed at obtaining insights into behaviors and outcomes that may be used by teachers for self-improvement.

B. Niles Township High Schools, Skokie, Illinois

Figure 7-6

B.1

STUDENT'S RATING OF A TEACHER

An honest rating of teachers by students can be very helpful to teachers in improving their teaching. You are being asked to give your opinion because your teachers are interested in this improvement.

Please rate your teacher as fairly as you can. Your teacher may make changes because of your opinions. Don't put your name on this rating sheet or in any way identify it with yourself. Your teacher is the only person who will see the rating unless he/she voluntarily chooses to share it with someone.

Circle the rating that represents your best opinion of the teacher's work in each category.

	Strongly Agree	Agree	Disagree	Strongly Disagree	No Opinion
1. The grading system was clear.	1	2	3	4	5
2. The instruction was intellectually stimulating.	1	2	3	4	5
3. Exams and/or papers covered important aspects of the course material.	1	2	3	4	5
4. The teacher was sensitive to the students' level of understanding.	1	2	3	4	5
5. I would recommend this course to a friend with similar interests.	1	2	3	4	5
6. The teacher had a thorough knowledge of the subject matter.	1	2	3	4	5
7. The workload in the course was too heavy.	1	2	3	4	5
8. The teacher sought and responded to student opinion.	1	2	3	4	5
9. The classes were to the point and time was well spent.	1	2	3	4	5
10. The teacher's policy toward discussing questions was agreeable.	1	2	3	4	5
11. The teacher showed enthusiasm for the course.	1	2	3	4	5
12. The lectures or discussions should have concerned themselves more with the readings.	1	2	3	4	5

	Strongly Agree	Agree	Disagree	Strongly Disagree	No Opinion
13. The teacher had sufficient evidence of a student's performance in terms of class participation, tests, and written work.	1	2	3	4	5
14. The lectures were presented in a clear and organized manner.	1	2	3	4	5
15. The books were good choices for the course.	1	2	3	4	5
16. The test questions covered the primary facts and concepts presented.	1	2	3	4	5
17. Taking this course has increased my knowledge of the course's subject area.	1	2	3	4	5
18. The teacher made good use of examples and illustrations and/or A-V materials.	1	2	3	4	5
19. Fellow students contributed to the value of this course.	1	2	3	4	5
20. The student found the teacher available after/outside of class for individual attention.	1	2	3	4	5
21. The student was presented with new or innovative ways of learning.	1	2	3	4	5
22. The teacher's objectives for the course have been made clear.	1	2	3	4	5
23. The teacher used class time well.	1	2	3	4	5
24. The teacher seemed to know when students didn't understand material.	1	2	3	4	5
25. The course description accurately describes the contents and method of the course.	1	2	3	4	5
26. I have been challenged by this course.	1	2	3	4	5
27. The teacher informed students how they would be evaluated in the course.	1	2	3	4	5
28. The teacher was generally well prepared for class.	1	2	3	4	5
29. Students were encouraged to think for themselves.	1	2	3	4	5
30. The instructor made helpful comments on papers or tests.	1	2	3	4	5

31. Compared to other teachers you have had, how effective has this teacher been?
    a. one of the most effective.
    b. more effective than most.
    c. not as effective as most.
    d. one of the least effective.

32. I would have preferred changes in: (stato reasons for changes indicated below).
    a. the amount and/or type of homework.
    b. the materials read.
    c. the method of instruction (discussion, lecture).
    d. the expectations of the teacher.
    e. my own scholarship, participation, time spent on the course.

Figure 7-7

B.2

The checklist you have just completed allows you to express your opinions, but affords no opportunity to make comments or suggestions. In this portion you are encouraged to make suggestions that you think will aid the instructor in his/her attempt to improve this course. When finished, please return the questionnaire to your instructor. Thank you.

1. How could this course be improved?

2. Which parts of the course did you enjoy most?

3. What part of the course will be most valuable to you?

4. If there were labs, did you learn from them?

5. How could the instructor best improve his/her teaching?

6. Why did you take the course?

7. Any other comments you wish to make:

Figure 7-8

C. Northfield Mount Herman[7]

STUDENT EVALUATION

INSTRUCTOR ____________________ ________ ____________ __________

Dept. Course Period

Circle the answer in each group that best answers each question.

1. Knowledge of Subject

Knowledge of field inadequate	Adequate	Knowledgeable	Expert

Comment:

2. Presentation of Material

Very hard to follow	Reasonably understandable	Makes subject very clear

Comment:

3. Balance of Breadth and Detail

Gets bogged down in trivia	Generalizes too much	Reasonable balance	Good balance of breadth and detail

Comment:

4. Enthusiasm for Subject

Seems disinterested	Mildly interested	Interested	Displays great enthusiasm

Comment:

5. Fairness in Marking

Partial and prejudiced	Reasonably fair	Very fair and impartial

Comment:

6. Attitude toward Student

Unsympathetic and intolerant	Reasonably good; average	Sympathetic and understanding

Comment:

7. Fairness of Workload

Unnecessarily light	Reasonably adequate	Excessively heavy

Comment:

8. Overall Summary as Instructor

Unsatisfactory	Average	Above average	Outstanding

General comment:

D. Student Evaluation Form (Suggested)

Figure 7-9

	Always	Sometimes	Never	Comments:
1. Do you work toward the completion of some objectives that are different from those of your classmates?				
2. Are you permitted to select your own: a. Objectives b. Learning resources c. Learning activities/experiences d. Assignments e. Learning partners or groups f. Method of learning g. Rate of learning h. Time and method of self-evaluation prior to teacher testing or checking?				
3. Do you know where and how to get help with your work when you need it?				

	Always	Sometimes	Never	Comments:
4. Do you know how to: a. locate ____ b. use ____ c. share ____ d. repair ____ learning resources?				
5. Do you know how the teacher rates your work?				
6. Do you agree with his rating of your work?				
7. Do you ever learn through: a. contracts b. instructional packages c. programmed learning d. task cards or sets of objectives e. games?				
8. Are the things you study in this class interesting to you?				
9. Would you recommend this teacher (or class) to a good friend?				
10. Did you look forward to attending this class?				
11. Did you learn a great deal during these class sessions?				
12. Did the instructor use a variety of teaching methods to reach you and other students in the class?				
[In addition, the comment questions from Niles Township High Schools (Figure 7-7) should be added to this suggested form.]				

Written comments, of course, are very helpful, especially when analyzed by a class or by groups of classes. Questions similar to those noted earlier under the Administrative Style Questionnaire (chapter 1) would be very helpful here:

What Is the Teacher's Greatest Strength(s)?	What Would Most Increase His or Her Effectiveness as a Teacher?

The composite results honestly given and openly received would sensitize the teacher to his strengths and weaknesses as perceived by his "clients," and would be likely to contribute toward change and improvement of his behavior as a teacher.

USING THE EXIT INTERVIEW TO IMPROVE EVALUATION

There are times, of course, when a teacher leaves because of extreme unhappiness with an individual principal or supervisor. Whether justified or not, it is extremely helpful to collect the reasons people give for leaving and to examine patterns in an effort to improve your personnel-administration behavior. A study of exit interviews may reveal the causes of either satisfaction or irritation with aspects of the evaluation procedures, and constructive comments also may be revealing. Therefore, an opportunity to express both positive and negative reactions should be provided in whichever document you elect to use.

Some companies like to interview at the time a person leaves to take advantage of the "heat of the moment" to obtain honest answers. It is sometimes preferable to solicit responses after any anger or hostility has cooled in the soothing waters of time and a new position. In either case, objectivity is to be desired because some people harbor antagonism throughout a lifetime.

The exit interview questionnaire[8] shown in Figure 7-10 was used with success in Texas. Butefish advises a personal interview using an independent agency to ensure anonymity and useful analyses that reveal patterns or trends if they exist. Some districts use the mails to obtain such information.

Figure 7-10

REASONS FOR TEACHER TURNOVER
A QUESTIONNAIRE

Responses to questions should be checked under E, H, M, S, or N. E indicates that the reason cited in the question was extremely instrumental in the move; H indicates highly instrumental; M, moderately instrumental; S, slightly instrumental; and N, not instrumental.

IMPORTANT: On each page of the questionnaire, answer questions first in the left column and then in the right column.

I. SUPERVISION OF INSTRUCTION	E	H	M	S	N
1. To what degree was the supervision of instruction too directive, thus becoming a contributing cause for your move?	____	____	____	____	____
2. To what degree was the supervision of instruction too general, thus becoming a contributing cause for your move?	____	____	____	____	____
3. To what degree was lack of supervision a contributing cause for your move?	____	____	____	____	____
4. To what degree was supervision that was not offered in a spirit of improvement a contributing cause for your move?	____	____	____	____	____
5. To what degree was poor supervision of a type not yet mentioned in this interview a contributing cause for your move?	____	____	____	____	____

II. WORKING CONDITIONS	E	H	M	S	N
1. To what degree were inadequate facilities a contributing cause for your move?	____	____	____	____	____
2. To what degree were inadequate instructional supplies a contributing cause for your move?	____	____	____	____	____
3. To what degree was a low salary scale a contributing cause for your move?	____	____	____	____	____
4. To what degree was a lack of opportunity for advancement a contributing cause for your move?	____	____	____	____	____
5. To what degree was a lack of academic freedom a contributing cause for your move?	____	____	____	____	____

	E	H	M	S	N
6. To what degree was the lack of a strong professional organization a contributing cause for your move?	___	___	___	___	___
7. To what degree was the lack of security in your position a contributing cause for your move?	___	___	___	___	___
8. To what degree was an inadequate sick-leave policy a contributing cause for your move?	___	___	___	___	___
9. To what degree was an inadequate orientation program a contributing cause for your move?	___	___	___	___	___
10. To what degree were working conditions other than those that have been previously mentioned in this interview a contributing cause for your move?	___	___	___	___	___

III. SCHOOL ADMINISTRATION

	E	H	M	S	N
1. To what degree was a lack of communication with the administration a contributing cause for your move?	___	___	___	___	___
2. To what degree was the administration's lack of professional abilities a contributing cause for your move?	___	___	___	___	___
3. To what degree was the administration's lack of consistency a contributing cause for your move?	___	___	___	___	___
4. To what degree was the administration's lack of dependability a contributing cause for your move?	___	___	___	___	___
5. To what degree was the administration's lack of recognition for the individual accomplishments of teachers a contributing cause for your move?	___	___	___	___	___
6. To what degree was the administration's lack of respect for individual teachers a contributing cause for your move?	___	___	___	___	___
7. To what degree was the lack of opportunities for consulting and sharing with the administration a contributing cause for your move?	___	___	___	___	___

	E	H	M	S	N
8. To what degree was the lack of opportunity for cooperative planning with the administration a contributing cause for your move?	____	____	____	____	____
9. To what degree was the lack of administrative support for particular parts of the school program a contributing cause for your move?	____	____	____	____	____
10. To what degree was the application of administrative pressure for effectiveness a contributing cause for your move?	____	____	____	____	____
11. To what degree was the lack of some aspect of administrative leadership not previously mentioned in this interview a contributing cause for your move?	____	____	____	____	____

IV. INSTRUCTIONAL PROGRAM

	E	H	M	S	N
1. To what degree was a lack of definite aims and goals for the instructional program a contributing cause for your move?	____	____	____	____	____
2. To what degree was the narrow limitation of the instructional program a contributing cause for your move?	____	____	____	____	____
3. To what degree was the lack of a progressive instructional program a contributing cause for your move?	____	____	____	____	____
4. To what degree was an instructional program lacking intellectual challenges for young people a contributing cause for your move?	____	____	____	____	____
5. To what degree were low academic standards a contributing cause for your move?	____	____	____	____	____
6. To what degree were standards that were too demanding on the students a contributing cause for your move?	____	____	____	____	____
7. To what degree was a part of the instructional program not yet mentioned in this interview a contributing cause for your move?	____	____	____	____	____

V. PERSONAL ASSIGNMENT AND RESPONSIBILITIES	E	H	M	S	N
1. To what degree was a teaching assignment in a subject area that you preferred not to teach a contributing cause for your move?	___	___	___	___	___
2. To what degree was a grade-level assignment that was unsatisfactory to you a contributing cause for your move?	___	___	___	___	___
3. To what degree was a heavy teaching load in total number of students taught a contributing cause for your move?	___	___	___	___	___
4. To what degree was a heavy teaching load in time spent in the classroom a contributing cause for your move?	___	___	___	___	___
5. To what degree was a heavy load of clerical duties a contributing cause for your move?	___	___	___	___	___
6. To what degree was an excessive amount of "extra duties" a contributing cause for your move?	___	___	___	___	___
7. To what degree was an unsatisfactory grouping arrangement a contributing cause for your move?	___	___	___	___	___
8. To what degree was a part of your personal assignment and responsibilities not yet mentioned in this interview a contributing cause for your move?	___	___	___	___	___

VI. INTERPERSONAL RELATIONSHIPS	E	H	M	S	N
1. To what degree was a poor relationship with another teacher or other teachers a contributing cause for your move?	___	___	___	___	___
2. To what degree was a poor relationship with a supervisor or department head a contributing cause for your move?	___	___	___	___	___
3. To what degree was a poor relationship with your building principal a contributing cause for your move?	___	___	___	___	___
4. To what degree was a poor relationship with the superintendent of schools a contributing cause for your move?	___	___	___	___	___

	E	H	M	S	N
5. To what degree was a poor relationship with school personnel other than professional personnel a contributing cause for your move?	___	___	___	___	___
6. To what degree was a poor relationship with students' parents a contributing cause for your move?	___	___	___	___	___
7. To what degree was a poor relationship with one or more members of the board of education a contributing cause for your move?	___	___	___	___	___
8. To what degree was a poor relationship with others than those previously mentioned in this interview a contributing cause for your move?	___	___	___	___	___

VII. STUDENT CHARACTERISTICS

	E	H	M	S	N
1. To what degree was the students' lack of moral values a contributing cause for your move?	___	___	___	___	___
2. To what degree was the students' lack of adequate academic standards a contributing cause for your move?	___	___	___	___	___
3. To what degree was the students' lack of self-control concerning order and discipline a contributing cause for your move?	___	___	___	___	___
4. To what degree was the students' lack of respect for authority a contributing cause for your move?	___	___	___	___	___
5. To what degree were student characteristics other than those previously mentioned in this interview a contributing cause for your move?	___	___	___	___	___

VIII. BOARD OF EDUCATION

	E	H	M	S	N
1. To what degree was the board of education's lack of awareness of the needs of youth a contributing cause for your move?	___	___	___	___	___
2. To what degree was the board of education's lack of concern for all parts of the school program a contributing cause for your move?	___	___	___	___	___
3. To what degree was a lack of written personnel policies by the board of education a contributing cause for your move?	___	___	___	___	___

	E	H	M	S	N
4. To what degree was a lack of clarity of the school board's personnel policies a contributing cause for your move?	___	___	___	___	___
5. To what degree was the school board's lack of recognition of teaching as a profession a contributing cause for your move?	___	___	___	___	___
6. To what degree was the school board's lack of respect for the dignity and worth of individual teachers a contributing cause for your move?	___	___	___	___	___
7. To what degree were characteristics of the school board other than those previously mentioned in this interview a contributing cause for your move?	___	___	___	___	___

IX. COMMUNITY RELATIONSHIPS

	E	H	M	S	N
1. To what degree was the poor image of teachers in the community a contributing cause for your move?	___	___	___	___	___
2. To what degree was the lack of support for all areas of education by the community a contributing cause for your move?	___	___	___	___	___
3. To what degree was the lack of support for particular areas of the school program by the community a contributing cause for your move?	___	___	___	___	___
4. To what degree was the degree of expectation by the community for participation by teachers in outside activities a contributing cause for your move?	___	___	___	___	___
5. To what degree were community relationships other than those previously mentioned in this interview a contributing cause for your move?	___	___	___	___	___

X. TEACHING STAFF

	E	H	M	S	N
1. To what degree was the lack of dedication to teaching of the teaching staff a contributing cause for your move?	___	___	___	___	___
2. To what degree was the lack of teaching competence of the teaching staff a contributing cause for your move?	___	___	___	___	___
3. To what degree was the lack of professional ethics of the teaching staff a contributing cause for your move?	___	___	___	___	___

	E	H	M	S	N
4. To what degree was the lack of willingness to cooperate by the teaching staff a contributing cause for your move?	____	____	____	____	____
5. To what degree was the lack of social experiences among members of the teaching staff a contributing cause for your move?	____	____	____	____	____
6. To what degree were characteristics of the teaching staff other than those previously mentioned in this interview a contributing cause for your move?	____	____	____	____	____

XI. COMMUNITY CONDITIONS

	E	H	M	S	N
1. To what degree was the limitation of recreational activities in the community a contributing cause for your move?	____	____	____	____	____
2. To what degree was the limitation of cultural activities that were available in the community a contributing cause for your move?	____	____	____	____	____
3. To what degree was the limitation of opportunities for making friends in the community a contributing cause for your move?	____	____	____	____	____
4. To what degree was the limitation of opportunities for making extra money in the community a contributing cause for your move?	____	____	____	____	____
5. To what degree was the distance to a graduate school a contributing cause for your move?	____	____	____	____	____
6. To what degree was the distance to your hometown a contributing cause for your move?	____	____	____	____	____
7. To what degree was the distance from this location to a metropolitan center a contributing cause for your move?	____	____	____	____	____
8. To what degree was the limitation of educational opportunities for your own children a contributing cause for your move?	____	____	____	____	____
9. To what degree was the absence of the religious denomination of your preference a contributing cause?	____	____	____	____	____
10. To what degree were conditions other than those previously mentioned in this interview a contributing cause for your move?	____	____	____	____	____

To these primarily hygienic, dissatisfying working condition questions, the authors would add those categories that Herzberg and Ford found so important in motivating and stimulating people within the job itself.

EXIT INTERVIEW—A

E—Extremely Instrumental
H—Highly Instrumental
M—Moderately Instrumental
S—Slightly Instrumental
N—Not Instrumental

	E	H	M	S	N
A. Achievement To what degree did a limitation on your ability to achieve results contribute to your desire to leave? Please comment	___	___	___	___	___
B. Recognition To what degree did the lack of recognition of your accomplishments contribute to your desire to leave? Please comment	___	___	___	___	___
C. Responsibility To what degree did restriction on your ability to assume responsibility for instruction or setting teaching objectives contribute to your desire to leave? Please comment	___	___	___	___	___
D. Advancement To what degree did the lack of opportunity to advance in title or role contribute to your desire to leave? Please comment	___	___	___	___	___
E. Growth To what degree did restrictions on your ability to grow and to become a better teacher contribute to your desire to leave? Please comment	___	___	___	___	___

Still another, briefer set of questions to ask people when they leave, or a few months later by an outside agency, are the inverse of questions cited at the beginning of chapter 3.

EXIT INTERVIEW—B

A. What were the things you were most happy about in your last position before you left?

1.
2.
3.
4.
5.

Comments____

B. What were the things you were most unhappy about and which contributed to your seeking employment elsewhere?

1.
2.
3.
4.
5.

Comments____

Even if a teacher were not granted tenure or were asked to leave, his comments in this area could be helpful if they were part of a branch or pattern.

GROWING AND LEARNING FOR ALL

The chart in Figure 7-11 suggests supervisory key behaviors in overcoming the obstacles to self-improvement.

Figure 7-11

TYPES OF EVALUATION PROGRAMS AND KEY SUPERVISORY BEHAVIORS TO ENHANCE SUCCESS

Behavior Obstacles to Self-improvement	*A. Typical Observation and Evaluation Writeups*	*B. Joint or Self-evaluation*	*C. Peer Evaluation*	*D. Student Evaluation*
1. People tend to react because of their attitudes, not facts.	A-1 Allow teacher to explain his view of the lesson or his teaching objectives.	B-1 Both parties must reveal all hidden agenda.	C-1 Build confidence through nonrating sessions to start.	D-1 Do not allow teacher to lose face or professionalism.
2. People become suspicious when confused.	A-2 Supervisor must be very clear and specific about his expectations.	B-2 Supervisor and teacher must agree and be clear about goals.	C-2 The procedures for peer evaluation must be agreed to and understood by all.	D-2 The roles and responses of administrator, teacher, and student must be agreed to and understood by all.
3. People judge from their own frame of reference.	A-3 Allow teacher to explain his view of the lesson or his teaching objectives.	B-3 Have teacher and supervisor switch roles or have teacher test goals with other teachers.	C-3 Prepare for peer evaluation through intervisits, informal discussion.	D-3 Have student evaluators teach and be appraised before they evaluate teachers.

4. There may be a hidden agenda.	A-4 Have supervisor and teacher discuss learning, administration, the school, etc., first.	B-4 Both parties must reveal all hidden agenda.	C-4 Attitudes toward the school and each other should be discussed first.	D-4 Pretraining and discussion should precede student evaluations.
5. People do not like to lose face.	A-5 Project attainable goals; measure progress against ability.	B-5 Encourage realistic, attainable goals; measure results against own ability and stage of development.	C-5 Build confidence through nonrating sessions to start.	D-5 Do not allow teacher to lose face or professionalism.
6. Stubbornness or stuffiness causes resentment.	A-6 Have teacher observe others, take the role of students; supervisors the role of teachers.	B-6 Have teacher and supervisor switch roles or have teacher test goals with other teachers.	C-6 Have group agree and work on group objective.	D-6 Teacher should be sensitized to role as open, friendly receiver of suggestions.
7. One-way directives block behavior change.	A-7 Allow teacher to explain his view of the lesson or his teaching objectives.	B-7 Agree to at least an equal role; have frequent meetings.	C-7 Have group indicate goals to overall supervisor.	D-7 Directions to students should be matched with questions from students.
8. People are interested in their own activities.	A-8 Have teacher observe others, take the role of students; supervisors the role of teachers.	B-8 Have teacher and supervisor switch roles or have teacher test goals with other teachers.	C-8 Have group agree and work on group objective.	D-8 Have student evaluators teach and be appraised before they evaluate teachers.

Living, growing, self-actualizing—the common desires of students, teachers, and supervisors—are more easily obtained if each recognizes the same goals in others.

And, a final note to principals, supervisors, teachers, parents and students:

> "The ultimate result of shielding men from the effects of folly is to fill the world with fools."
>
> *Herbert Spencer*
> *Essays* (1891). "State Tampering with Money Banks."

NOTES FOR CHAPTER 7

1. *Education USA*. Washington, D.C., Vol. 17, No. 47 (July 14, 1975).
2. "Composition Grades: A Study of Consistency Among Raters." *The Education Council for School Research and Development*. New York, New York: AEVAC, Inc. (1968).
3. "Composition Grades: A Study of Consistency Among Raters": 10, 11.
4. "Composition Grades: A Study of Consistency Among Raters": 29-36.
5. "The Week in Review." *New York Times,* Section IV (June 8, 1975).
6. "Evaluating Teachers for Professional Growth." Arlington, Virginia: National School Public Relations Association (1974): 24.
7. David Mallery. "The Strengths of a Good School Faculty." Boston: National Association of Independent Schools (1975): 42-44.
8. William L. Butefish. *School Management*. (May, 1971): 16-20.

Appendix

Selected Bibliography and Sources of Additional Information

Abramson, Ted. "Development of Improved Techniques for Establishing the Reliability of Observation Ratings." New York: Fordham University, United States Department of Health, Education and Welfare Project No. 9-b-070, Grant No. OEC-2-9-400070-1039 (010).

Apple, Michael W., Michael J. Subkoviak, and Henry S. Lufler, Jr. *Educational Evaluation: Analysis and Responsibility*. Berkeley, California: McCutchan Publishing Corporation, 1974.

Bennie, William A. *Supervising Clinical Experiences in the Classroom*. New York: Harper & Row, 1972.

Berman, Louise M. *Supervision, Staff Development and Leadership*. Columbus, Ohio: Charles E. Merrill Company, 1971.

Block, James (ed.). *Schools, Society, and Mastery Learning*. New York: Holt, Rinehart, and Winston, 1974.

Bolton, Dale L. *Selection and Evaluation of Teachers*. Berkeley, California: McCutchan Publishing Corporation, 1973.

Culver, Carmen, and Gary Hoban. *Power to Change*. New York: McGraw-Hill Book Company, Inc., 1973.

Cunningham, Lavern L., and William J. Gephart. *Leadership: The Science and the Art Today*. Ithica, Illinois: F. F. Peacock, 1973.

Dowling, W. F. *How Managers Motivate*. New York: McGraw-Hill Book Company, Inc., 1971.

Dunkin, M. J., and B.J. Biddle. *The Study of Teaching*. New York: Holt, Rinehart, and Winston, 1974.

Dunn, Rita, and Kenneth Dunn. *Educator's Self-Teaching Guide to Individualizing Instructional Programs*. West Nyack, New York: Parker Publishing Company, Inc., 1975.

"Elementary School Evaluative Criteria." Arlington, Virginia: National Study of School Evaluation, 1973.

"Evaluating Administrative Performance." Arlington, Virginia: Educational Research Service, Inc., 1974.

"Evaluating Teachers for Professional Growth: Current Trends in School Policies and Programs." Arlington, Virginia: National School Public Relations Association, 1974.

Frymier, Jack R. *A School for Tomorrow.* Berkeley, California: McCutchan Publishing Corporation, 1973.

Greene, Robert E. "Administrative Appraisal: A Step to Improved Leadership." Washington, D.C.: National Association of Secondary School Principals, 1972.

Hankins, Norman. *Psychology for Contemporary Education.* Columbus, Ohio: Charles Merrill Publishers, 1973.

Haubrich, Vernon F., and Michael W. Apple. *Schooling and the Rights of Children.* Berkeley, California: McCutchan Publishing Corporation, 1975.

Herman, Jerry J. *Developing an Effective School Staff Evaluation Program.* West Nyack, New York: Parker Publishing Company, Inc., 1973.

Hyman, Ronald T. *School Administrator's Handbook of Teacher Supervision and Evaluation Methods.* Englewood Cliffs, New Jersey: Prentice-Hall, Inc., 1975.

Ianni, Francis (ed.). *Conflict and Change in Education.* Glenview, Illinois: Scott Foresman & Company, 1975.

"Improving School Staffs: An Administrator's Guide to Staff Development," Volume III. Arlington, Virginia: American Association of School Administrators, 1974.

Kibler, Robert J., Larry L. Barker, David T. Miles, and Donald J. Cegala. *Objectives for Instruction and Evaluation.* Rockleigh, New Jersey: Allyn and Bacon, Inc., 1975.

Mackenzie, R. Alec. *The Time Trap.* New York: American Management Association, 1972.

Mager, Robert F., and Peter Pipe. *Analyzing Performance Problems.* Belmont, California: Fearon Publishers, 1970.

Mallery, David. "The Strengths of a Good School Faculty: Notes on Evaluation, Growth, and Professional Partnership of Teachers." Boston, Massachusetts: National Association of Independent Schools, 1975.

Mosher, Ralph L. *Supervision: The Reluctant Profession.* New York: Houghton Mifflin, 1972.

Popham, James W. *Educational Evaluation.* Englewood Cliffs, New Jersey: Prentice-Hall, Inc., 1975.

Price, James. *Handbook of Organizational Measurement.* Lexington, Mass.: D. C. Heath & Company, 1972.

Raths, James. "Problems Associated with Describing Activities," in Charles W. Beegle and Richard M. Brandt (eds.) *Observational Methods in the Schools.* Washington, D.C.: Association for Supervision and Curriculum Development, 1973.

Reeves, Eltor T. *So You Want to Be a Supervisor.* New York: American Management Association, 1971.

Rosenshine, B., and N. Furst. "Research on Teacher Performance Criteria," in B. O. Smith (ed.) *Research on Teacher Education: A Symposium.* Englewood Cliffs, N. J.: Prentice-Hall, Inc., 1971.

Sabine, Gordon A. "How Students Rate Their Schools and Teachers." Washington, D.C.: National Association of Secondary School Principals, 1971.

Scribner, Harvey B. *Make Your Schools Work.* New York: Simon and Schuster, 1975.

Townsend, Robert. *Up the Organization.* Conn.: Fawcett Crest Books, 1971.

Tyler, Ralph, and Richard Wold (eds.). *Crucial Issues in Testing.* Berkeley, California: McCutchan Publishers, 1974.

Walberg, Herbert J. *Evaluating Educational Performance: A Sourcebook of Methods, Instruments and Examples.* Berkeley, California: McCutchan Publishers, 1974.

"What Research Says About Improving Student Performance." Albany, New York: The University of the State of New York, The State Education Department, Bureau of School Programs Evaluation, 1973.

Wick, B. *Evaluation for Decision-Making in the Schools.* New York: Houghton Mifflin, 1971.

Wick, J. W., and D. L. Beggs. "Evaluating Teacher Effectiveness," in *Evaluation for Decision-Making in the Schools.* Boston: Houghton Mifflin Company, 1971.

Wittrock, M. and D. Wiley. (eds.). *The Evaluation of Instruction: Issues and Problems.* New York: Holt, Rinehart and Winston, 1970.

Index

A

B

C

D

E

L

M

N

O

P

Q

R

S